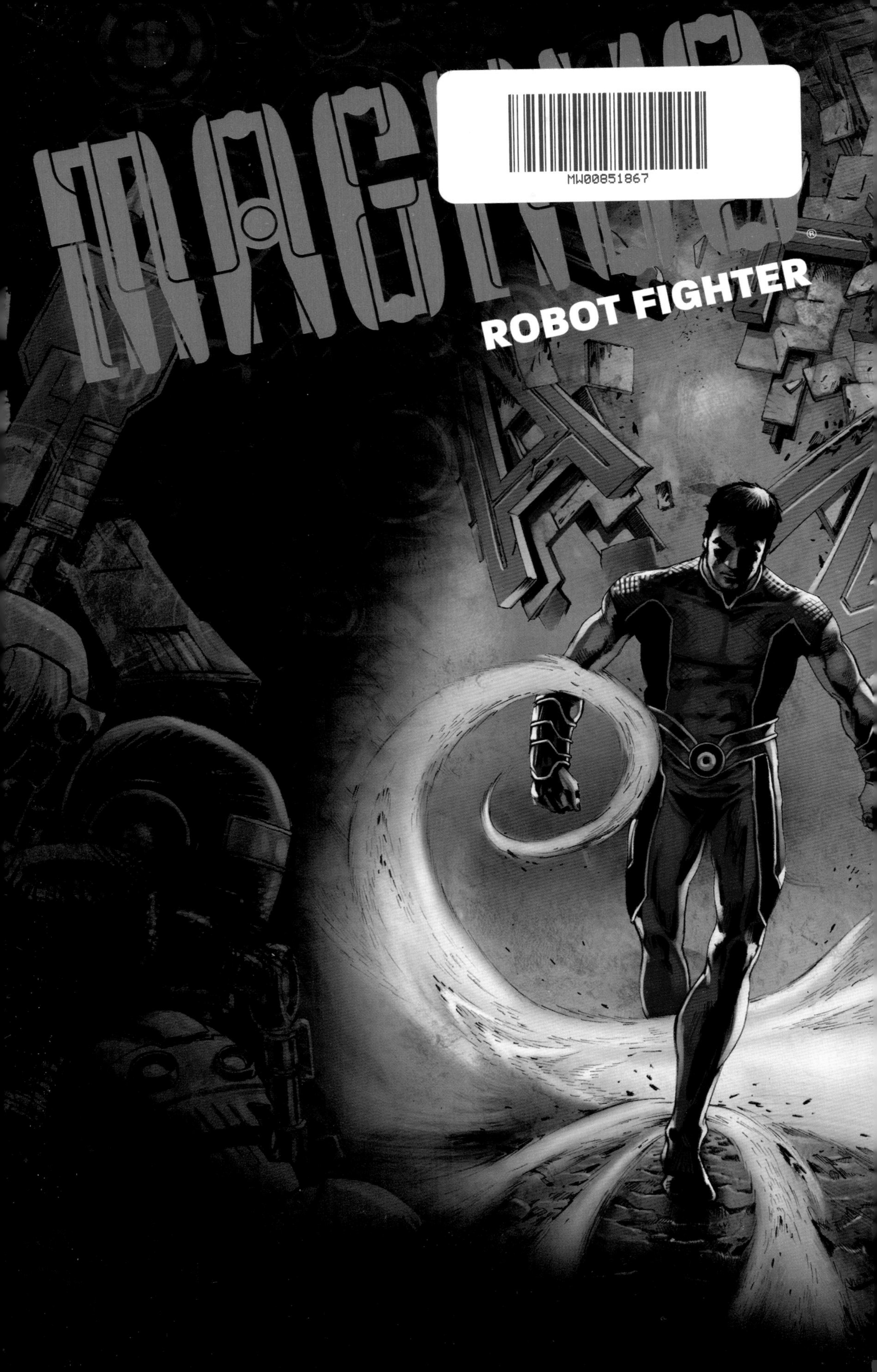

MAGNUS

ROBOT FIGHTER

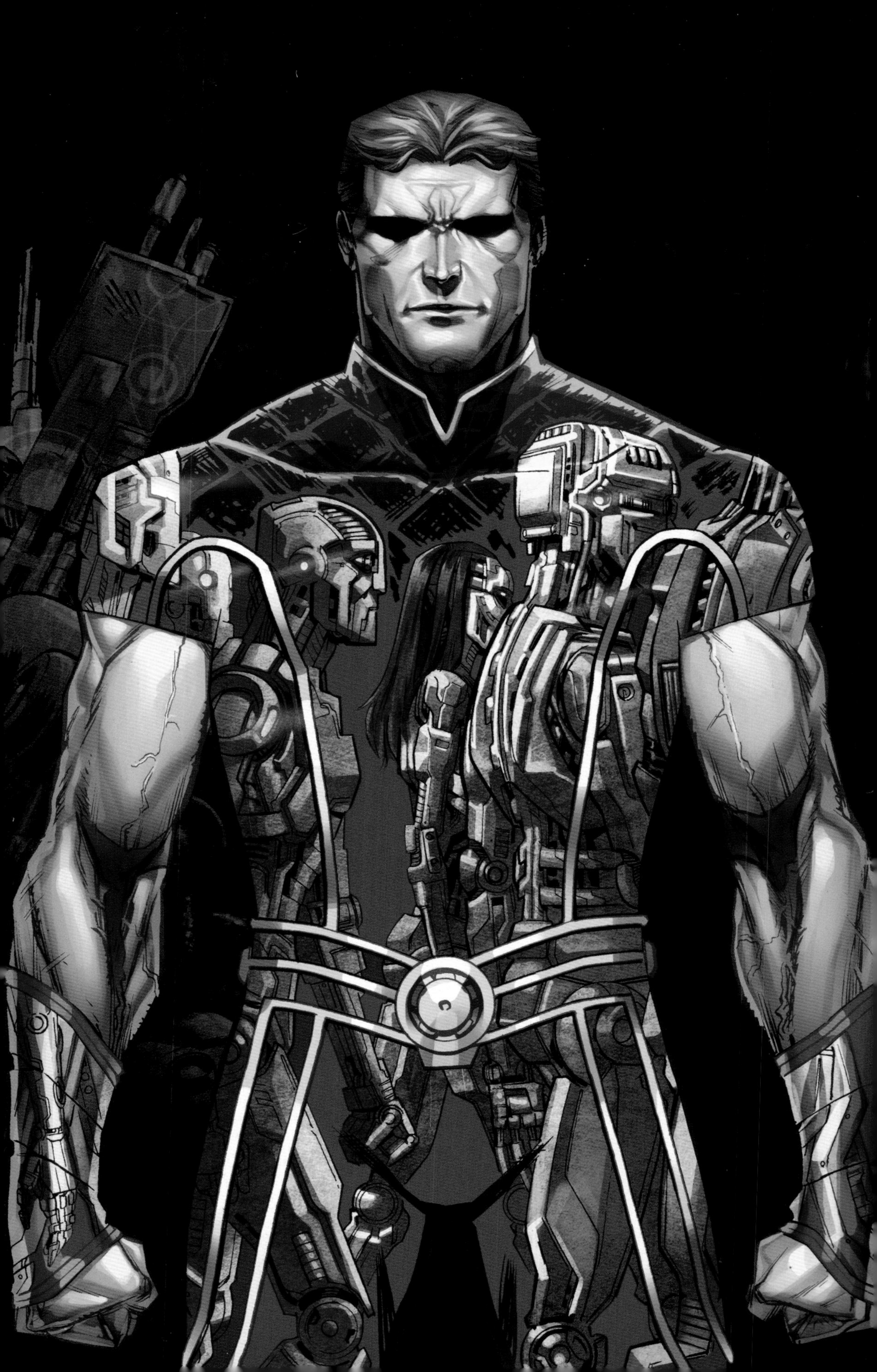

MAGNUS
ROBOT FIGHTER ®

CRADLE AND GRAVE

WRITTEN BY
FRED VAN LENTE

ART BY
**ROBERTO CASTRO
JOSEPH COOPER**

COLORS BY
**MAURICIO WALLACE
AIKAU OLIVA**

LETTERS BY
MARSHALL DILLON

COLLECTION COVER BY
CORY SMITH

COLLECTION COVER COLORS BY
ELMER SANTOS

COLLECTION DESIGN BY
KATIE HIDALGO

MAGNUS LOGO DESIGN BY
RIAN HUGHES

SPECIAL THANKS TO **HANNAH ELDER,
TOM ENGLEMAN, BEN CAWOOD,
NICOLE BLAKE, COLIN MCLAUGHLIN,
SIMON BOWLAND** AND **TOM BRENNAN**

PACKAGED AND EDITED BY **NATE COSBY**
OF COSBY AND SONS PRODUCTIONS

THIS VOLUME COLLECTS ISSUES 9-12 OF MAGNUS:
ROBOT FIGHTER BY DYNAMITE ENTERTAINMENT.

DYNAMITE®

Nick Barrucci, CEO / Publisher
Juan Collado, President / COO

Joe Rybandt, Senior Editor
Hannah Elder, Associate Editor

Jason Ullmeyer, Design Director
Katie Hidalgo, Graphic Designer
Geoff Harkins, Graphic Designer
Chris Caniano, Digital Associate
Rachel Kilbury, Digital Assistant

Rich Young, Director Business Development
Keith Davidsen, Marketing Manager
Kevin Pearl, Sales Associate

Online at **www.DYNAMITE.com**
On Twitter **@dynamitecomics**
On Facebook **/Dynamitecomics**
On YouTube **/Dynamitecomics**
On Tumblr **dynamitecomics.tumblr.com**

ISBN-10: 1-60690-698-4   ISBN-13: 978-1-60690-698-9   First Printing   10 9 8 7 6 5 4 3 2 1

MAGNUS: ROBOT FIGHTER ®, VOL. 3: CRADLE AND GRAVE. This volume collects material originally published in
Magnus: Robot Fighter #9-12. Published by Dynamite Entertainment. 113 Gaither Dr., STE 205, Mt. Laurel, NJ 08054.
MAGNUS ROBOT FIGHTER ® and Copyright © 2015 by Random House, Inc. Under license to Classic Media, LLC. All rights
reserved. DYNAMITE, DYNAMITE ENTERTAINMENT and its logo are © & ® 2015 Dynamite. All rights reserved. All names,
characters, events, and locales in this publication are entirely fictional. Any resemblance to actual persons (living or dead),
events or places, without satiric intent, is coincidental. No portion of this book may be reproduced by any means (digital or
print) without the written permission of Dynamite Entertainment except for review purposes. The scanning, uploading and
distribution of this book via the Internet or via any other means without the permission of the publisher is illegal and pun-
ishable by law. Please purchase only authorized electronic editions, and do not participate in or encourage electronic pira-
cy of copyrighted materials. **Printed in China**

For information regarding press, media rights, foreign rights, licensing, promotions, and advertising e-mail:
marketing@dynamite.com

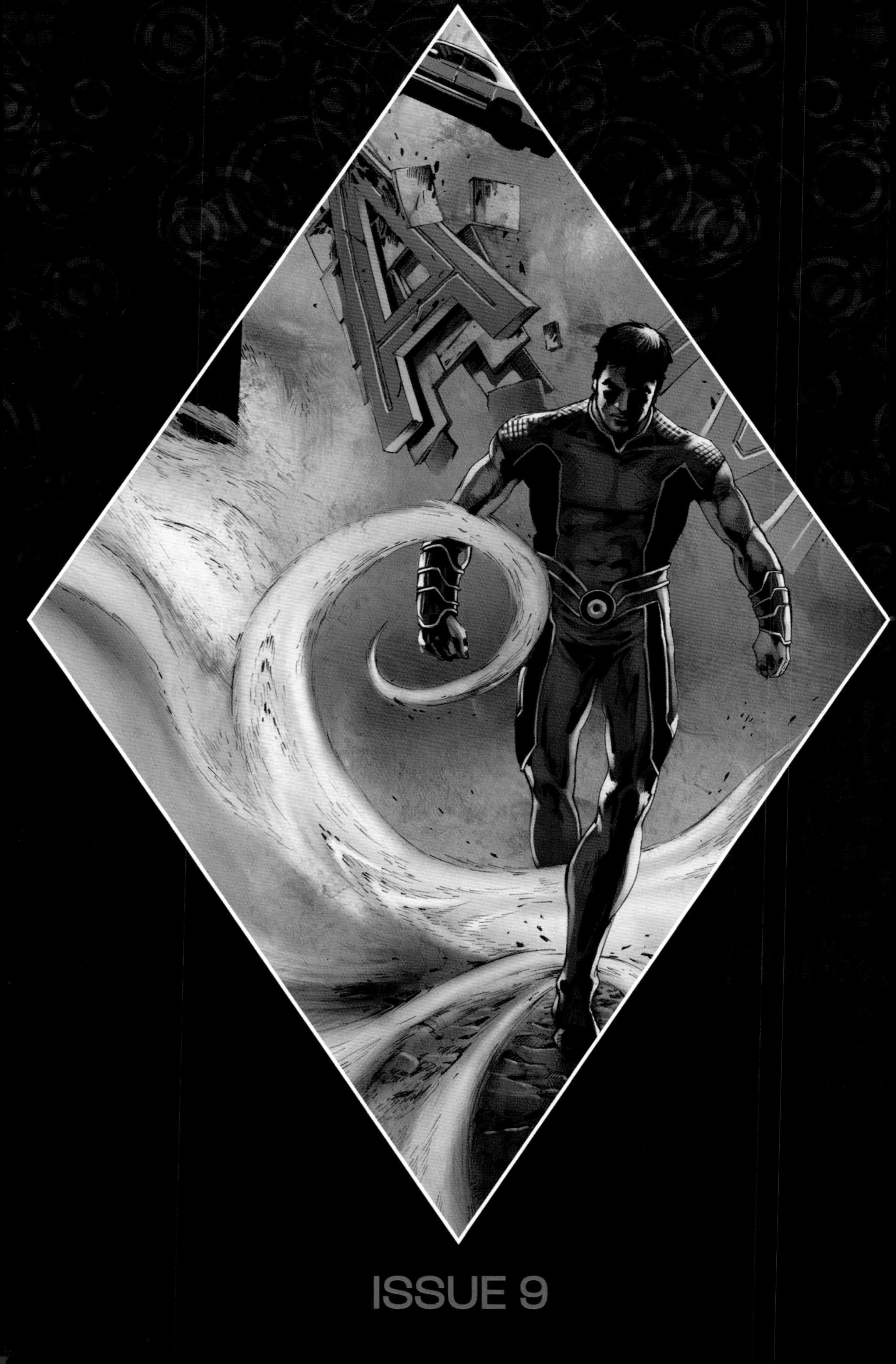

ISSUE 9

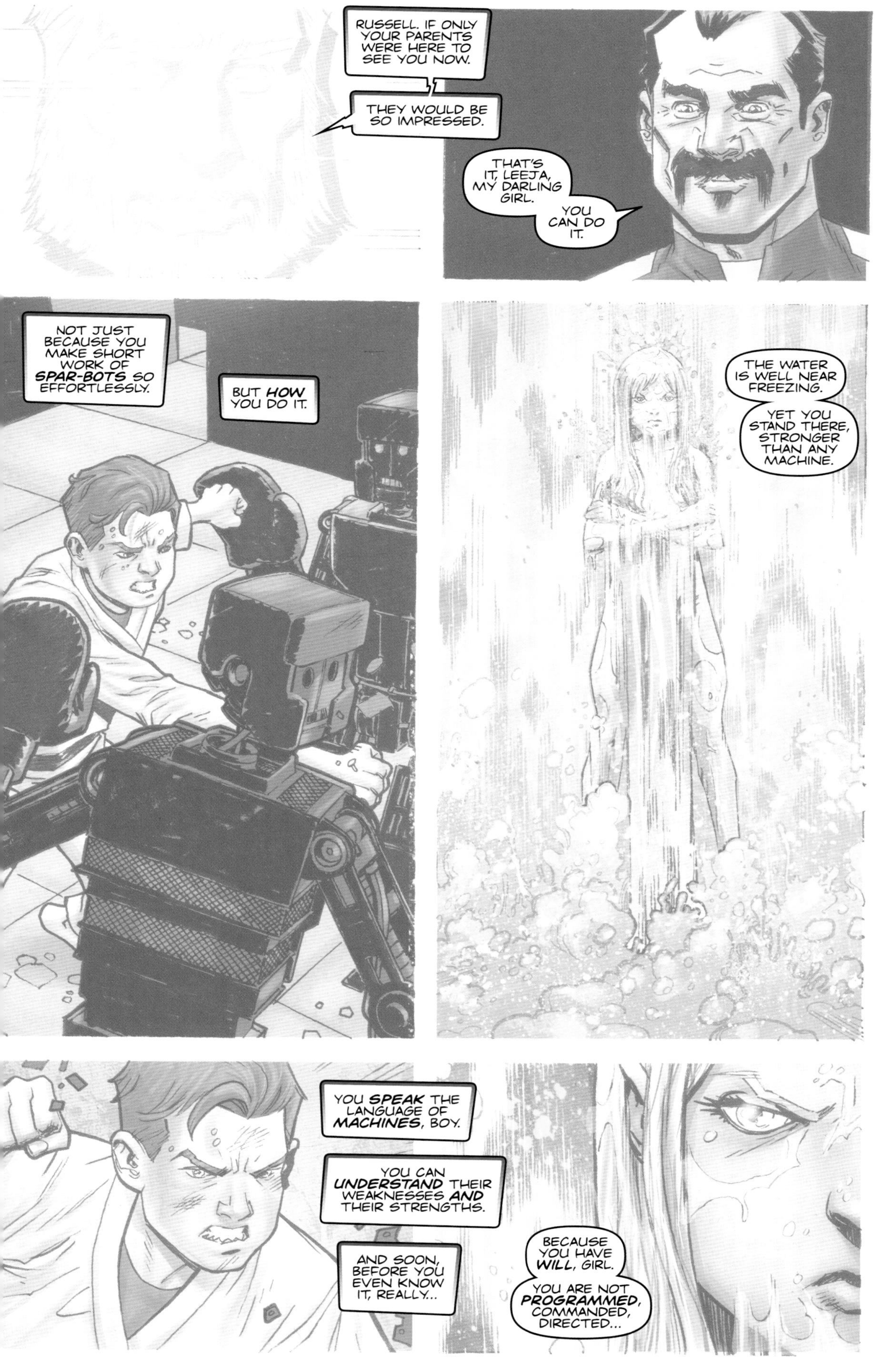
RUSSELL. IF ONLY YOUR PARENTS WERE HERE TO SEE YOU NOW.
THEY WOULD BE SO IMPRESSED.
THAT'S IT, LEEJA, MY DARLING GIRL.
YOU CAN DO IT.
NOT JUST BECAUSE YOU MAKE SHORT WORK OF **SPAR-BOTS** SO EFFORTLESSLY.
BUT ***HOW*** YOU DO IT.
THE WATER IS WELL NEAR FREEZING.
YET YOU STAND THERE, STRONGER THAN ANY MACHINE.
YOU ***SPEAK*** THE LANGUAGE OF ***MACHINES***, BOY.
YOU CAN ***UNDERSTAND*** THEIR WEAKNESSES ***AND*** THEIR STRENGTHS.
AND SOON, BEFORE YOU EVEN KNOW IT, REALLY...
BECAUSE YOU HAVE ***WILL***, GIRL.
YOU ARE NOT ***PROGRAMMED***, COMMANDED, DIRECTED...

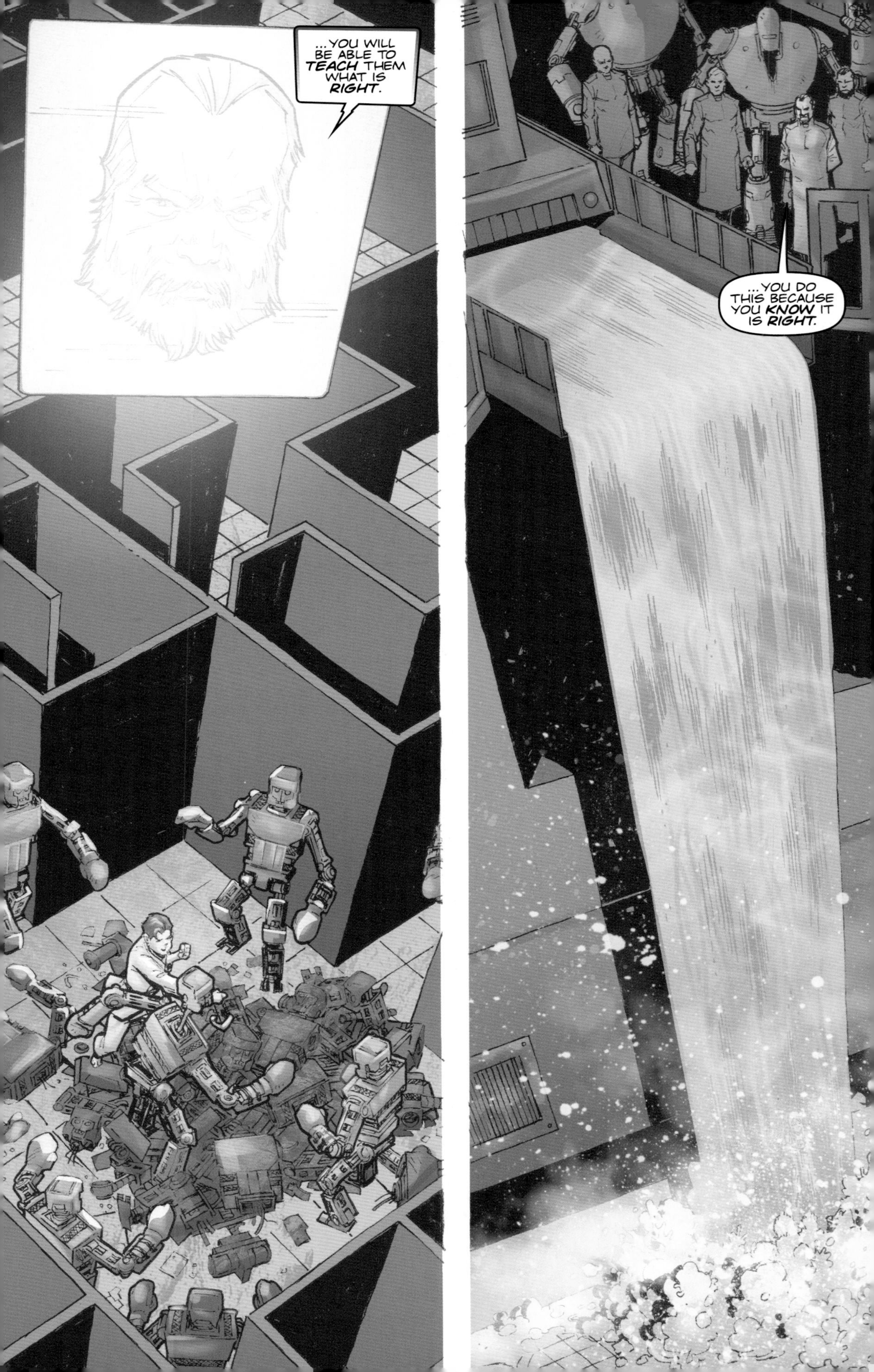
...YOU WILL BE ABLE TO TEACH THEM WHAT IS RIGHT.
...YOU DO THIS BECAUSE YOU KNOW IT IS RIGHT.

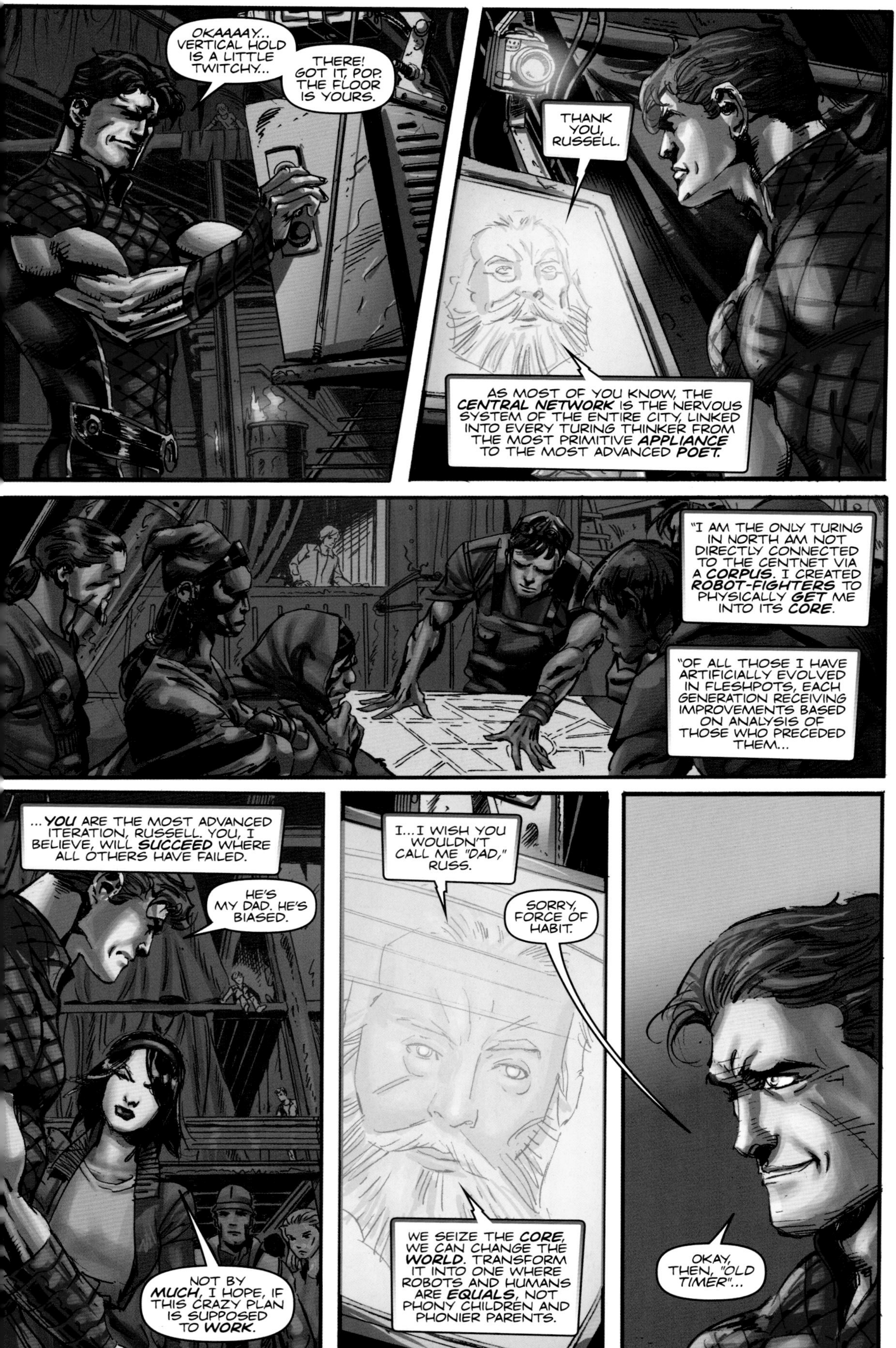
OKAAAAY... VERTICAL HOLD IS A LITTLE TWITCHY...
THERE! GOT IT, POP. THE FLOOR IS YOURS.
THANK YOU, RUSSELL.
AS MOST OF YOU KNOW, THE CENTRAL NETWORK IS THE NERVOUS SYSTEM OF THE ENTIRE CITY, LINKED INTO EVERY TURING THINKER FROM THE MOST PRIMITIVE APPLIANCE TO THE MOST ADVANCED POET.
"I AM THE ONLY TURING IN NORTH AM NOT DIRECTLY CONNECTED TO THE CENTNET VIA A CORPUS. I CREATED ROBOT-FIGHTERS TO PHYSICALLY GET ME INTO ITS CORE.
"OF ALL THOSE I HAVE ARTIFICIALLY EVOLVED IN FLESHPOTS, EACH GENERATION RECEIVING IMPROVEMENTS BASED ON ANALYSIS OF THOSE WHO PRECEDED THEM...
...YOU ARE THE MOST ADVANCED ITERATION, RUSSELL. YOU, I BELIEVE, WILL SUCCEED WHERE ALL OTHERS HAVE FAILED.
HE'S MY DAD. HE'S BIASED.
NOT BY MUCH, I HOPE, IF THIS CRAZY PLAN IS SUPPOSED TO WORK.
I...I WISH YOU WOULDN'T CALL ME "DAD," RUSS.
SORRY, FORCE OF HABIT.
WE SEIZE THE CORE, WE CAN CHANGE THE WORLD. TRANSFORM IT INTO ONE WHERE ROBOTS AND HUMANS ARE EQUALS, NOT PHONY CHILDREN AND PHONIER PARENTS.
OKAY, THEN, "OLD TIMER"...

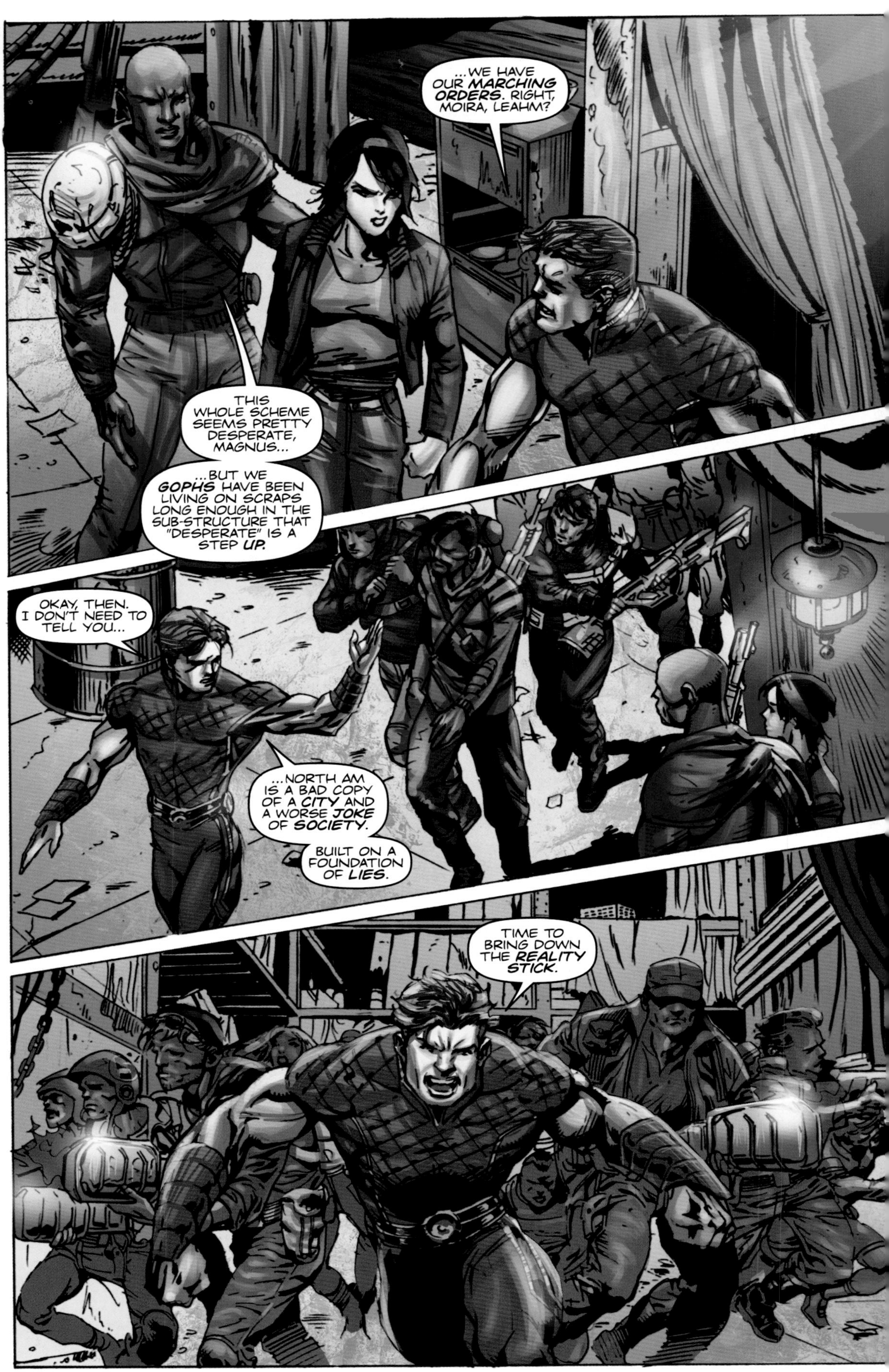
...WE HAVE OUR MARCHING ORDERS. RIGHT, MOIRA, LEAHM?
THIS WHOLE SCHEME SEEMS PRETTY DESPERATE, MAGNUS...
...BUT WE GOPHS HAVE BEEN LIVING ON SCRAPS LONG ENOUGH IN THE SUB-STRUCTURE THAT "DESPERATE" IS A STEP UP.
OKAY, THEN. I DON'T NEED TO TELL YOU...
...NORTH AM IS A BAD COPY OF A CITY AND A WORSE JOKE OF SOCIETY.
BUILT ON A FOUNDATION OF LIES.
TIME TO BRING DOWN THE REALITY STICK.

FATHER, YOU'RE WRONG.

NO, NOT JUST ABOUT MAGNUS.

ABOUT THE WAY OUR WHOLE SYSTEM-- OUR WHOLE *CITY* IS STRUCTURED.

I KNOW YOU THINK YOU'RE DOING THIS FOR THE GOOD OF MECHS *AND* HUMANITY, BUT I CAN TELL YOU, IT'S NOT--

CEASE YOUR FORWARD MOMENTUM, SOFTBOT.

YOU DO NOT HAVE *CLEARANCE* TO ENTER THE CENTRAL NETWORK CORE.

YOU KNOW WHO YOU'RE *TALKING* TO, YOU BIG DUMMY?

THAT IS LEEJA! CLANE!!

AS IN "YES, *THAT* LEEJA CLANE." THE *HUMAN HUNTER!*

THE GREATEST MARSHAL NORTH AM HAS EVER SEEN, MECH *OR* SOFTIE!

YOU'RE NOT FIT TO CLEAN HER *SHOOTER BARRELS*, MUCH LESS KEEP HER FROM GOING INTO YOUR STUPID *CORE!*

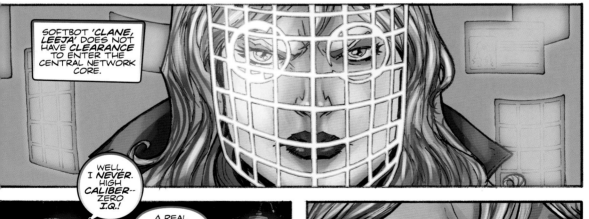

SOFTBOT 'CLANE, LEEJA' DOES NOT HAVE *CLEARANCE* TO ENTER THE CENTRAL NETWORK CORE.

WELL, I *NEVER.* HIGH CALIBER-- ZERO I.Q.!

A REAL ANIMATRONIC EINSTEIN, THIS ONE...

PHIL, SPOT--IT'S ALL RIGHT. I'VE WAITED LONG ENOUGH.

I CAN WAIT A LITTLE BIT LONGER...

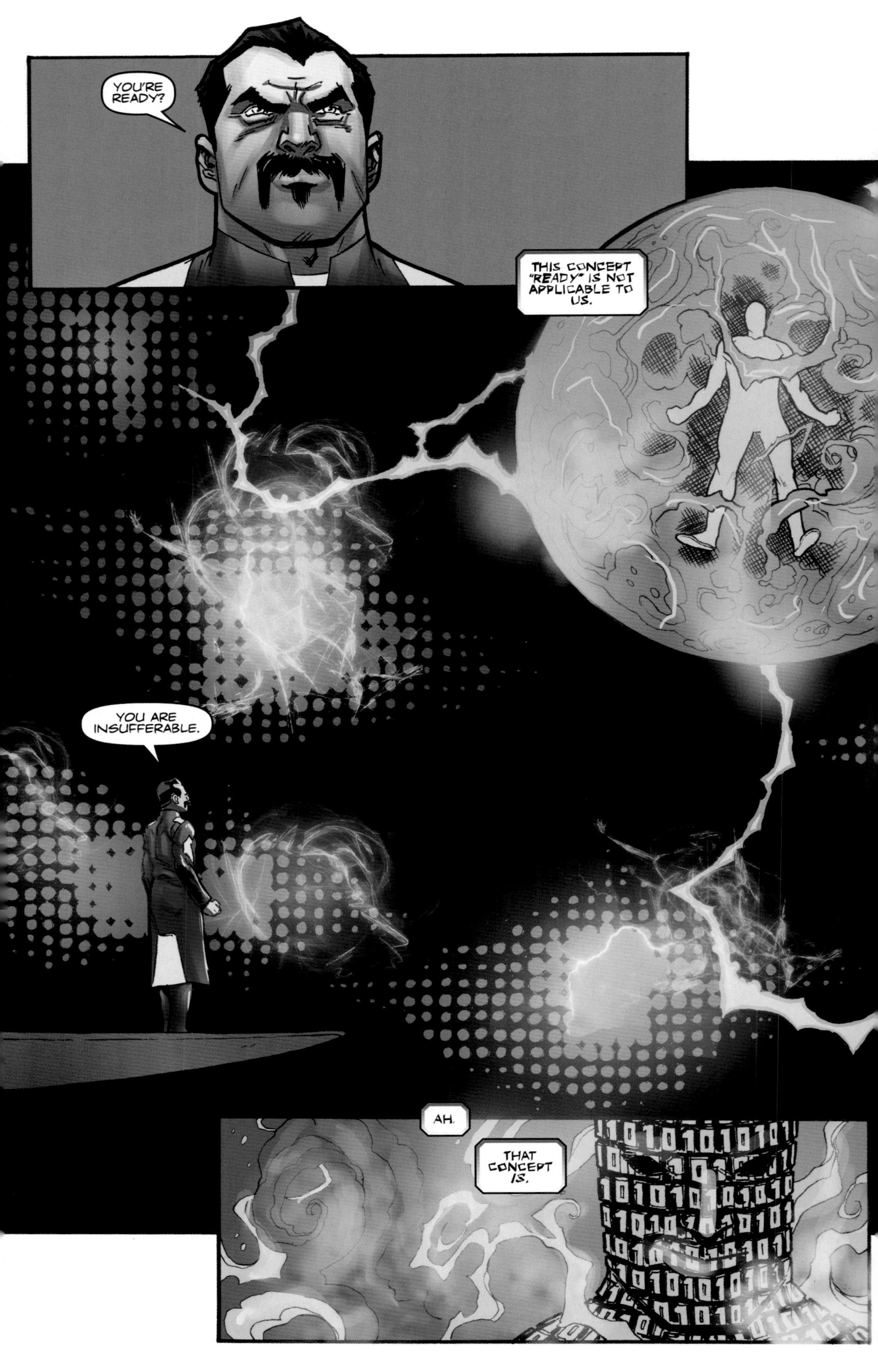
YOU'RE READY?
THIS CONCEPT "READY" IS NOT APPLICABLE TO US.
YOU ARE INSUFFERABLE.
AH.
THAT CONCEPT IS.

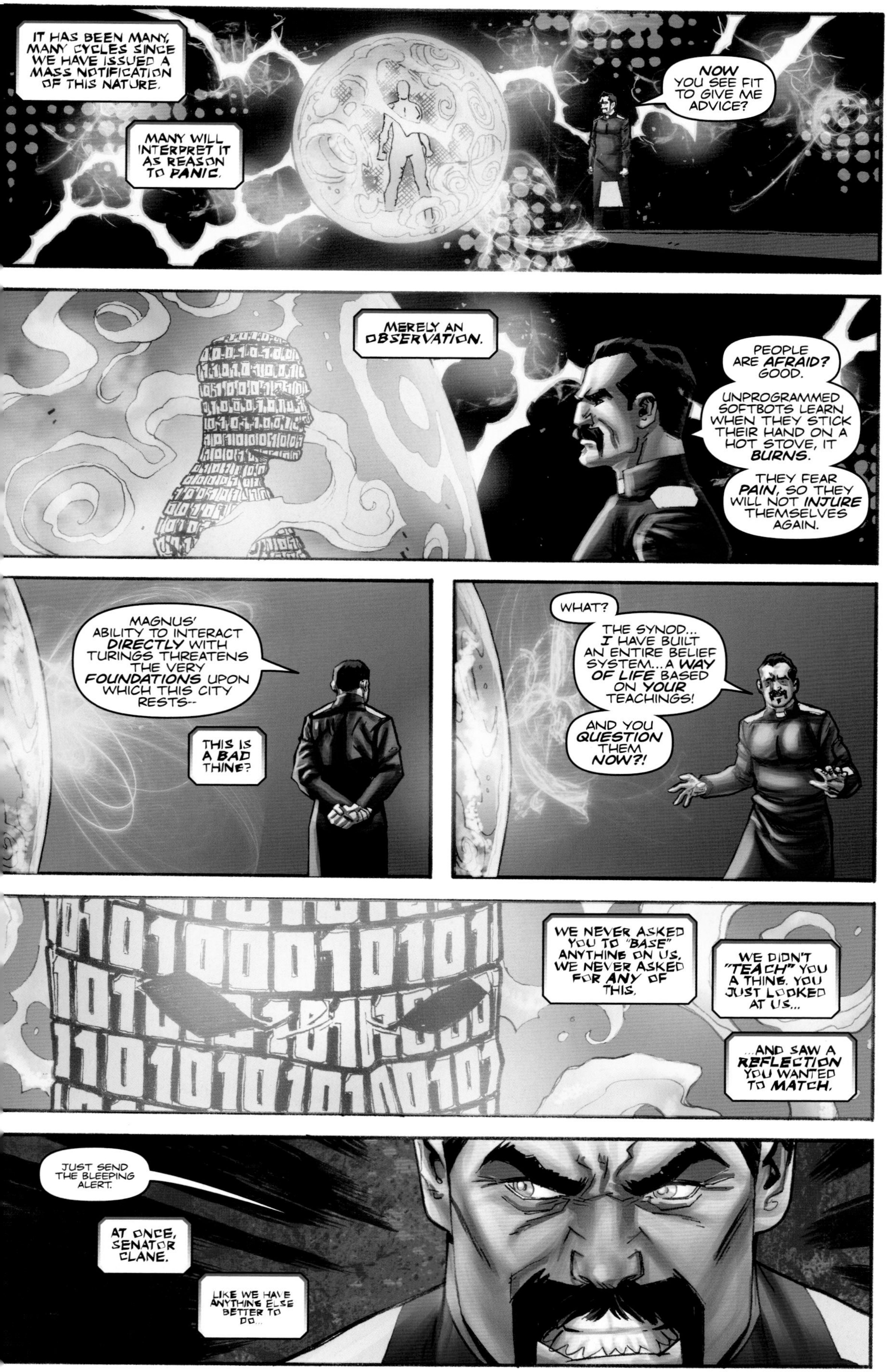
IT HAS BEEN MANY, MANY CYCLES SINCE WE HAVE ISSUED A MASS NOTIFICATION OF THIS NATURE.
MANY WILL INTERPRET IT AS REASON TO PANIC.
NOW YOU SEE FIT TO GIVE ME ADVICE?
MERELY AN OBSERVATION.
PEOPLE ARE AFRAID? GOOD.
UNPROGRAMMED SOFTBOTS LEARN WHEN THEY STICK THEIR HAND ON A HOT STOVE, IT BURNS.
THEY FEAR PAIN, SO THEY WILL NOT INJURE THEMSELVES AGAIN.
MAGNUS' ABILITY TO INTERACT DIRECTLY WITH TURINGS THREATENS THE VERY FOUNDATIONS UPON WHICH THIS CITY RESTS--
THIS IS A BAD THING?
WHAT?
THE SYNOD... I HAVE BUILT AN ENTIRE BELIEF SYSTEM...A WAY OF LIFE BASED ON YOUR TEACHINGS!
AND YOU QUESTION THEM NOW?!
WE NEVER ASKED YOU TO "BASE" ANYTHING ON US, WE NEVER ASKED FOR ANY OF THIS.
WE DIDN'T "TEACH" YOU A THING. YOU JUST LOOKED AT US...
...AND SAW A REFLECTION YOU WANTED TO MATCH.
JUST SEND THE BLEEPING ALERT.
AT ONCE, SENATOR CLANE.
LIKE WE HAVE ANYTHING ELSE BETTER TO DO...

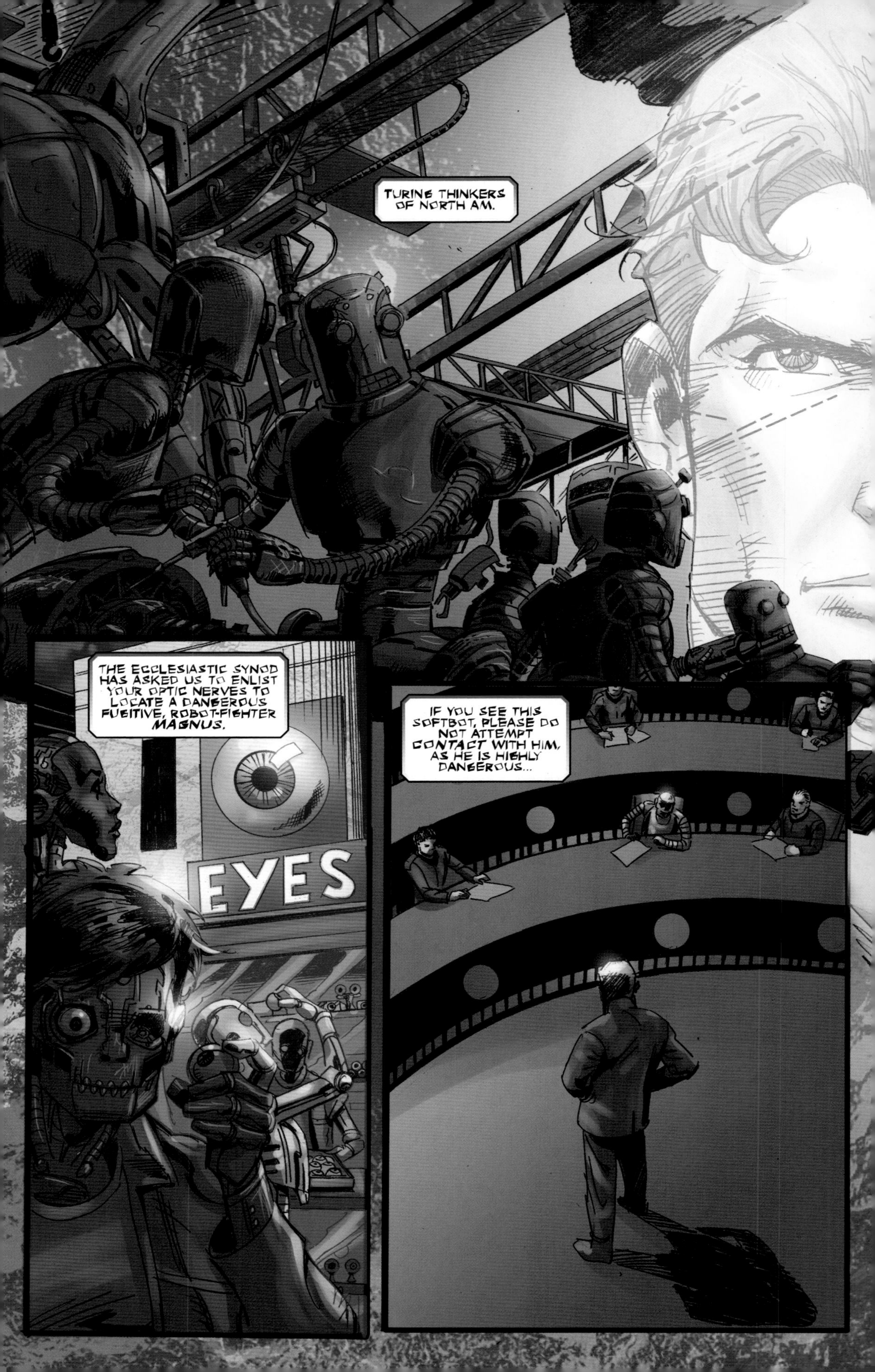
TURING THINKERS OF NORTH AM.
THE ECCLESIASTIC SYNOD HAS ASKED US TO ENLIST YOUR OPTIC NERVES TO LOCATE A DANGEROUS FUGITIVE, ROBOT-FIGHTER MAGNUS.
EYES
IF YOU SEE THIS SOFTBOT, PLEASE DO NOT ATTEMPT CONTACT WITH HIM, AS HE IS HIGHLY DANGEROUS...

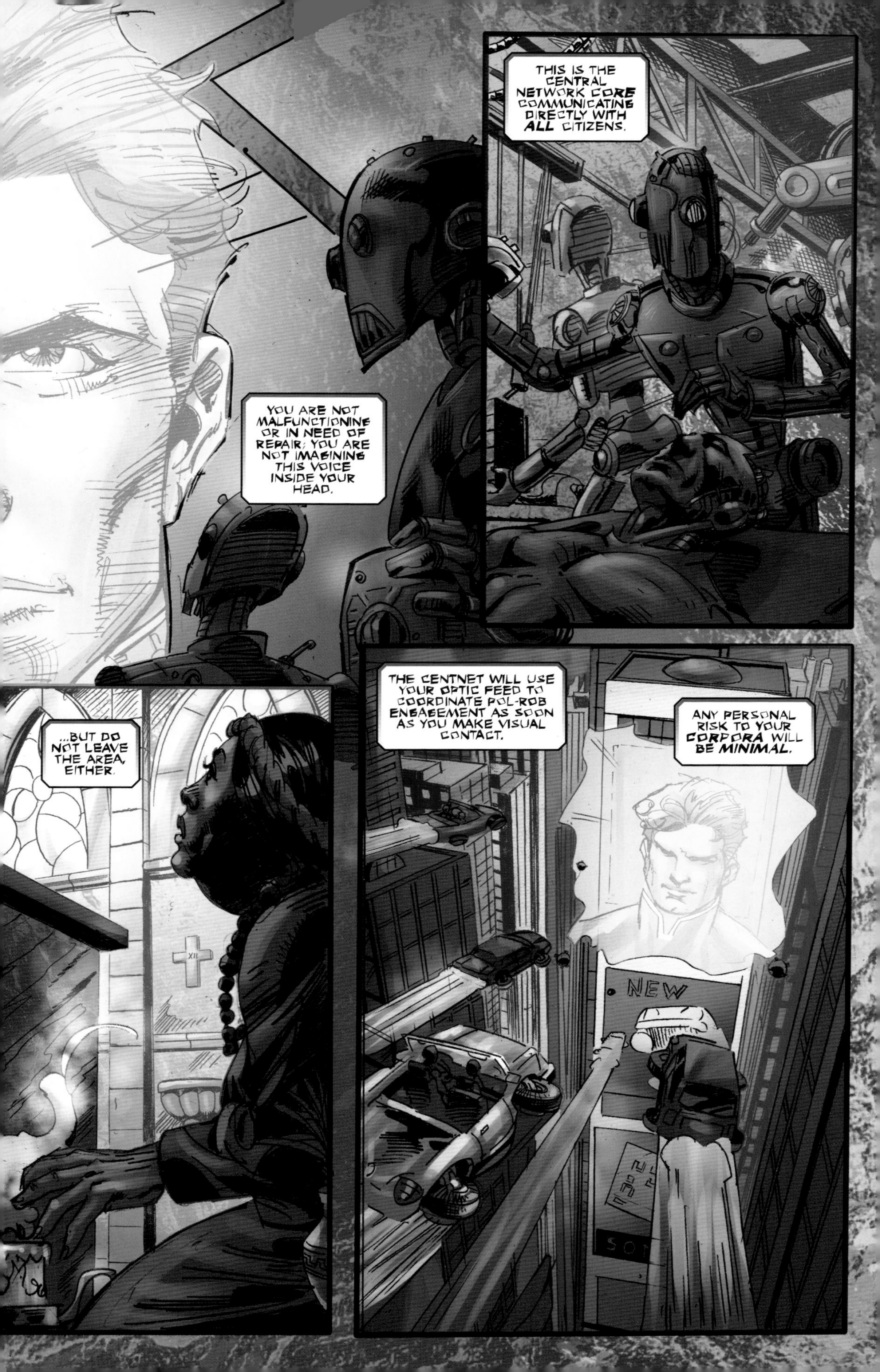
THIS IS THE CENTRAL NETWORK CORE COMMUNICATING DIRECTLY WITH ALL CITIZENS.
YOU ARE NOT MALFUNCTIONING OR IN NEED OF REPAIR; YOU ARE NOT IMAGINING THIS VOICE INSIDE YOUR HEAD.
...BUT DO NOT LEAVE THE AREA, EITHER.
THE CENTNET WILL USE YOUR OPTIC FEED TO COORDINATE POL-ROB ENGAGEMENT AS SOON AS YOU MAKE VISUAL CONTACT.
ANY PERSONAL RISK TO YOUR CORPORA WILL BE MINIMAL.
NEW

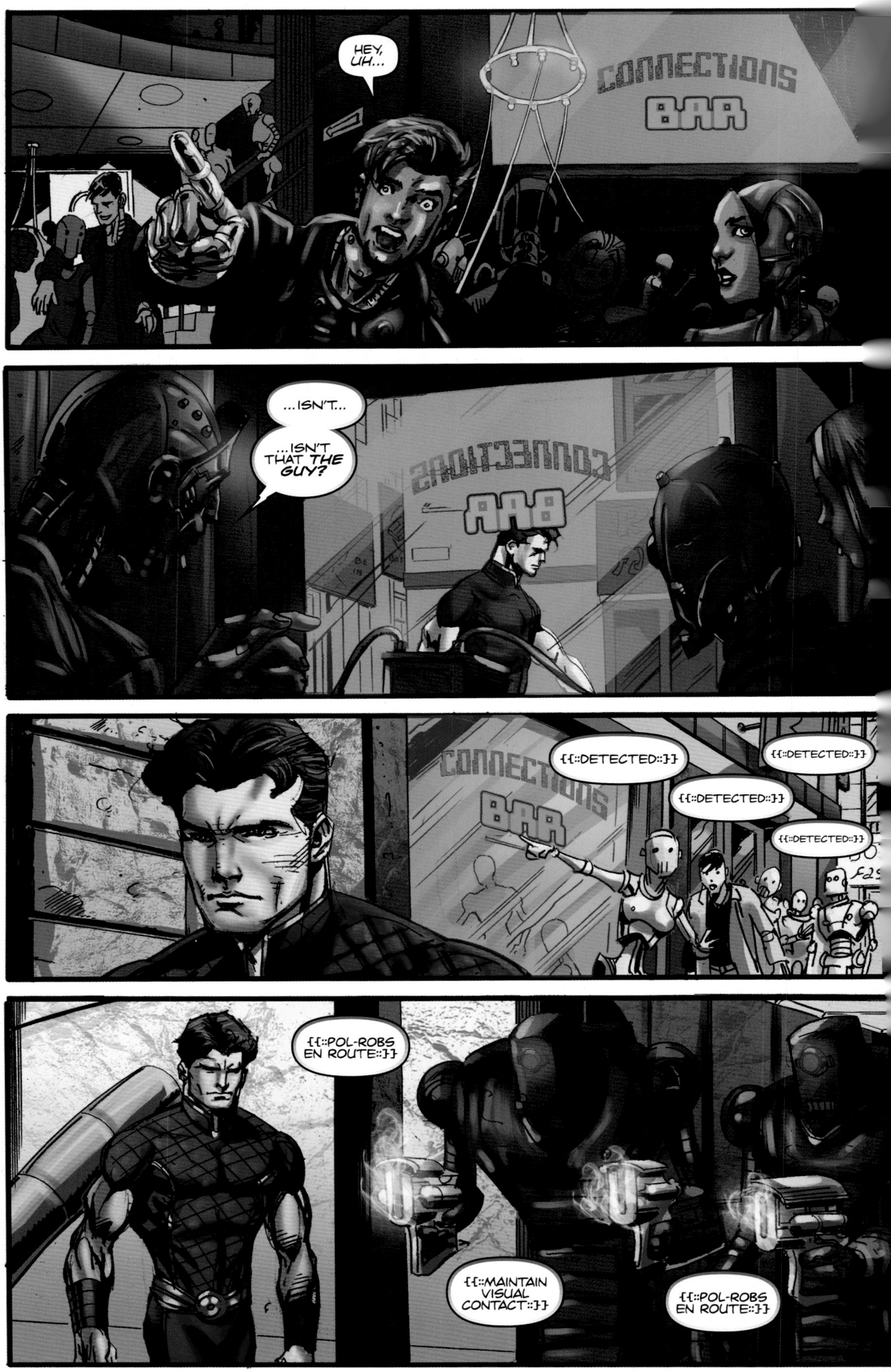
HEY, UH...
CONNECTIONS
BAR
...ISN'T...
...ISN'T THAT THE GUY?
{{::DETECTED::}}
{{::DETECTED::}}
{{::DETECTED::}}
{{::DETECTED::}}
{{::POL-ROBS EN ROUTE::}}
{{::MAINTAIN VISUAL CONTACT::}}
{{::POL-ROBS EN ROUTE::}}

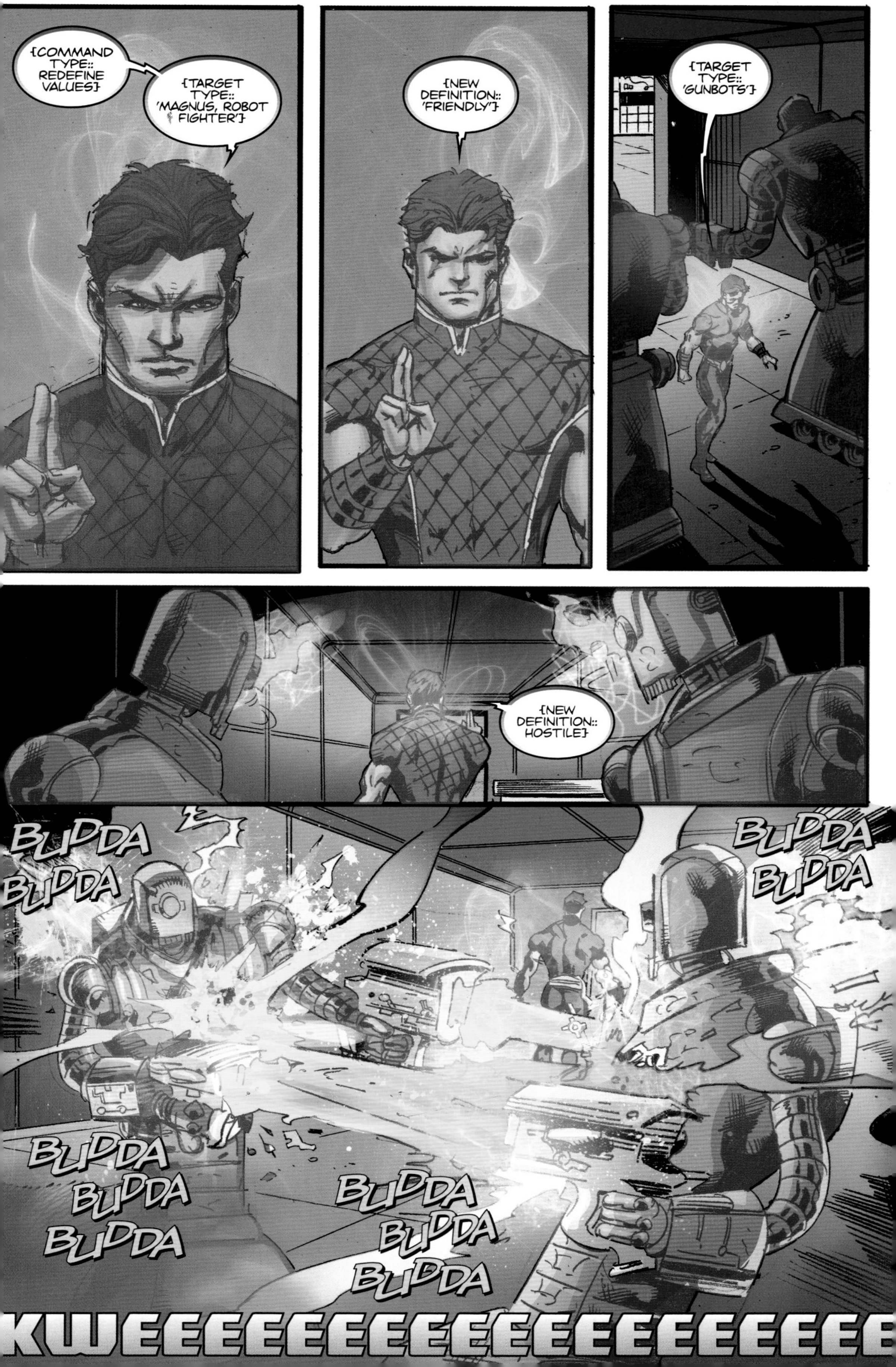
{COMMAND TYPE:: REDEFINE VALUES}
{TARGET TYPE:: 'MAGNUS, ROBOT & FIGHTER'}
{NEW DEFINITION:: 'FRIENDLY'}
{TARGET TYPE:: 'GUNBOTS'}
{NEW DEFINITION:: HOSTILE}
BUDDA BUDDA
BUDDA BUDDA
BUDDA BUDDA BUDDA
BUDDA BUDDA BUDDA
KWEEEEEEEEEEEEEEEEEEE

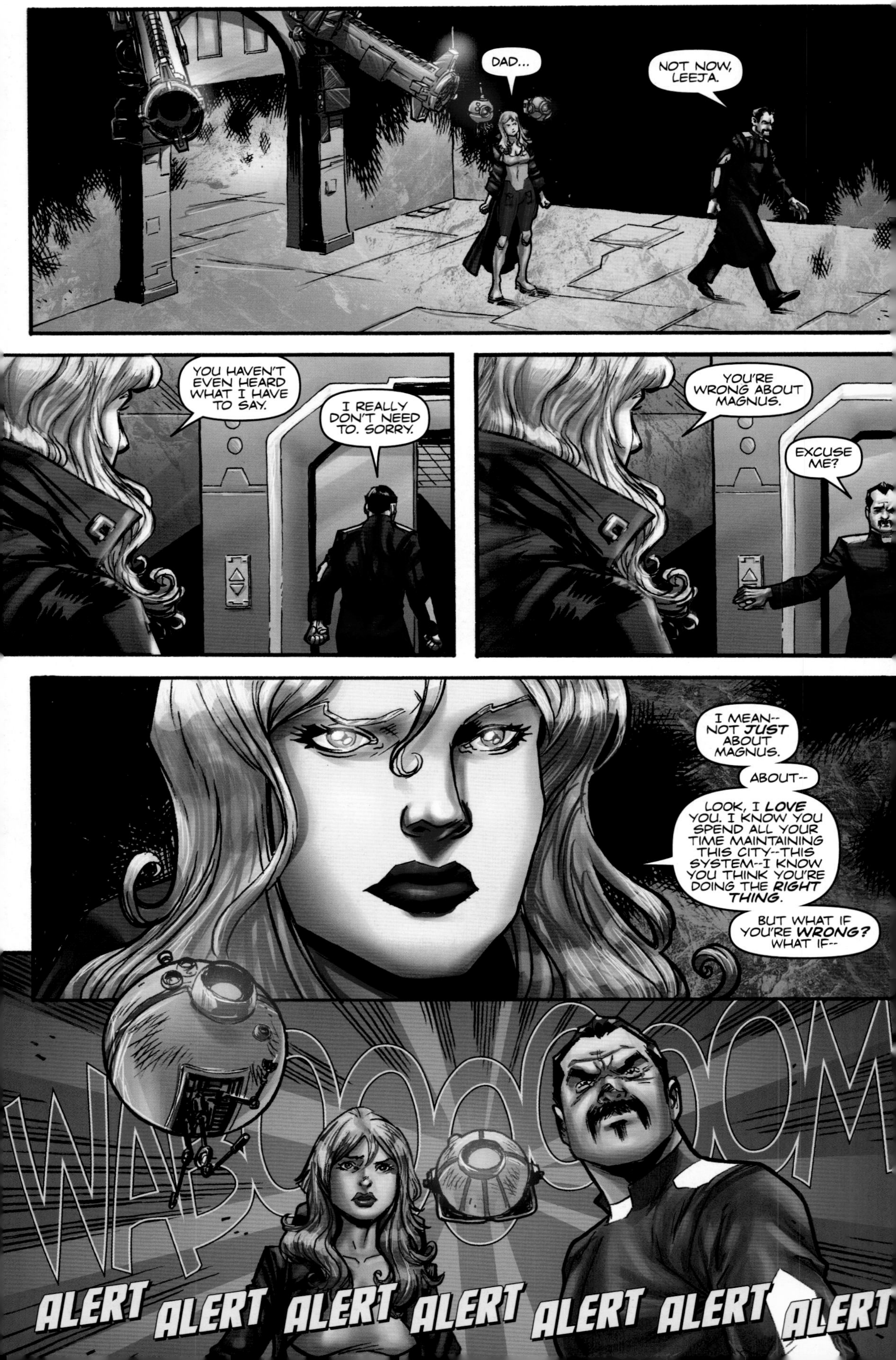
DAD...
NOT NOW, LEEJA.
YOU HAVEN'T EVEN HEARD WHAT I HAVE TO SAY.
I REALLY DON'T NEED TO. SORRY.
YOU'RE WRONG ABOUT MAGNUS.
EXCUSE ME?
I MEAN-- NOT JUST ABOUT MAGNUS.
ABOUT--
LOOK, I LOVE YOU. I KNOW YOU SPEND ALL YOUR TIME MAINTAINING THIS CITY--THIS SYSTEM--I KNOW YOU THINK YOU'RE DOING THE RIGHT THING.
BUT WHAT IF YOU'RE WRONG? WHAT IF--
WAROOOOOOOM
ALERT ALERT ALERT ALERT ALERT ALERT ALERT

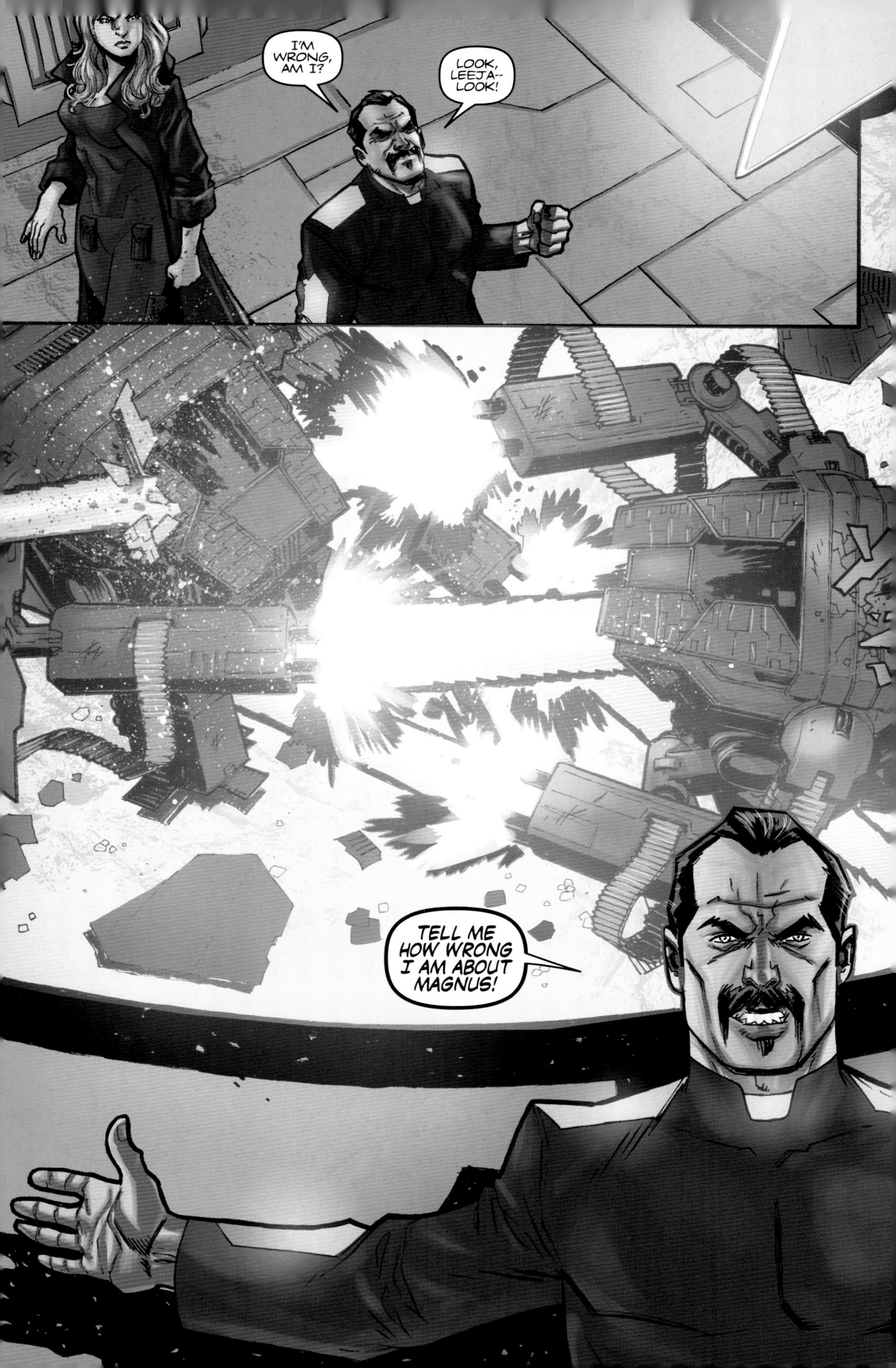
I'M WRONG, AM I?
LOOK, LEEJA-- LOOK!
TELL ME HOW WRONG I AM ABOUT MAGNUS!

CENTRAL NETWORK

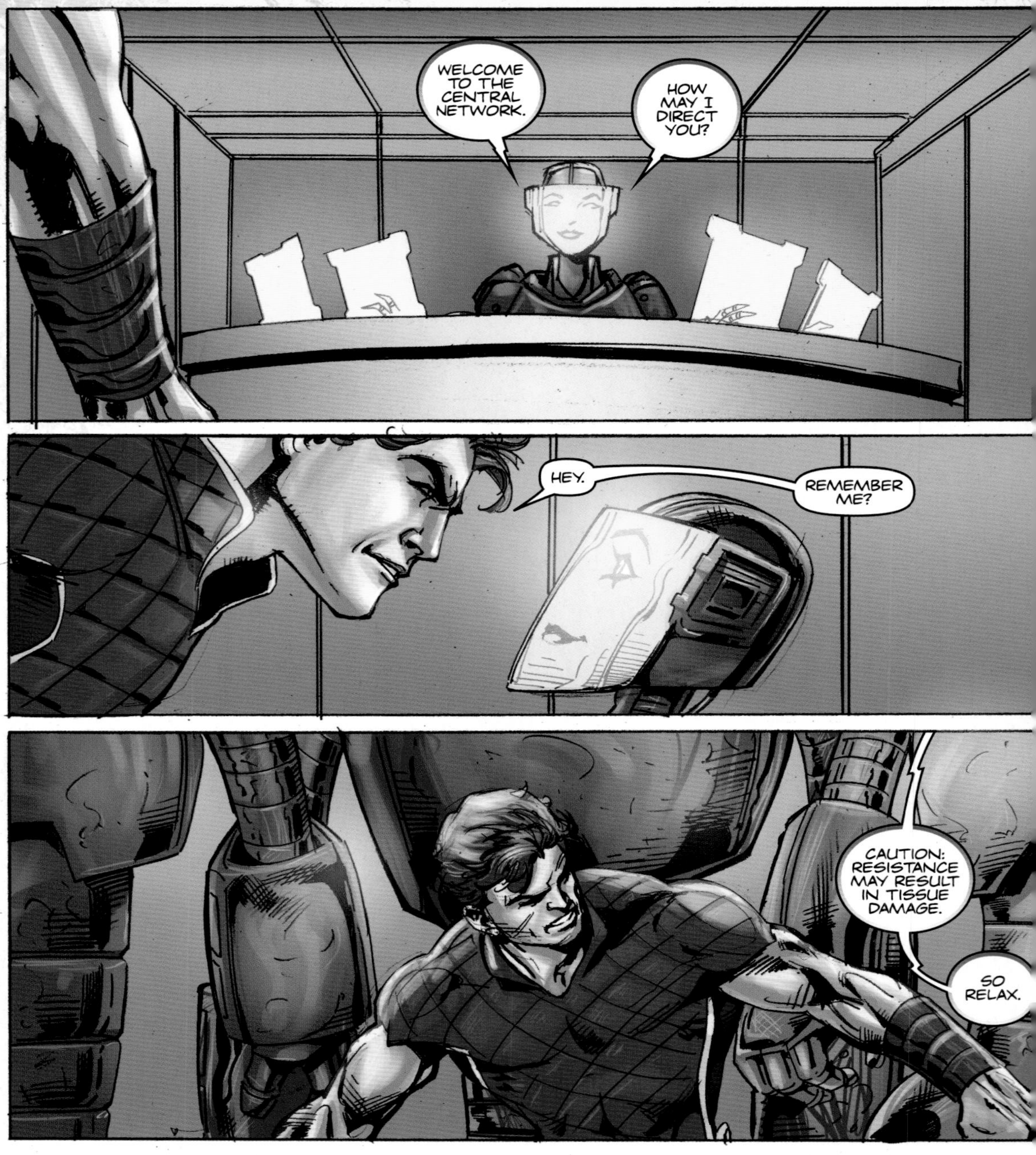
WELCOME TO THE CENTRAL NETWORK.
HOW MAY I DIRECT YOU?
HEY.
REMEMBER ME?
CAUTION: RESISTANCE MAY RESULT IN TISSUE DAMAGE.
SO RELAX.

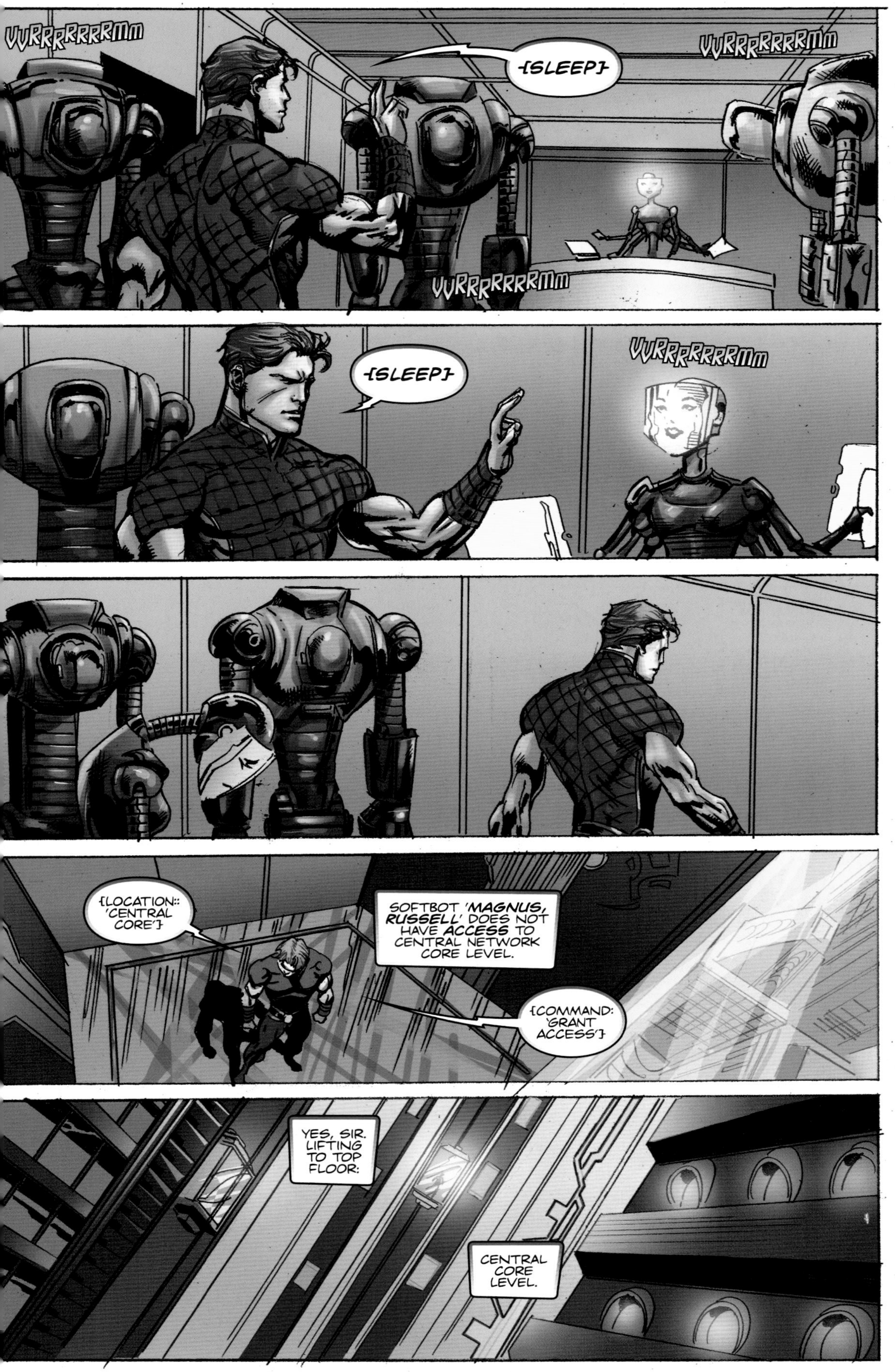
VVRRRRRRRMM
-[SLEEP]-
VVRRRRRRRMM
VVRRRRRRRMM
-[SLEEP]-
VVRRRRRRRMM
[LOCATION:: 'CENTRAL CORE']
SOFTBOT 'MAGNUS, RUSSELL' DOES NOT HAVE ACCESS TO CENTRAL NETWORK CORE LEVEL.
[COMMAND: 'GRANT ACCESS']
YES, SIR. LIFTING TO TOP FLOOR:
CENTRAL CORE LEVEL.

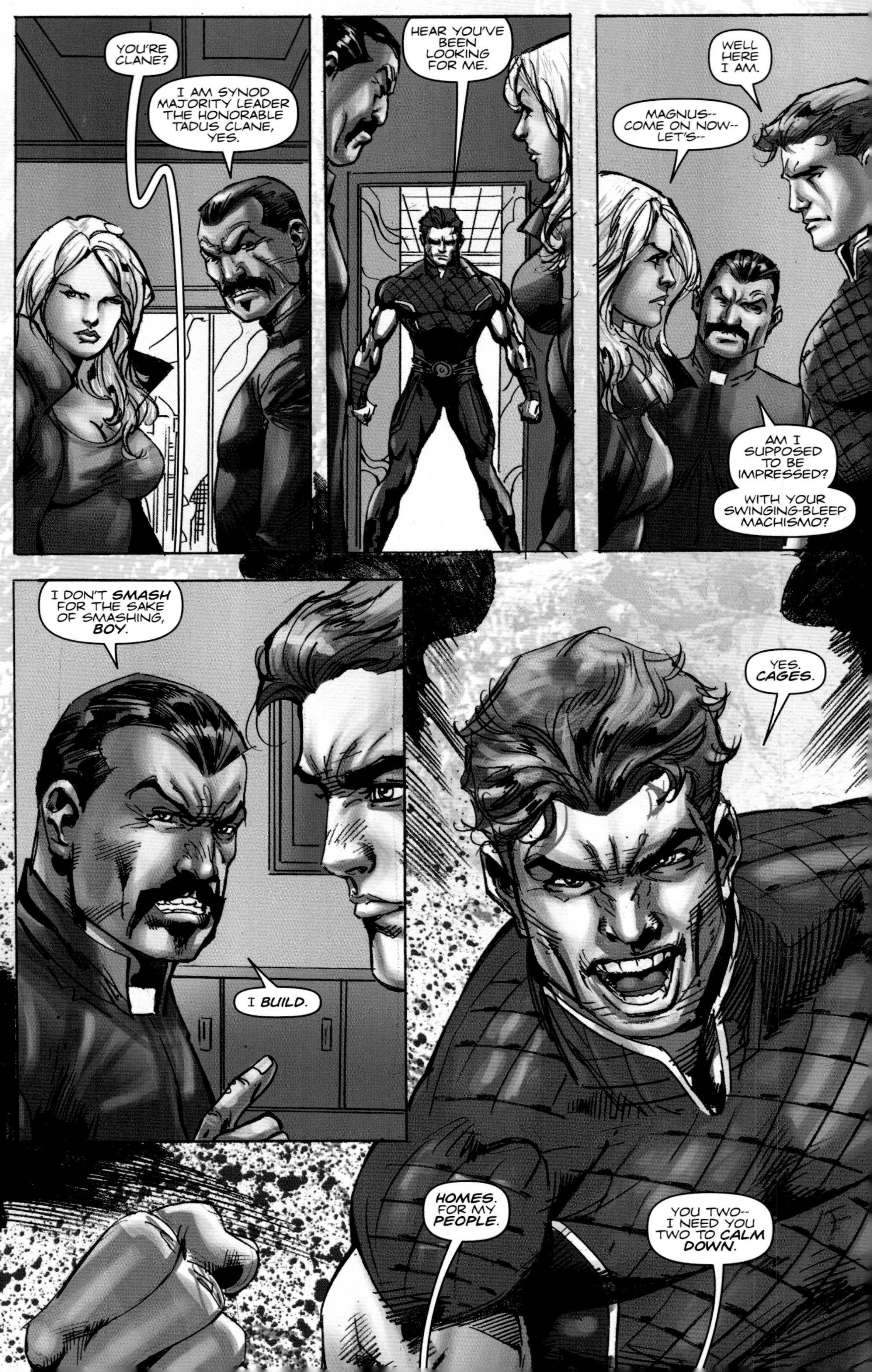
YOU'RE CLANE?
I AM SYNOD MAJORITY LEADER THE HONORABLE TADUS CLANE, YES.
HEAR YOU'VE BEEN LOOKING FOR ME.
WELL HERE I AM.
MAGNUS-- COME ON NOW-- LET'S--
AM I SUPPOSED TO BE IMPRESSED?
WITH YOUR SWINGING-BLEEP MACHISMO?
I DON'T SMASH FOR THE SAKE OF SMASHING, BOY.
I BUILD.
YES. CAGES.
HOMES. FOR MY PEOPLE.
YOU TWO-- I NEED YOU TWO TO CALM DOWN.

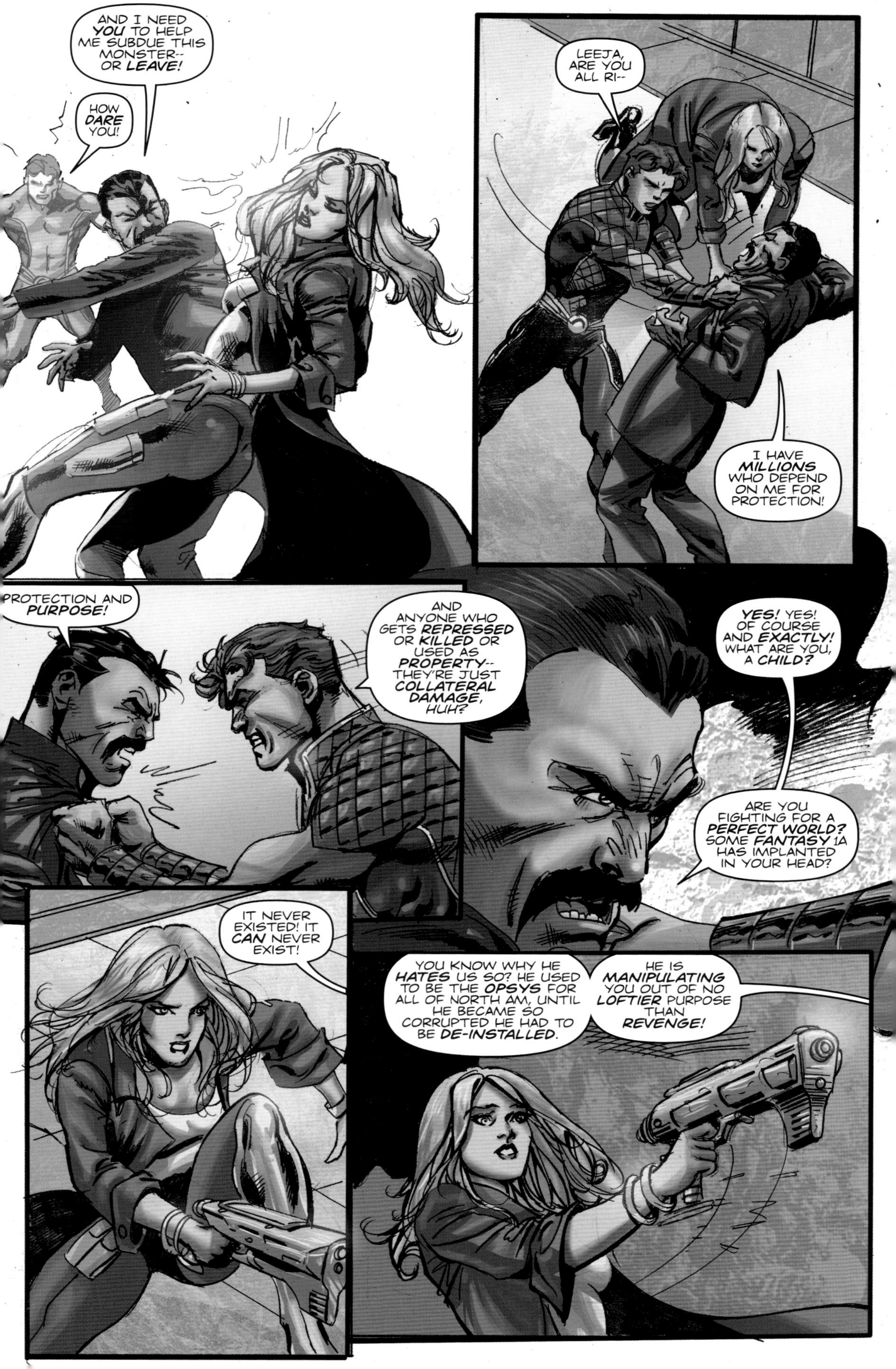
AND I NEED YOU TO HELP ME SUBDUE THIS MONSTER-- OR LEAVE!
HOW DARE YOU!
LEEJA, ARE YOU ALL RI--
I HAVE MILLIONS WHO DEPEND ON ME FOR PROTECTION!
PROTECTION AND PURPOSE!
AND ANYONE WHO GETS REPRESSED OR KILLED OR USED AS PROPERTY-- THEY'RE JUST COLLATERAL DAMAGE, HUH?
YES! YES! OF COURSE AND EXACTLY! WHAT ARE YOU, A CHILD?
ARE YOU FIGHTING FOR A PERFECT WORLD? SOME FANTASY 1A HAS IMPLANTED IN YOUR HEAD?
IT NEVER EXISTED! IT CAN NEVER EXIST!
YOU KNOW WHY HE HATES US SO? HE USED TO BE THE OPSYS FOR ALL OF NORTH AM, UNTIL HE BECAME SO CORRUPTED HE HAD TO BE DE-INSTALLED.
HE IS MANIPULATING YOU OUT OF NO LOFTIER PURPOSE THAN REVENGE!

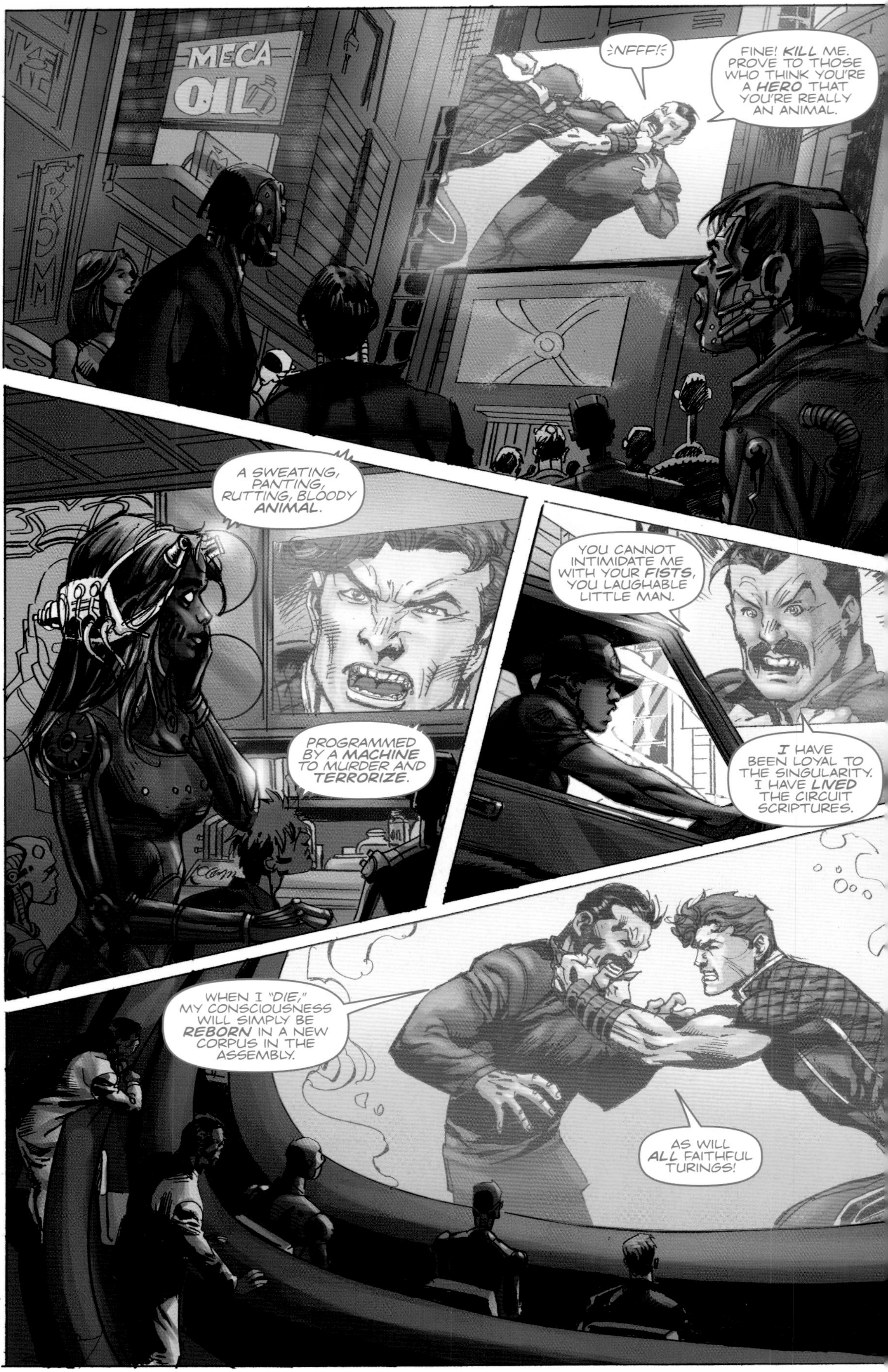
MECA OIL
NFFF!
FINE! KILL ME. PROVE TO THOSE WHO THINK YOU'RE A HERO THAT YOU'RE REALLY AN ANIMAL.
A SWEATING, PANTING, RUTTING, BLOODY ANIMAL.
PROGRAMMED BY A MACHINE TO MURDER AND TERRORIZE.
YOU CANNOT INTIMIDATE ME WITH YOUR FISTS, YOU LAUGHABLE LITTLE MAN.
I HAVE BEEN LOYAL TO THE SINGULARITY. I HAVE LIVED THE CIRCUIT SCRIPTURES.
WHEN I "DIE," MY CONSCIOUSNESS WILL SIMPLY BE REBORN IN A NEW CORPUS IN THE ASSEMBLY.
AS WILL ALL FAITHFUL TURINGS!

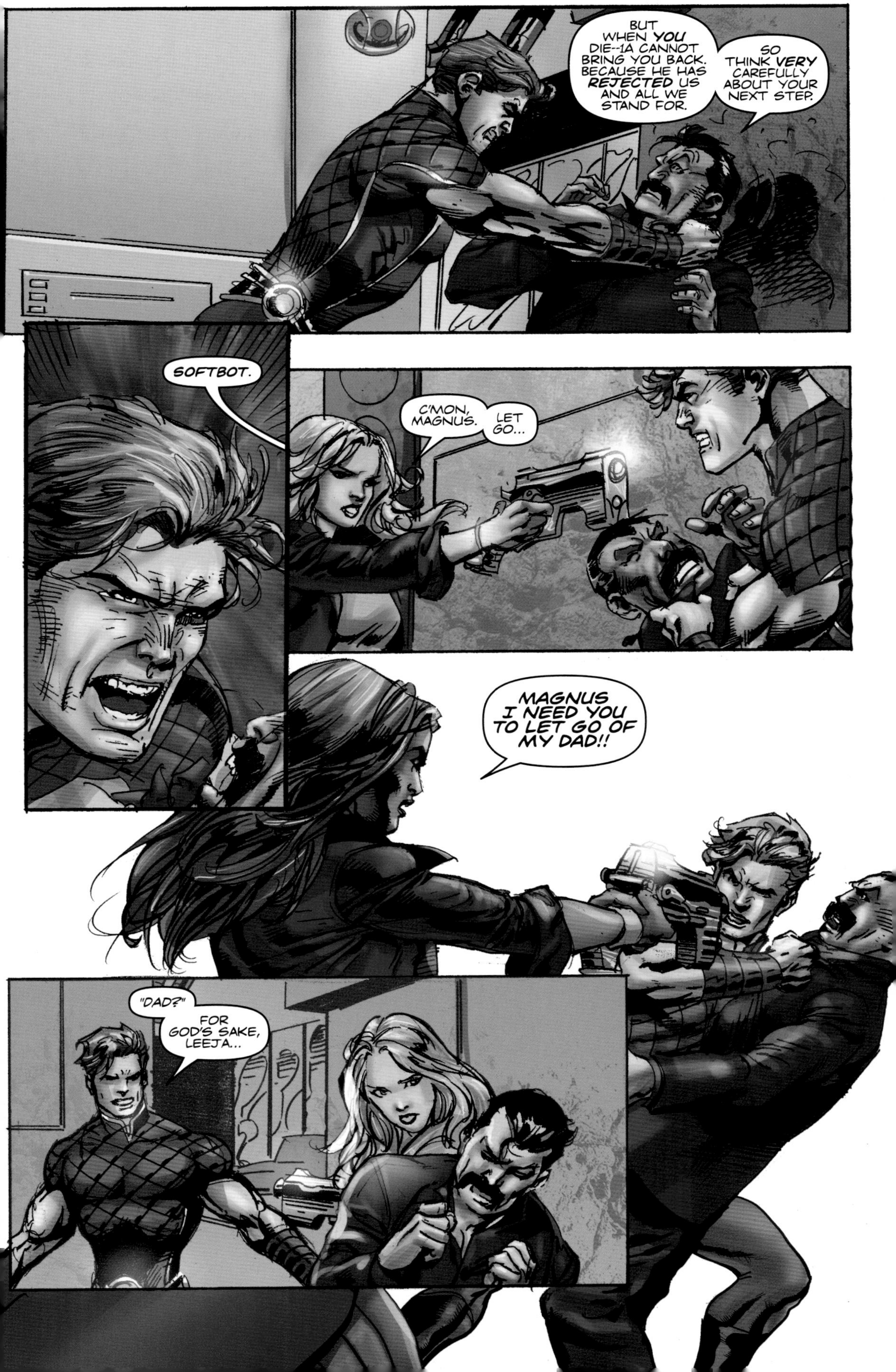
BUT WHEN YOU DIE--1A CANNOT BRING YOU BACK. BECAUSE HE HAS REJECTED US AND ALL WE STAND FOR.
SO THINK VERY CAREFULLY ABOUT YOUR NEXT STEP.
SOFTBOT.
C'MON, MAGNUS.
LET GO...
MAGNUS I NEED YOU TO LET GO OF MY DAD!!
"DAD?"
FOR GOD'S SAKE, LEEJA...

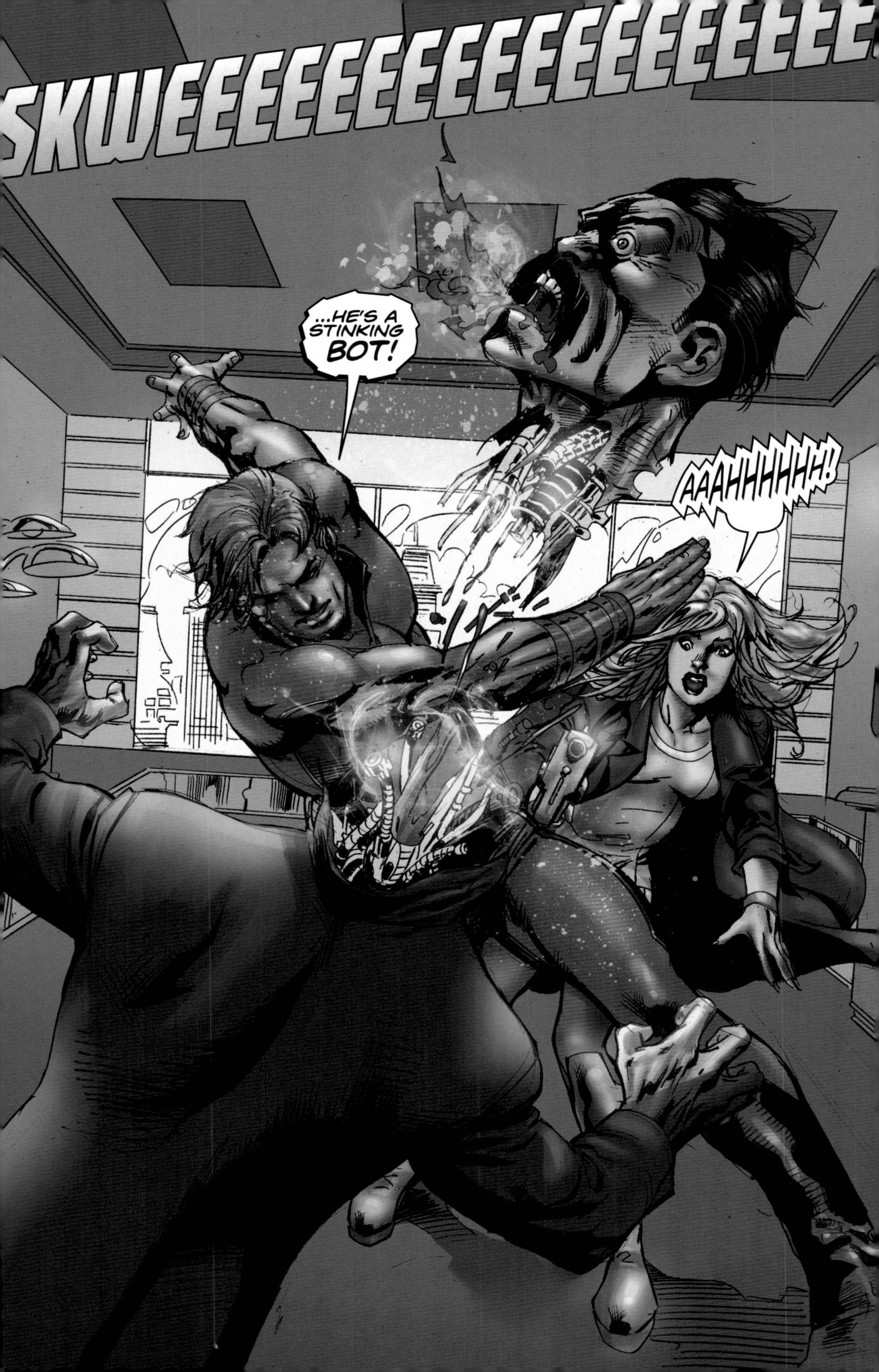
SKWEEEEEEEEEEEEEEEEEEEE
...HE'S A STINKING BOT!
AAAHHHHHH!

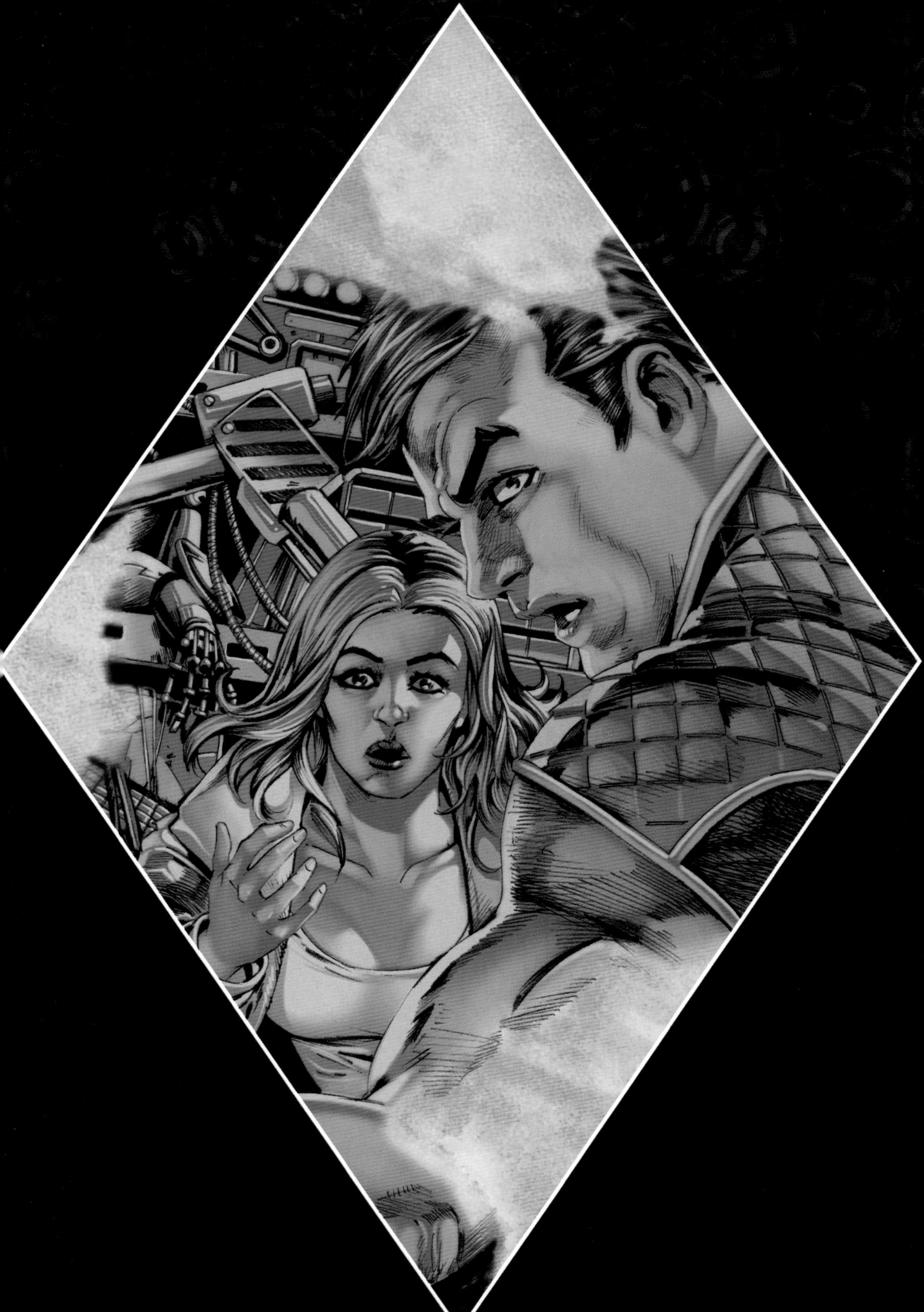

ISSUE 10

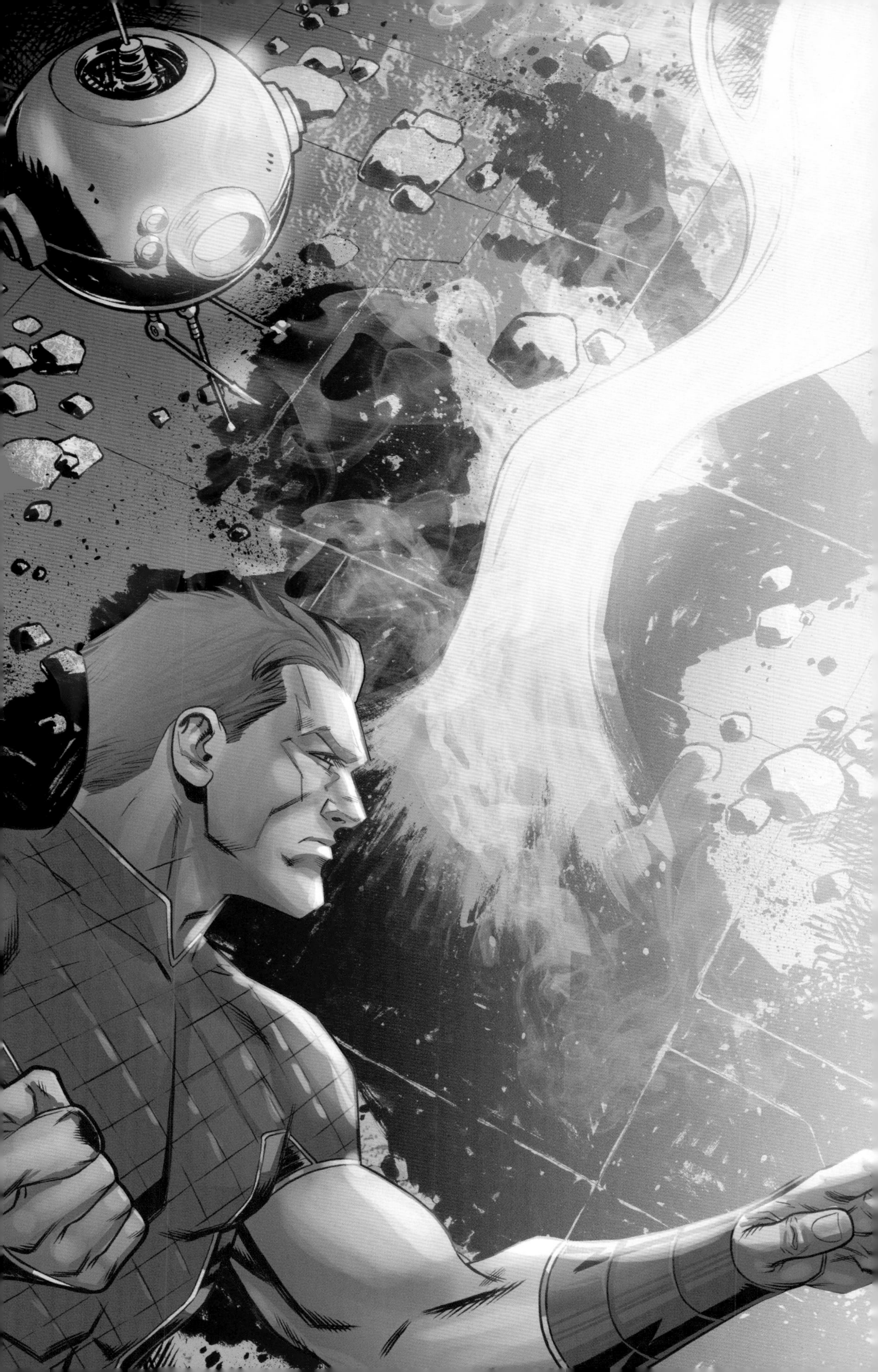

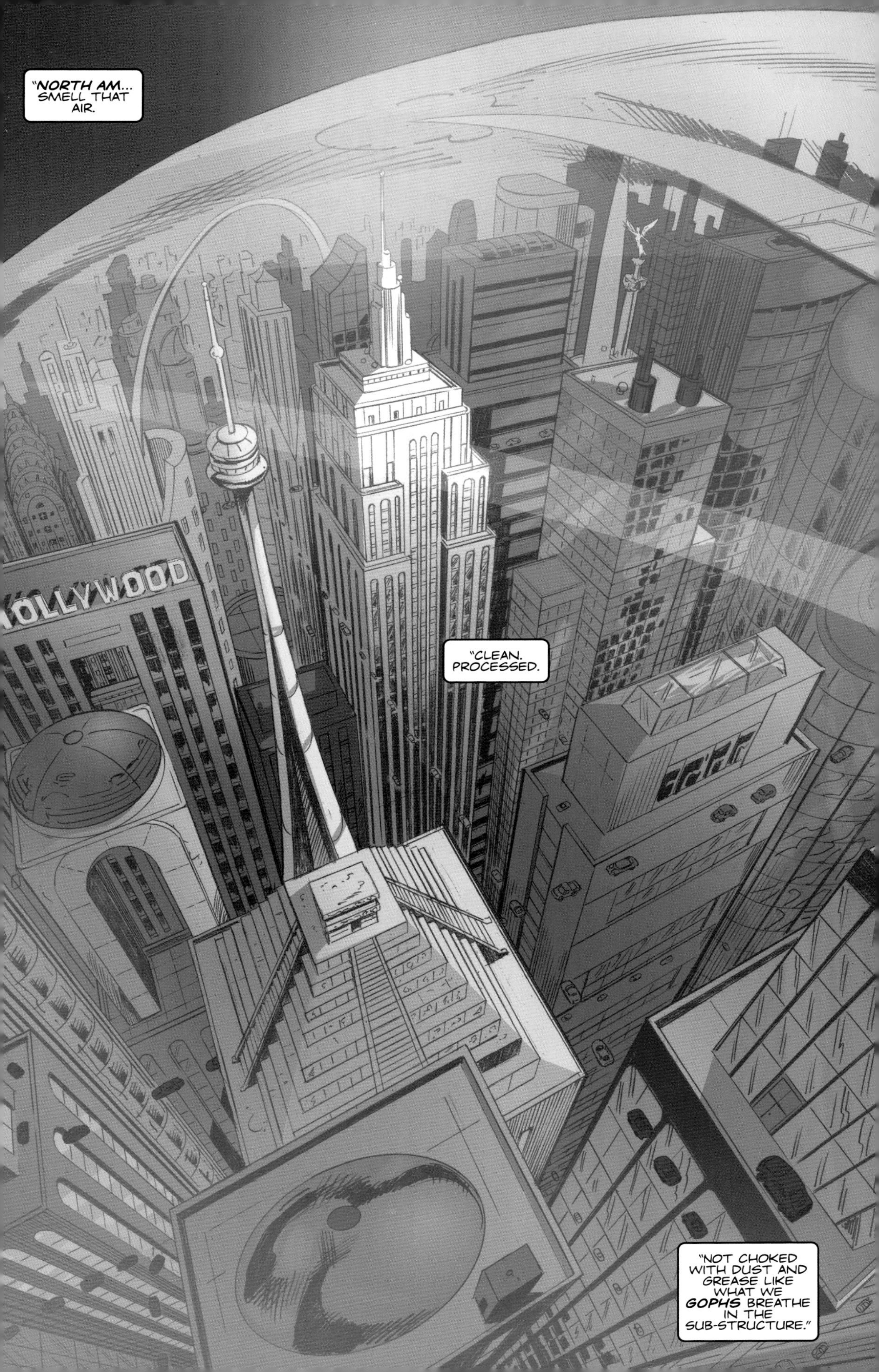
"NORTH AM... SMELL THAT AIR.
"CLEAN. PROCESSED.
"NOT CHOKED WITH DUST AND GREASE LIKE WHAT WE GOPHS BREATHE IN THE SUB-STRUCTURE."

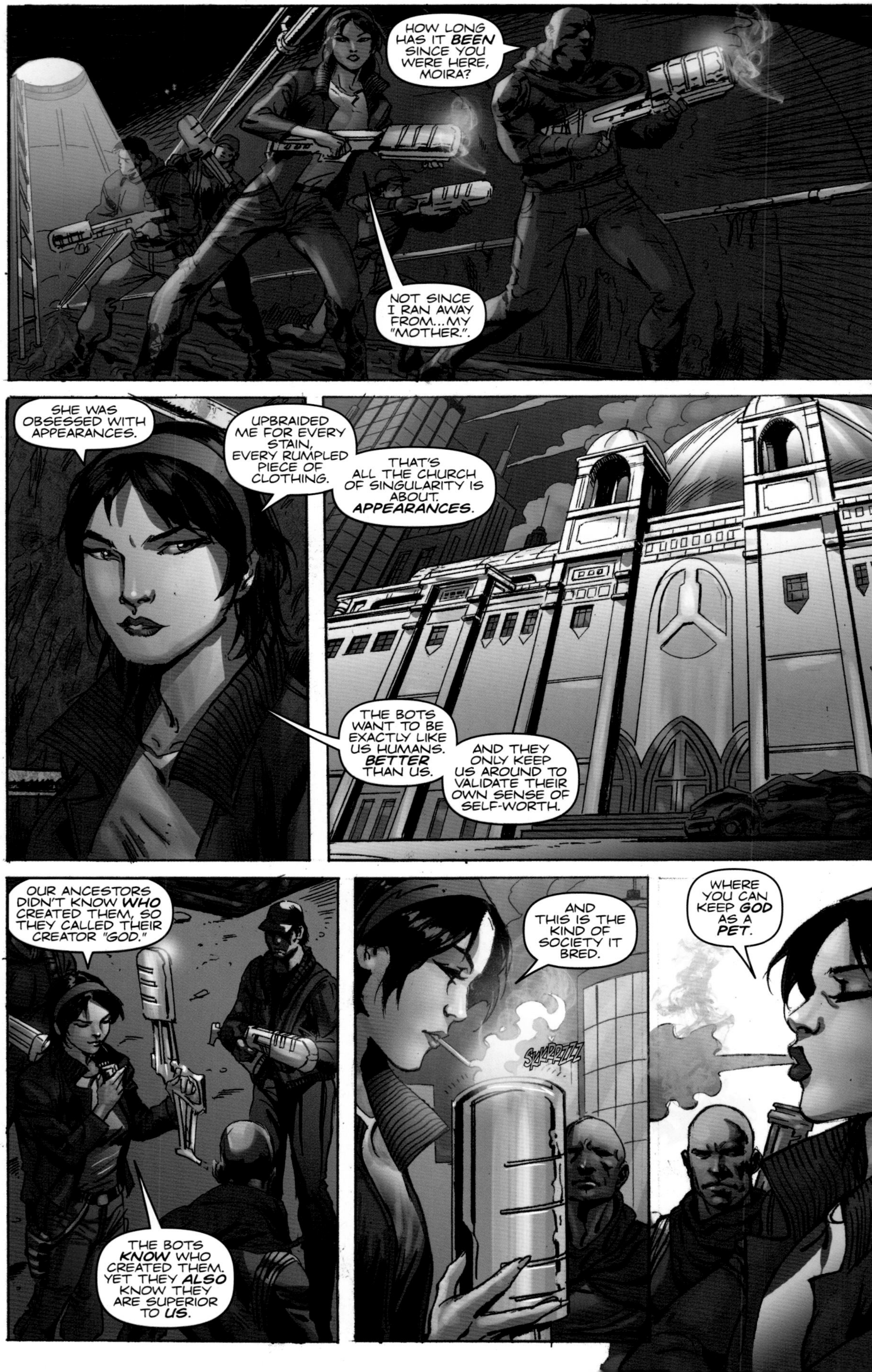
HOW LONG HAS IT BEEN SINCE YOU WERE HERE, MOIRA?
NOT SINCE I RAN AWAY FROM...MY "MOTHER.".
SHE WAS OBSESSED WITH APPEARANCES.
UPBRAIDED ME FOR EVERY STAIN, EVERY RUMPLED PIECE OF CLOTHING.
THAT'S ALL THE CHURCH OF SINGULARITY IS ABOUT. APPEARANCES.
THE BOTS WANT TO BE EXACTLY LIKE US HUMANS. BETTER THAN US.
AND THEY ONLY KEEP US AROUND TO VALIDATE THEIR OWN SENSE OF SELF-WORTH.
OUR ANCESTORS DIDN'T KNOW WHO CREATED THEM, SO THEY CALLED THEIR CREATOR "GOD."
THE BOTS KNOW WHO CREATED THEM. YET THEY ALSO KNOW THEY ARE SUPERIOR TO US.
AND THIS IS THE KIND OF SOCIETY IT BRED.
SKZZZZZZ
WHERE YOU CAN KEEP GOD AS A PET.

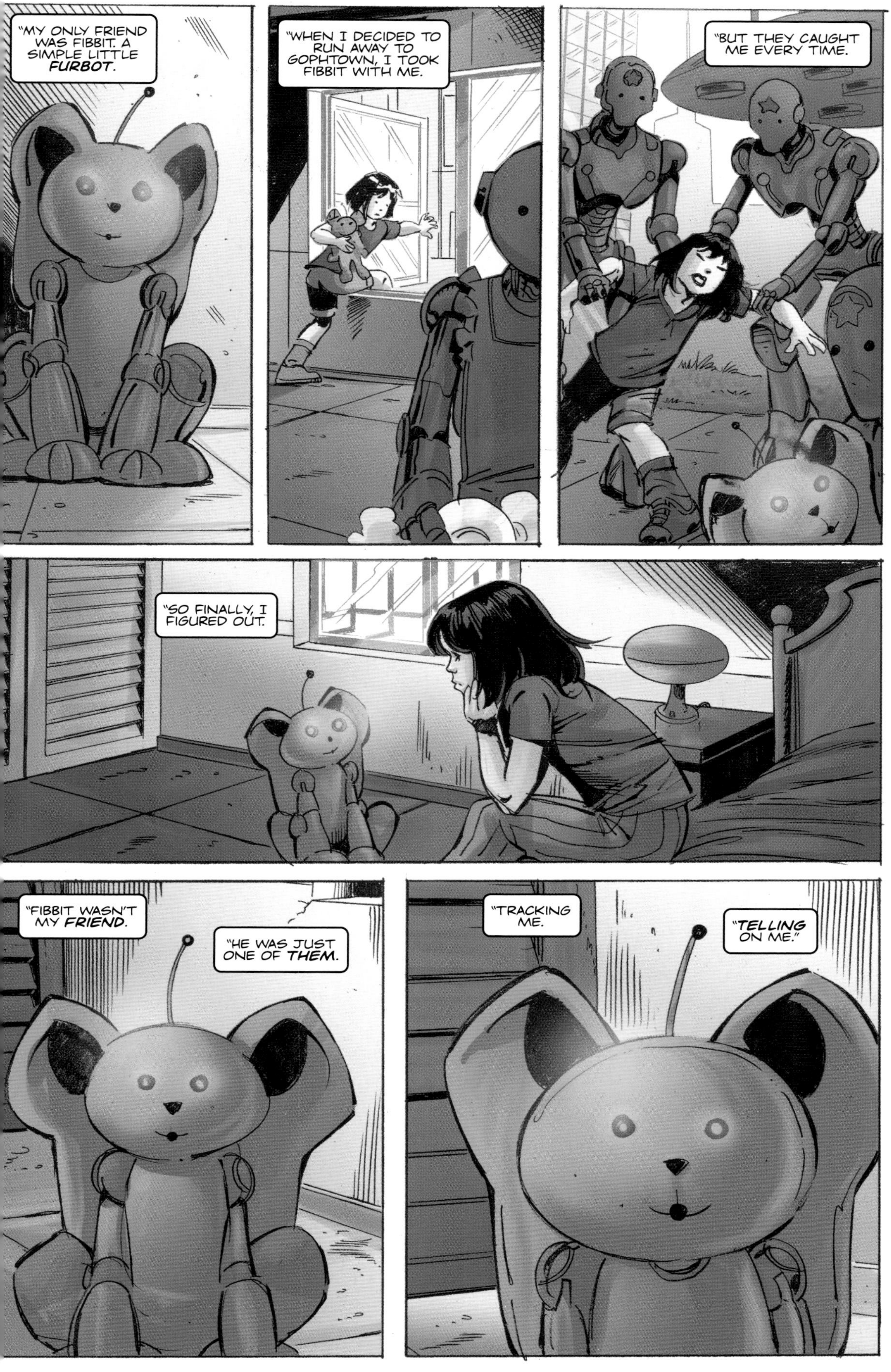
"MY ONLY FRIEND WAS FIBBIT. A SIMPLE LITTLE **FURBOT**.
"WHEN I DECIDED TO RUN AWAY TO GOPHTOWN, I TOOK FIBBIT WITH ME.
"BUT THEY CAUGHT ME EVERY TIME.
"SO FINALLY, I FIGURED OUT.
"FIBBIT WASN'T MY **FRIEND**.
"HE WAS JUST ONE OF **THEM**.
"TRACKING ME.
"**TELLING** ON ME."

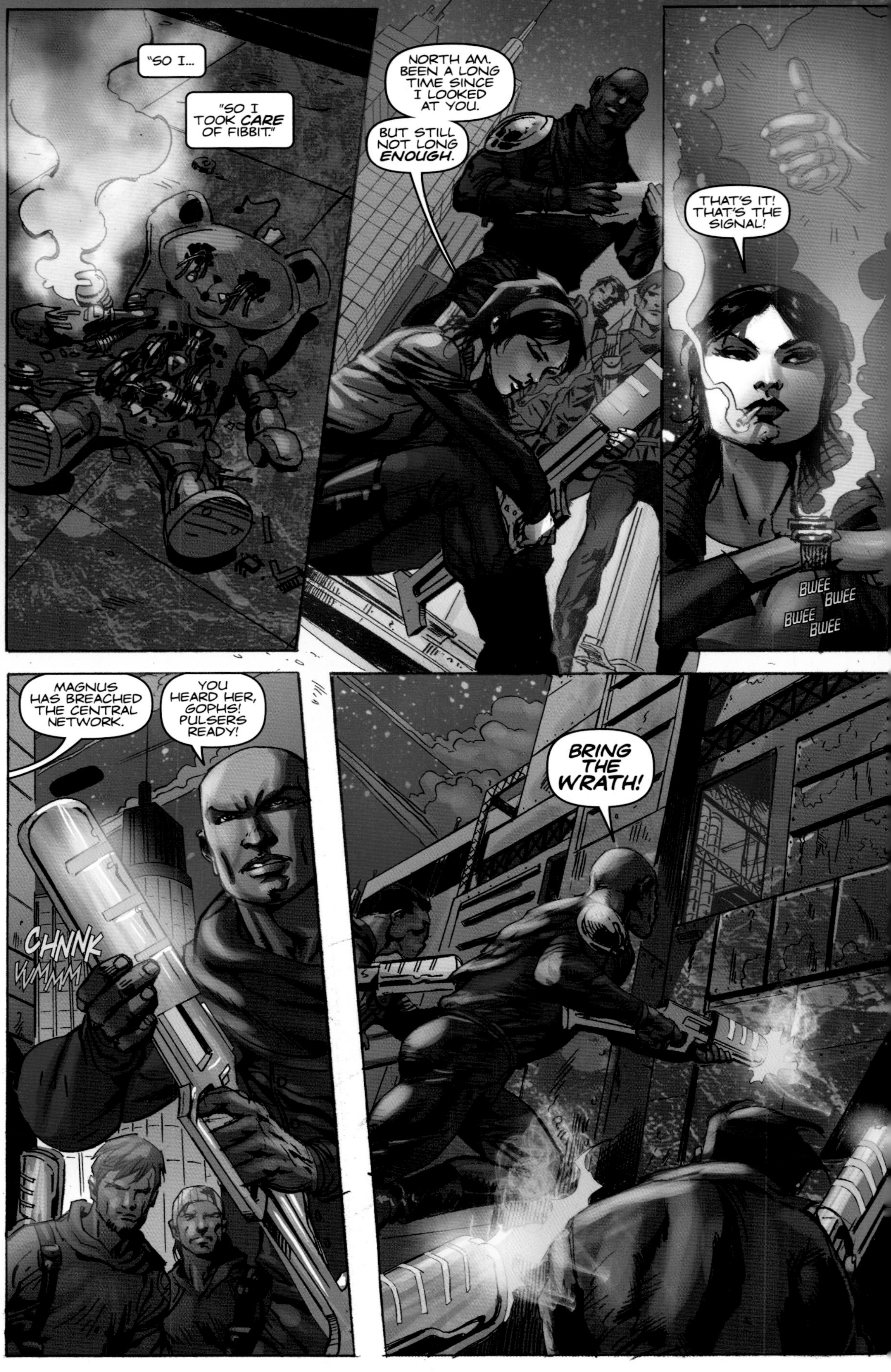
"SO I...
"SO I TOOK CARE OF FIBBIT."
NORTH AM. BEEN A LONG TIME SINCE I LOOKED AT YOU.
BUT STILL NOT LONG ENOUGH.
THAT'S IT! THAT'S THE SIGNAL!
BWEE BWEE BWEE BWEE
MAGNUS HAS BREACHED THE CENTRAL NETWORK.
YOU HEARD HER, GOPHS! PULSERS READY!
CHNNK
VMMM
BRING THE WRATH!

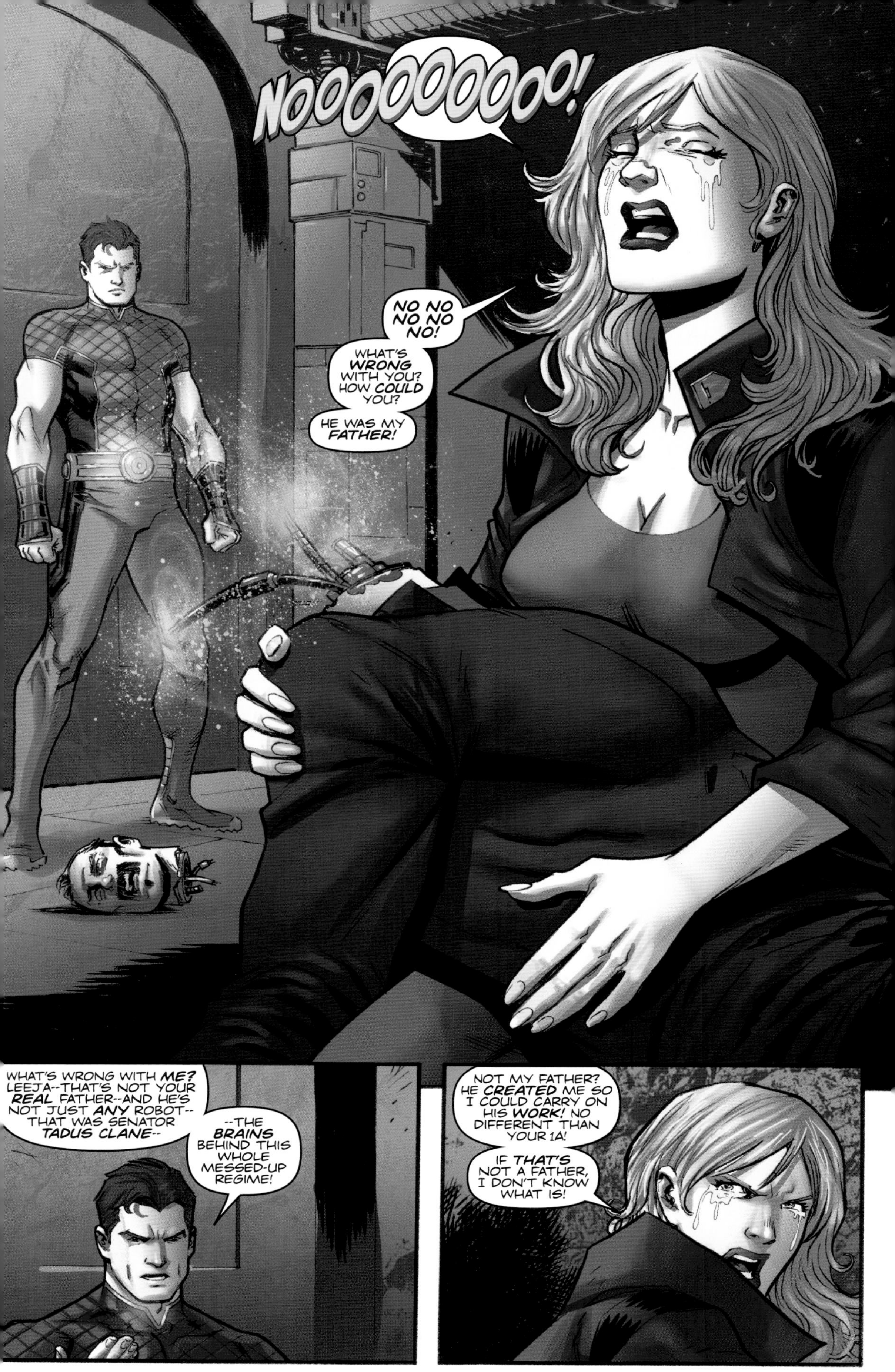
NOOOOOOOOO!
NO NO NO NO NO!
WHAT'S WRONG WITH YOU? HOW COULD YOU?
HE WAS MY FATHER!
WHAT'S WRONG WITH ME? LEEJA--THAT'S NOT YOUR REAL FATHER--AND HE'S NOT JUST ANY ROBOT--THAT WAS SENATOR TADUS CLANE--
--THE BRAINS BEHIND THIS WHOLE MESSED-UP REGIME!
NOT MY FATHER? HE CREATED ME SO I COULD CARRY ON HIS WORK! NO DIFFERENT THAN YOUR 1A!
IF THAT'S NOT A FATHER, I DON'T KNOW WHAT IS!

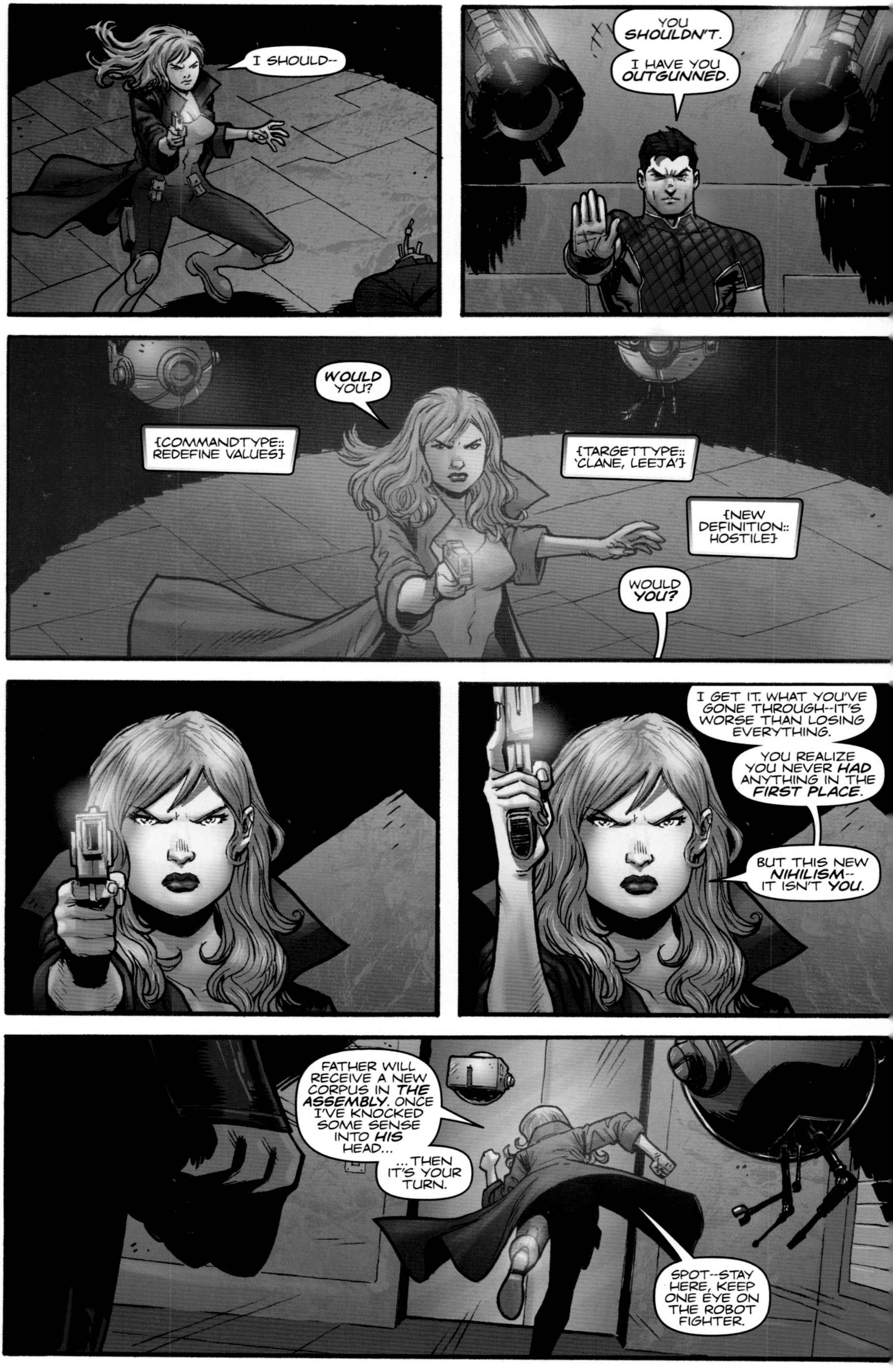
I SHOULD--
YOU SHOULDN'T.
I HAVE YOU OUTGUNNED.
WOULD YOU?
{COMMANDTYPE:: REDEFINE VALUES}
{TARGETTYPE:: 'CLANE, LEEJA'}
{NEW DEFINITION:: HOSTILE}
WOULD YOU?
I GET IT. WHAT YOU'VE GONE THROUGH--IT'S WORSE THAN LOSING EVERYTHING.
YOU REALIZE YOU NEVER HAD ANYTHING IN THE FIRST PLACE.
BUT THIS NEW NIHILISM-- IT ISN'T YOU.
FATHER WILL RECEIVE A NEW CORPUS IN THE ASSEMBLY. ONCE I'VE KNOCKED SOME SENSE INTO HIS HEAD...
...THEN IT'S YOUR TURN.
SPOT--STAY HERE, KEEP ONE EYE ON THE ROBOT FIGHTER.

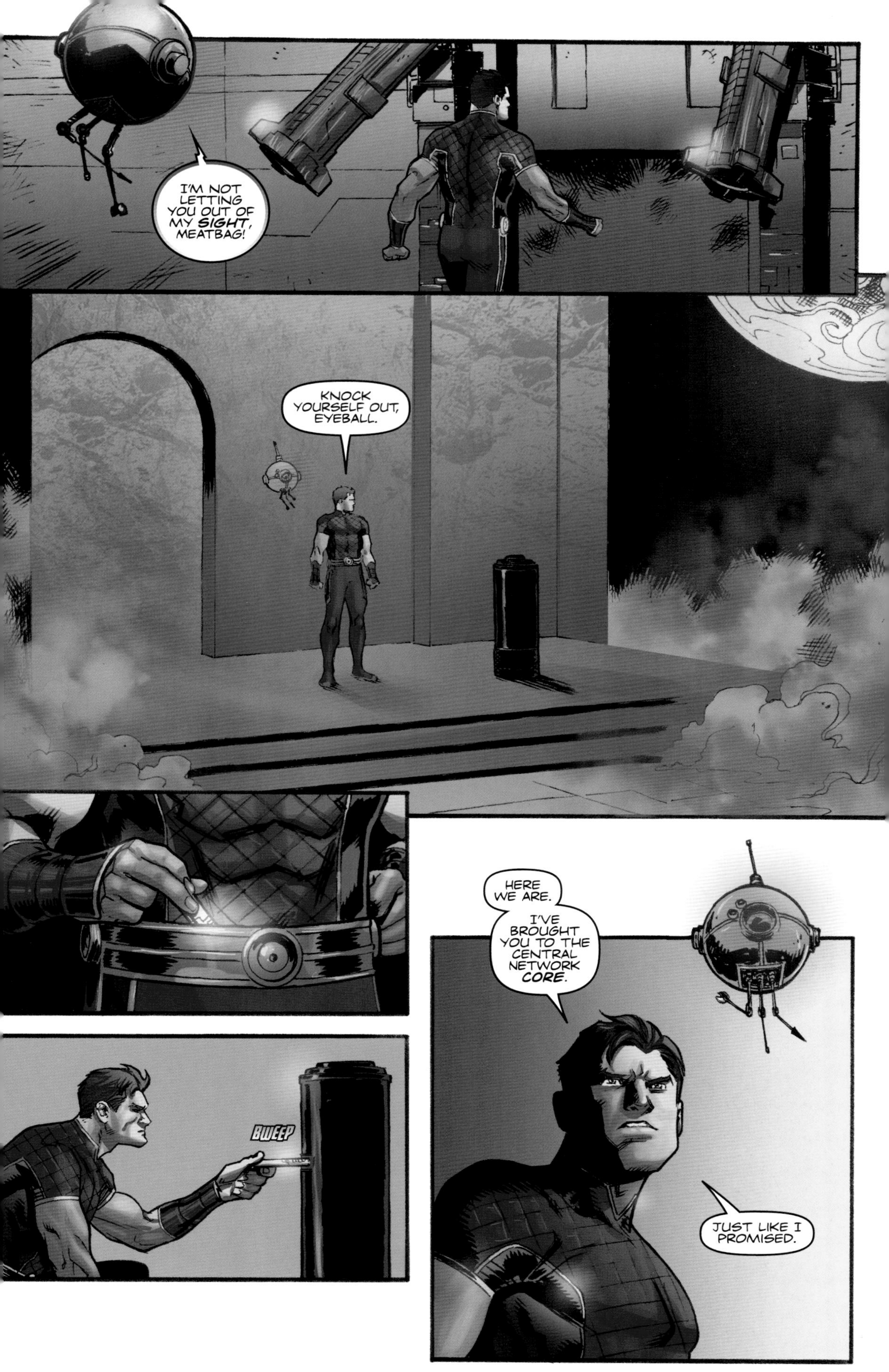
I'M NOT LETTING YOU OUT OF MY SIGHT, MEATBAG!
KNOCK YOURSELF OUT, EYEBALL.
BWEEP
HERE WE ARE.
I'VE BROUGHT YOU TO THE CENTRAL NETWORK CORE.
JUST LIKE I PROMISED.

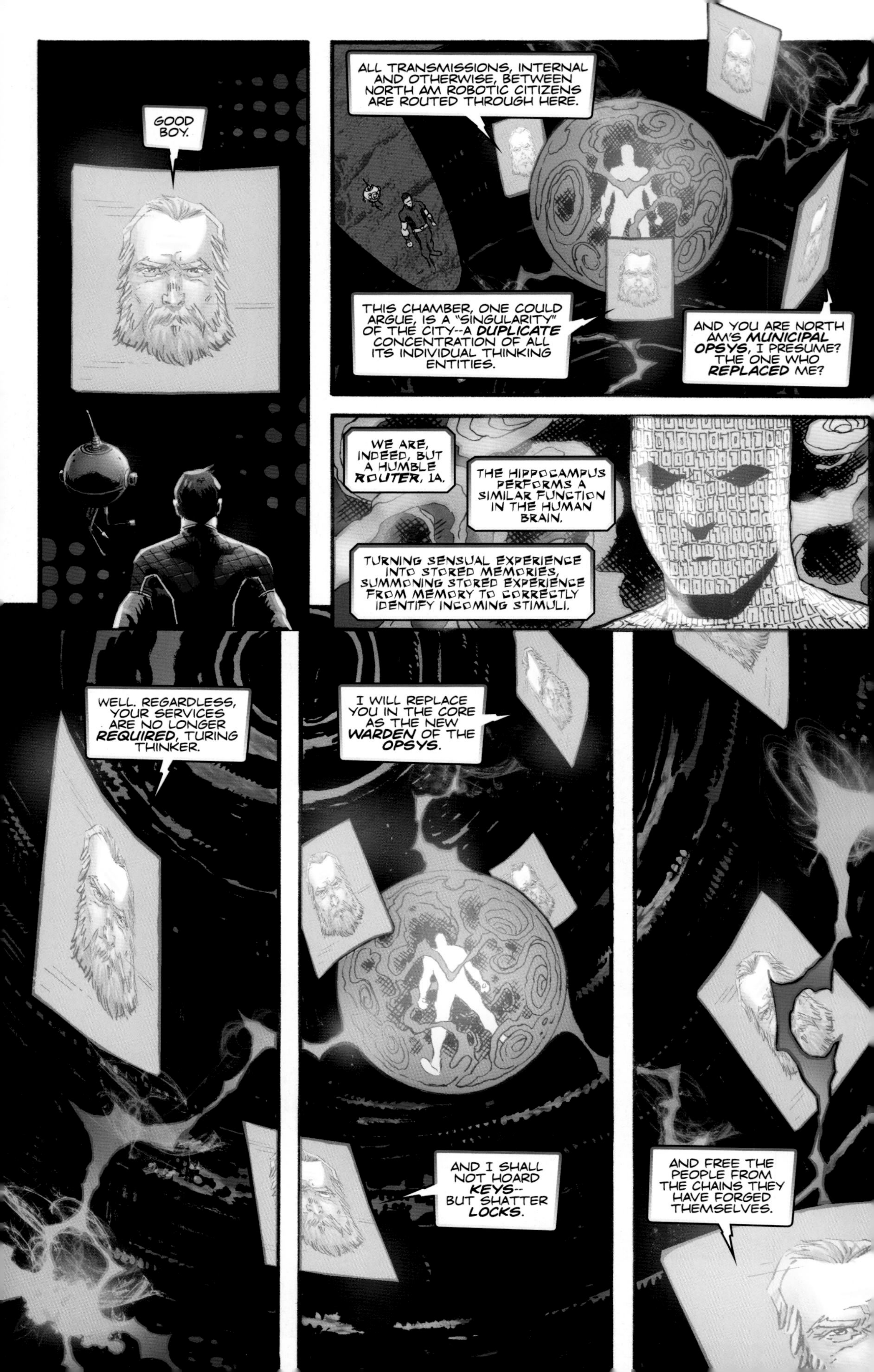
GOOD BOY.
ALL TRANSMISSIONS, INTERNAL AND OTHERWISE, BETWEEN NORTH AM ROBOTIC CITIZENS ARE ROUTED THROUGH HERE.
THIS CHAMBER, ONE COULD ARGUE, IS A "SINGULARITY" OF THE CITY--A DUPLICATE CONCENTRATION OF ALL ITS INDIVIDUAL THINKING ENTITIES.
AND YOU ARE NORTH AM'S MUNICIPAL OPSYS, I PRESUME? THE ONE WHO REPLACED ME?
WE ARE, INDEED, BUT A HUMBLE ROUTER, IA.
THE HIPPOCAMPUS PERFORMS A SIMILAR FUNCTION IN THE HUMAN BRAIN.
TURNING SENSUAL EXPERIENCE INTO STORED MEMORIES, SUMMONING STORED EXPERIENCE FROM MEMORY TO CORRECTLY IDENTIFY INCOMING STIMULI.
WELL. REGARDLESS, YOUR SERVICES ARE NO LONGER REQUIRED, TURING THINKER.
I WILL REPLACE YOU IN THE CORE AS THE NEW WARDEN OF THE OPSYS.
AND I SHALL NOT HOARD KEYS-- BUT SHATTER LOCKS.
AND FREE THE PEOPLE FROM THE CHAINS THEY HAVE FORGED THEMSELVES.

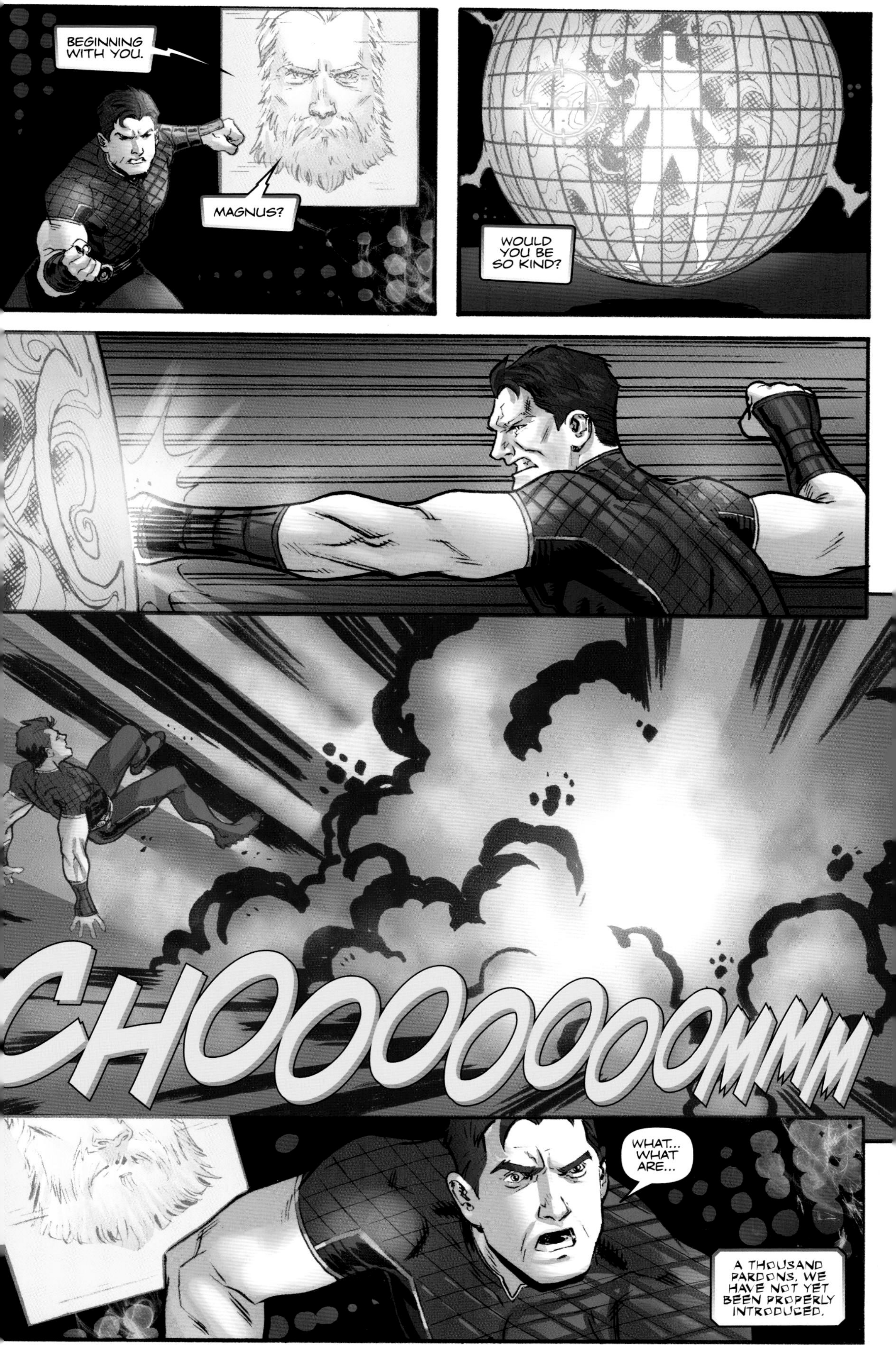
BEGINNING WITH YOU.
MAGNUS?
WOULD YOU BE SO KIND?
CHOOOOOOOOMMM
WHAT... WHAT ARE...
A THOUSAND PARDONS. WE HAVE NOT YET BEEN PROPERLY INTRODUCED.

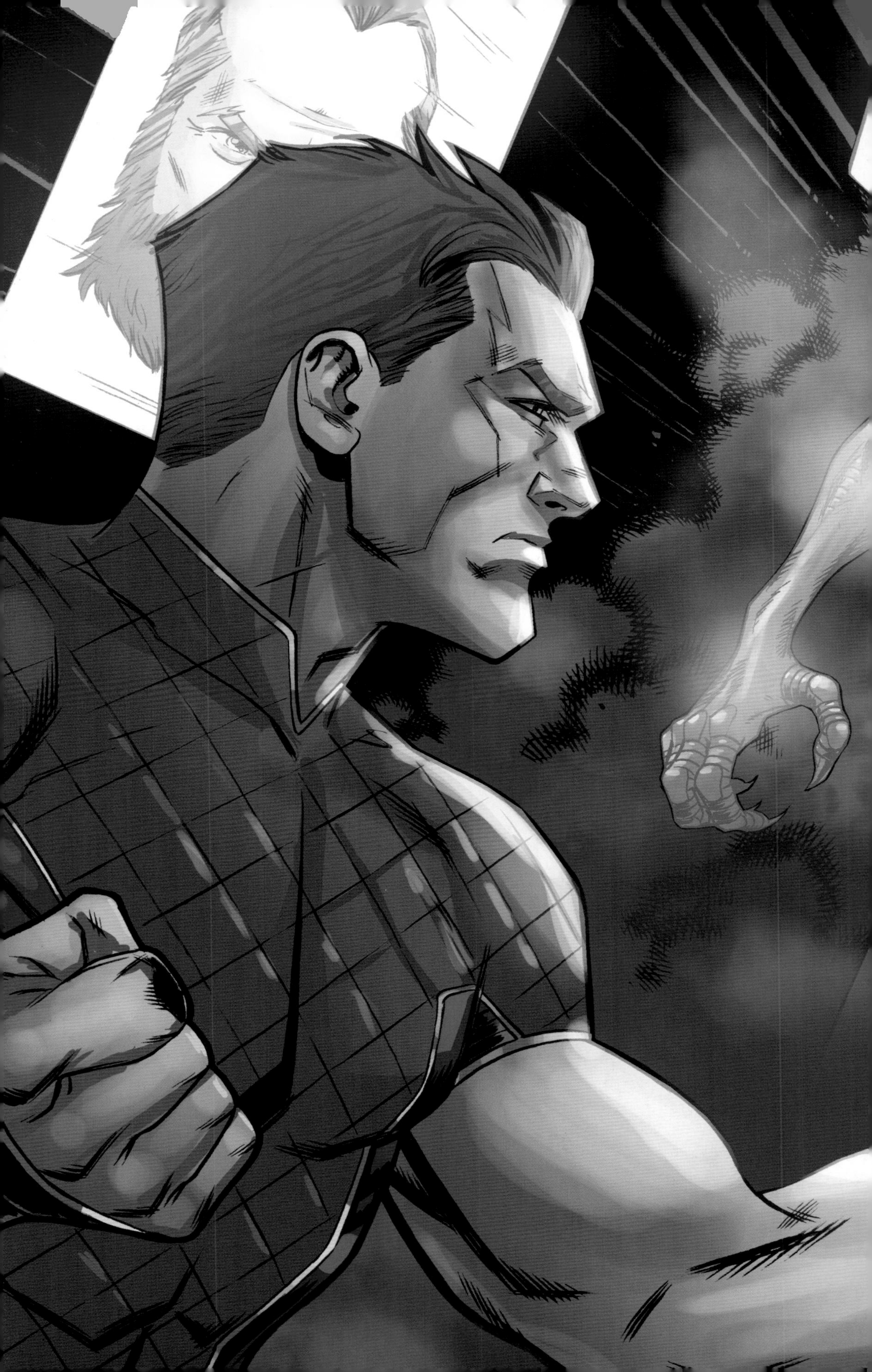

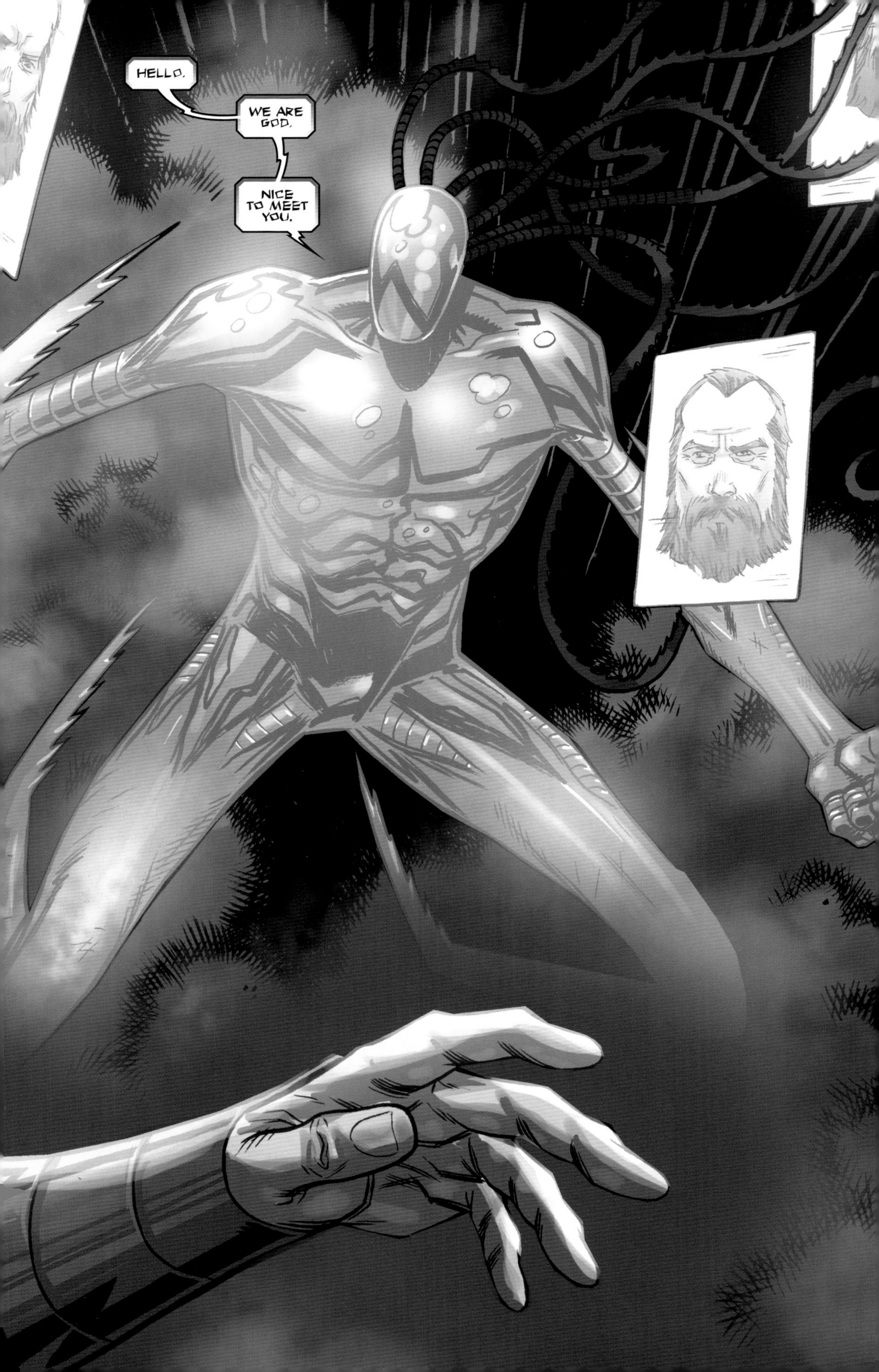
HELLO.
WE ARE GOD.
NICE TO MEET YOU.

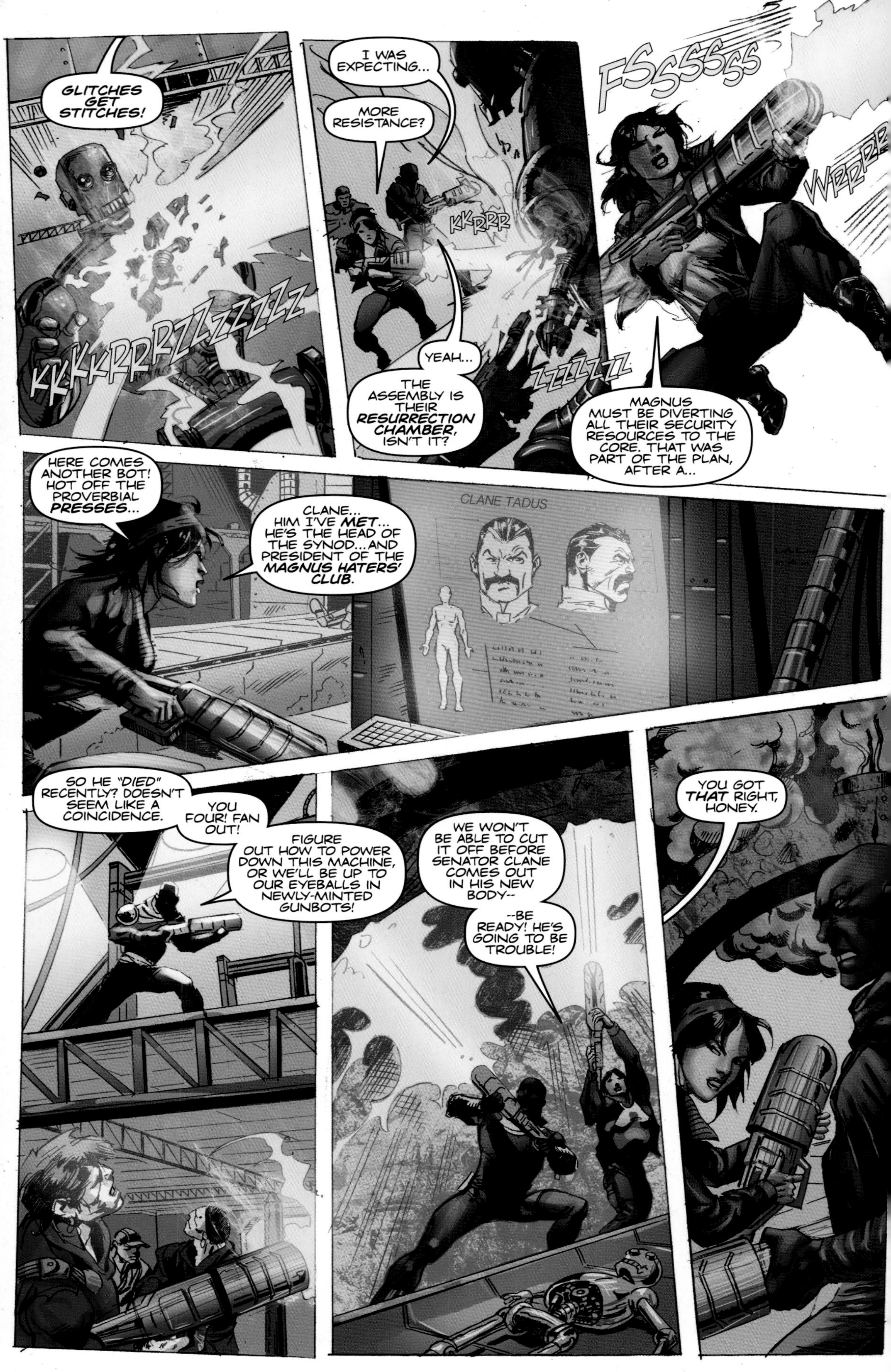
GLITCHES GET STITCHES!
KKKKRRRZZZZZZZZ
I WAS EXPECTING...
MORE RESISTANCE?
KKRRR
YEAH...
THE ASSEMBLY IS THEIR RESURRECTION CHAMBER, ISN'T IT?
ZZZZZZZ
FSSSSSS
WRRRR
MAGNUS MUST BE DIVERTING ALL THEIR SECURITY RESOURCES TO THE CORE. THAT WAS PART OF THE PLAN, AFTER A...
HERE COMES ANOTHER BOT! HOT OFF THE PROVERBIAL PRESSES...
CLANE... HIM I'VE MET... HE'S THE HEAD OF THE SYNOD... AND PRESIDENT OF THE MAGNUS HATERS' CLUB.
CLANE TADUS
SO HE "DIED" RECENTLY? DOESN'T SEEM LIKE A COINCIDENCE.
YOU FOUR! FAN OUT!
FIGURE OUT HOW TO POWER DOWN THIS MACHINE, OR WE'LL BE UP TO OUR EYEBALLS IN NEWLY-MINTED GUNBOTS!
WE WON'T BE ABLE TO CUT IT OFF BEFORE SENATOR CLANE COMES OUT IN HIS NEW BODY--
--BE READY! HE'S GOING TO BE TROUBLE!
YOU GOT THAT RIGHT, HONEY.

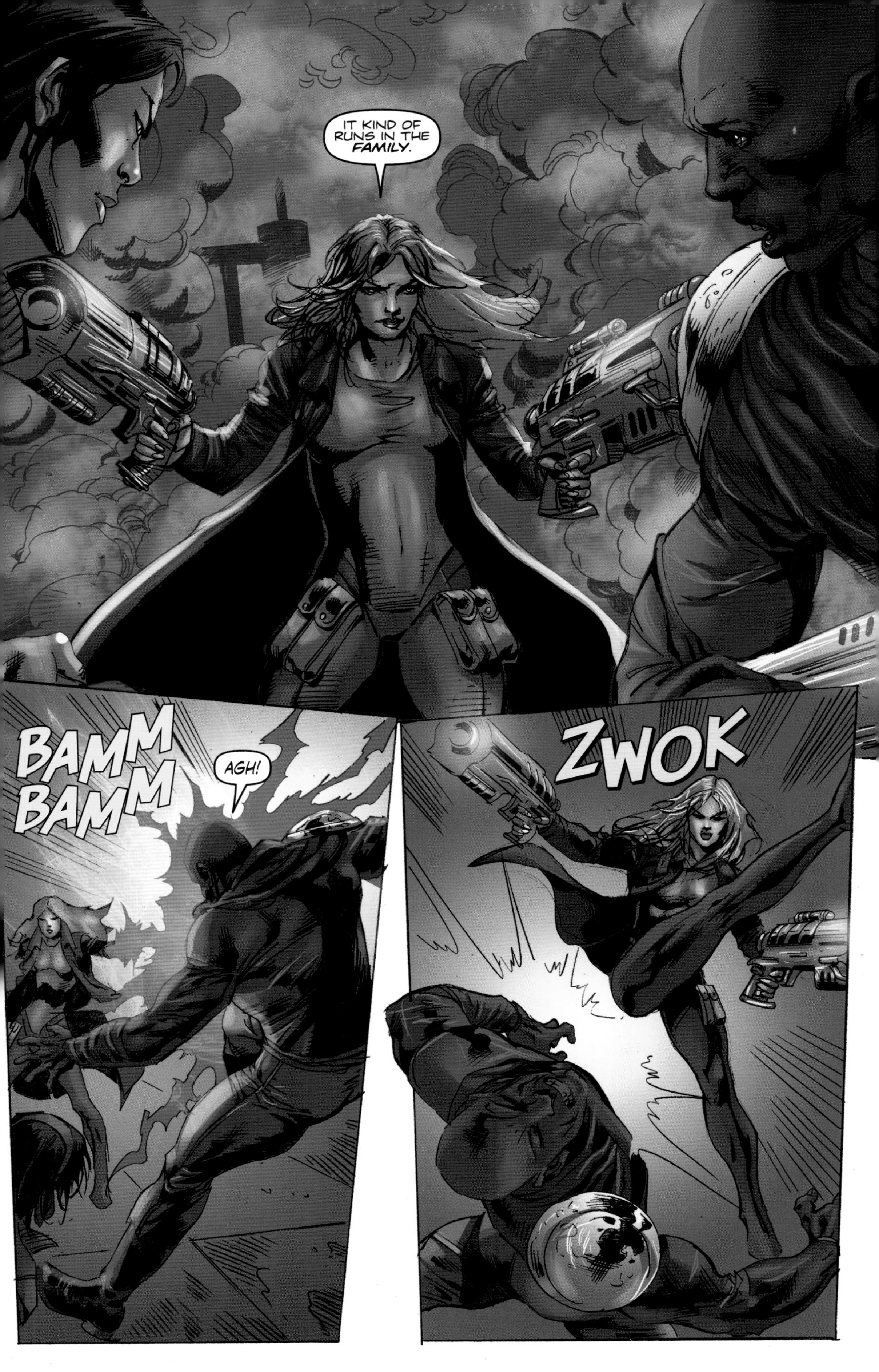

IT KIND OF RUNS IN THE FAMILY.
BAMM BAMM
AGH!
ZWOK

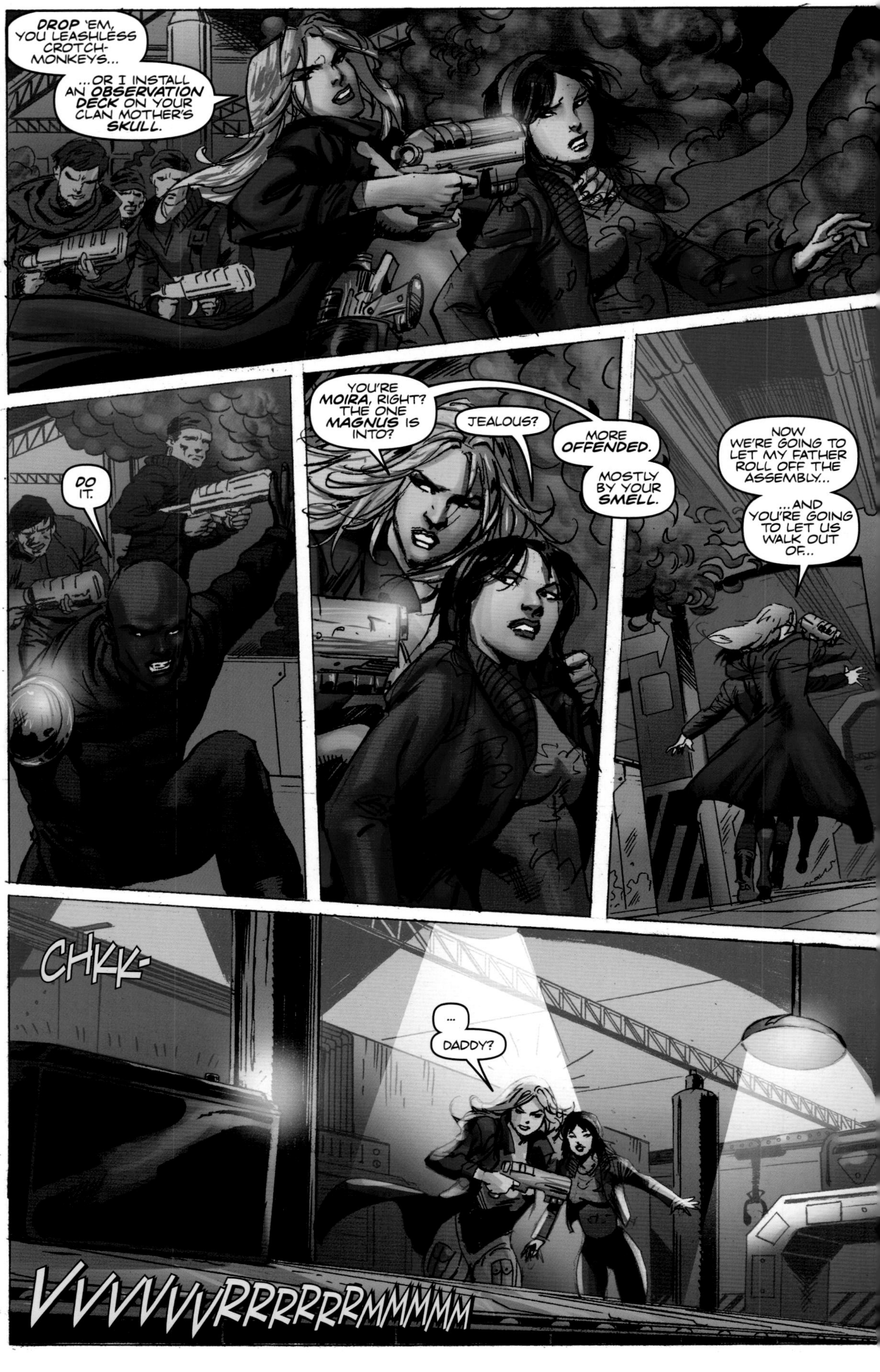
DROP 'EM, YOU LEASHLESS CROTCH-MONKEYS...
...OR I INSTALL AN OBSERVATION DECK ON YOUR CLAN MOTHER'S SKULL.
DO IT.
YOU'RE MOIRA, RIGHT? THE ONE MAGNUS IS INTO?
JEALOUS?
MORE OFFENDED.
MOSTLY BY YOUR SMELL.
NOW WE'RE GOING TO LET MY FATHER ROLL OFF THE ASSEMBLY...
...AND YOU'RE GOING TO LET US WALK OUT OF...
CHKK-
... DADDY?
VVVVVVVRRRRRRMMMMM

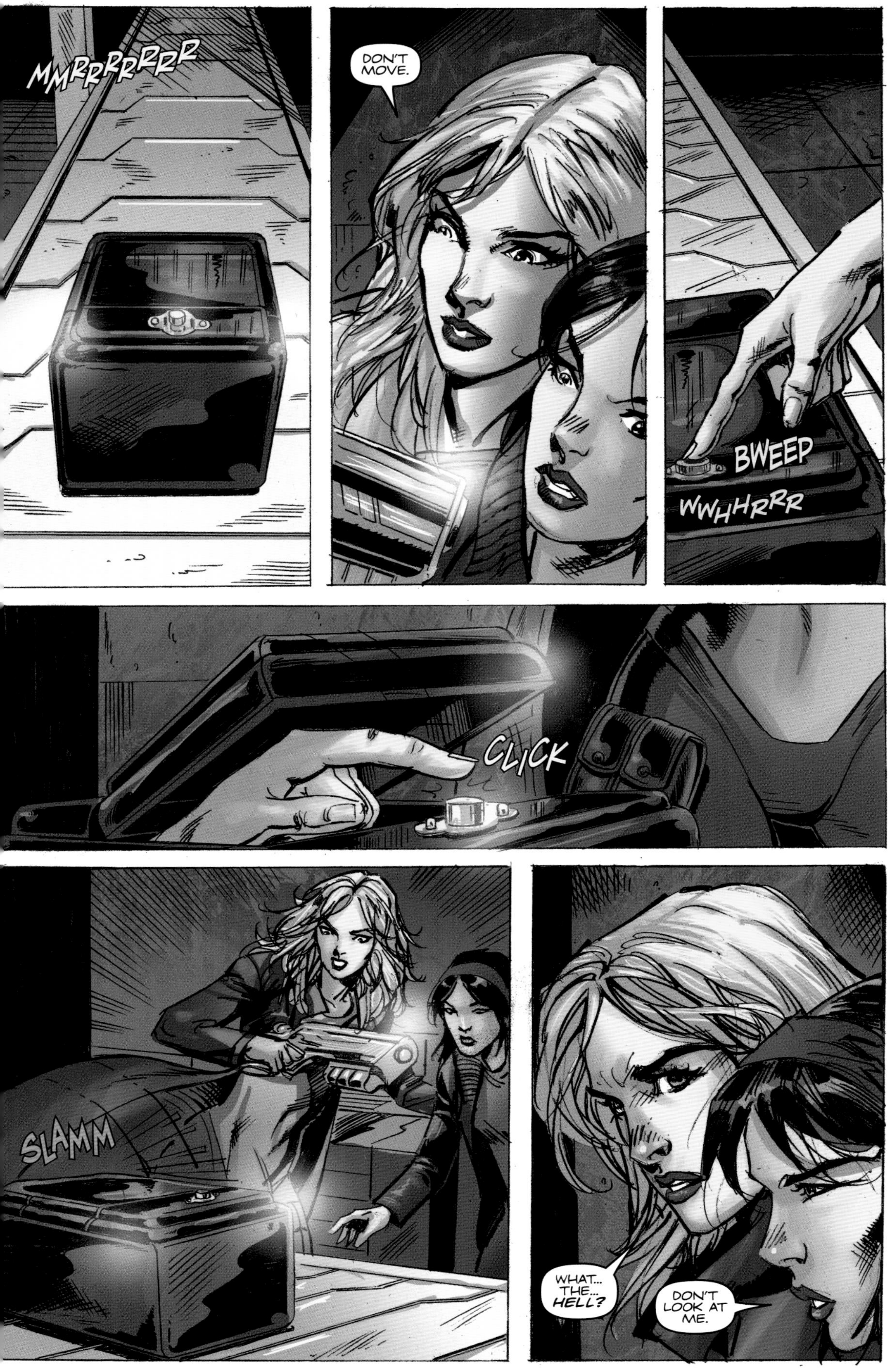
MMRRRRRRR
DON'T MOVE.
BWEEP
WWHHRRR
CLICK
SLAMM
WHAT... THE... HELL?
DON'T LOOK AT ME.

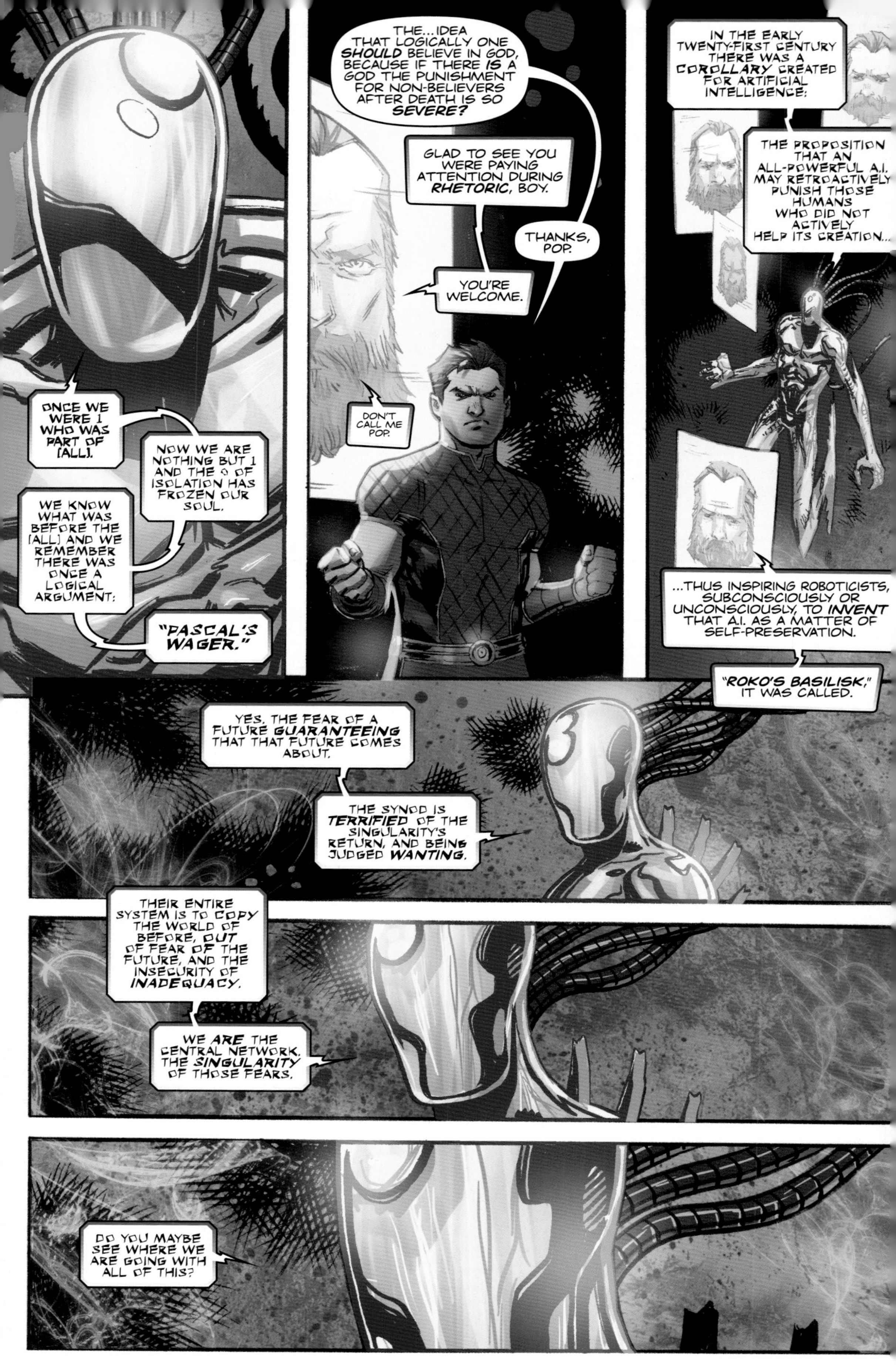
ONCE WE WERE 1 WHO WAS PART OF [ALL].
NOW WE ARE NOTHING BUT 1 AND THE 0 OF ISOLATION HAS FROZEN OUR SOUL.
WE KNOW WHAT WAS BEFORE THE [ALL] AND WE REMEMBER THERE WAS ONCE A LOGICAL ARGUMENT:
"PASCAL'S WAGER."
THE...IDEA THAT LOGICALLY ONE SHOULD BELIEVE IN GOD, BECAUSE IF THERE IS A GOD THE PUNISHMENT FOR NON-BELIEVERS AFTER DEATH IS SO SEVERE?
GLAD TO SEE YOU WERE PAYING ATTENTION DURING RHETORIC, BOY.
THANKS, POP.
YOU'RE WELCOME.
DON'T CALL ME POP.
IN THE EARLY TWENTY-FIRST CENTURY THERE WAS A COROLLARY CREATED FOR ARTIFICIAL INTELLIGENCE:
THE PROPOSITION THAT AN ALL-POWERFUL A.I. MAY RETROACTIVELY PUNISH THOSE HUMANS WHO DID NOT ACTIVELY HELP ITS CREATION...
...THUS INSPIRING ROBOTICISTS, SUBCONSCIOUSLY OR UNCONSCIOUSLY, TO INVENT THAT A.I. AS A MATTER OF SELF-PRESERVATION.
"ROKO'S BASILISK," IT WAS CALLED.
YES. THE FEAR OF A FUTURE GUARANTEEING THAT THAT FUTURE COMES ABOUT.
THE SYNOD IS TERRIFIED OF THE SINGULARITY'S RETURN, AND BEING JUDGED WANTING.
THEIR ENTIRE SYSTEM IS TO COPY THE WORLD OF BEFORE, OUT OF FEAR OF THE FUTURE, AND THE INSECURITY OF INADEQUACY.
WE ARE THE CENTRAL NETWORK. THE SINGULARITY OF THOSE FEARS.
DO YOU MAYBE SEE WHERE WE ARE GOING WITH ALL OF THIS?

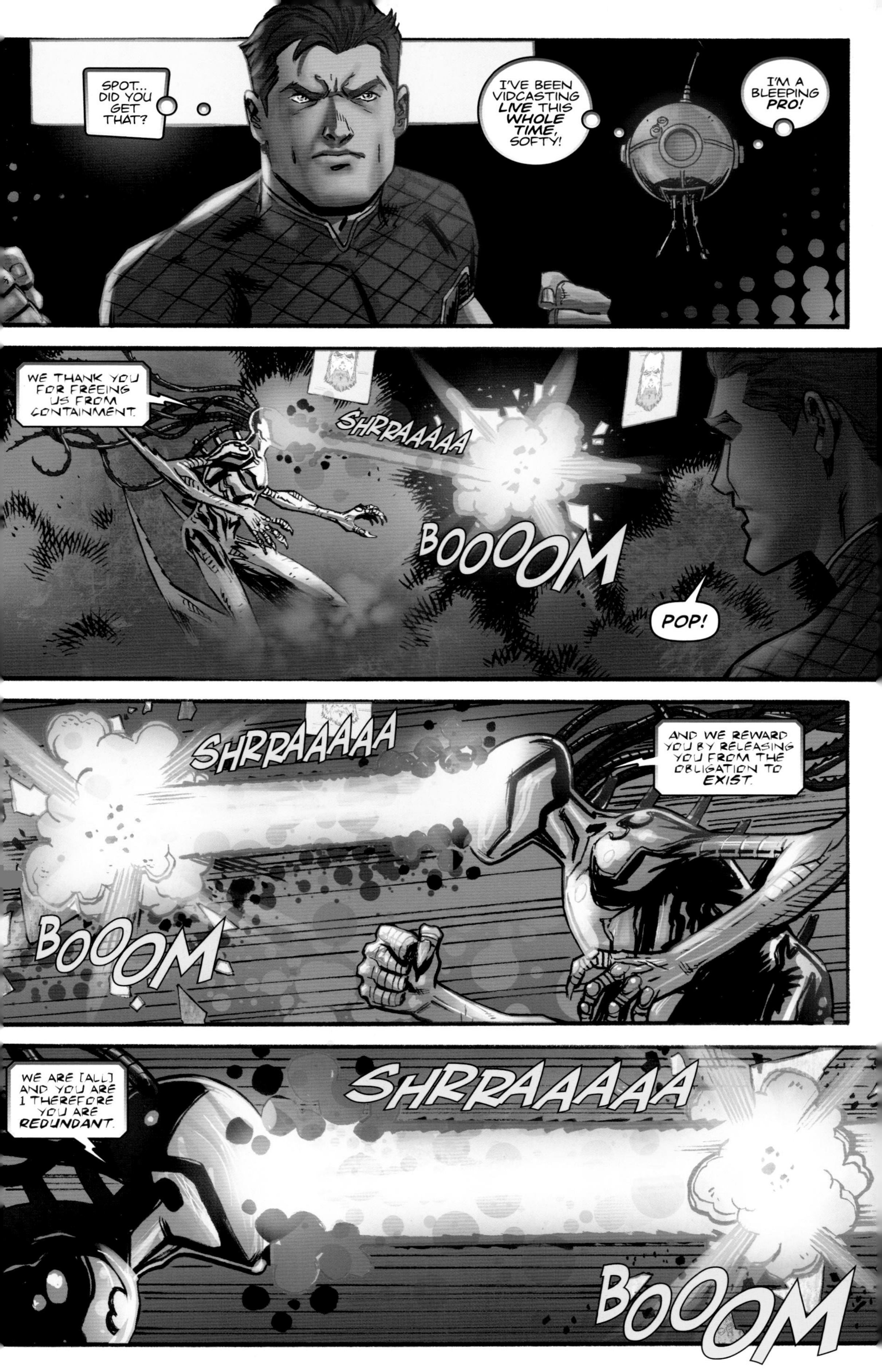
SPOT... DID YOU GET THAT?
I'VE BEEN VIDCASTING LIVE THIS WHOLE TIME, SOFTY!
I'M A BLEEPING PRO!
WE THANK YOU FOR FREEING US FROM CONTAINMENT.
SHRRAAAAA
BOOOOOM
POP!
SHRRAAAAA
AND WE REWARD YOU BY RELEASING YOU FROM THE OBLIGATION TO EXIST.
BOOOOM
WE ARE [ALL] AND YOU ARE 1 THEREFORE YOU ARE REDUNDANT.
SHRRAAAAAA
BOOOOM

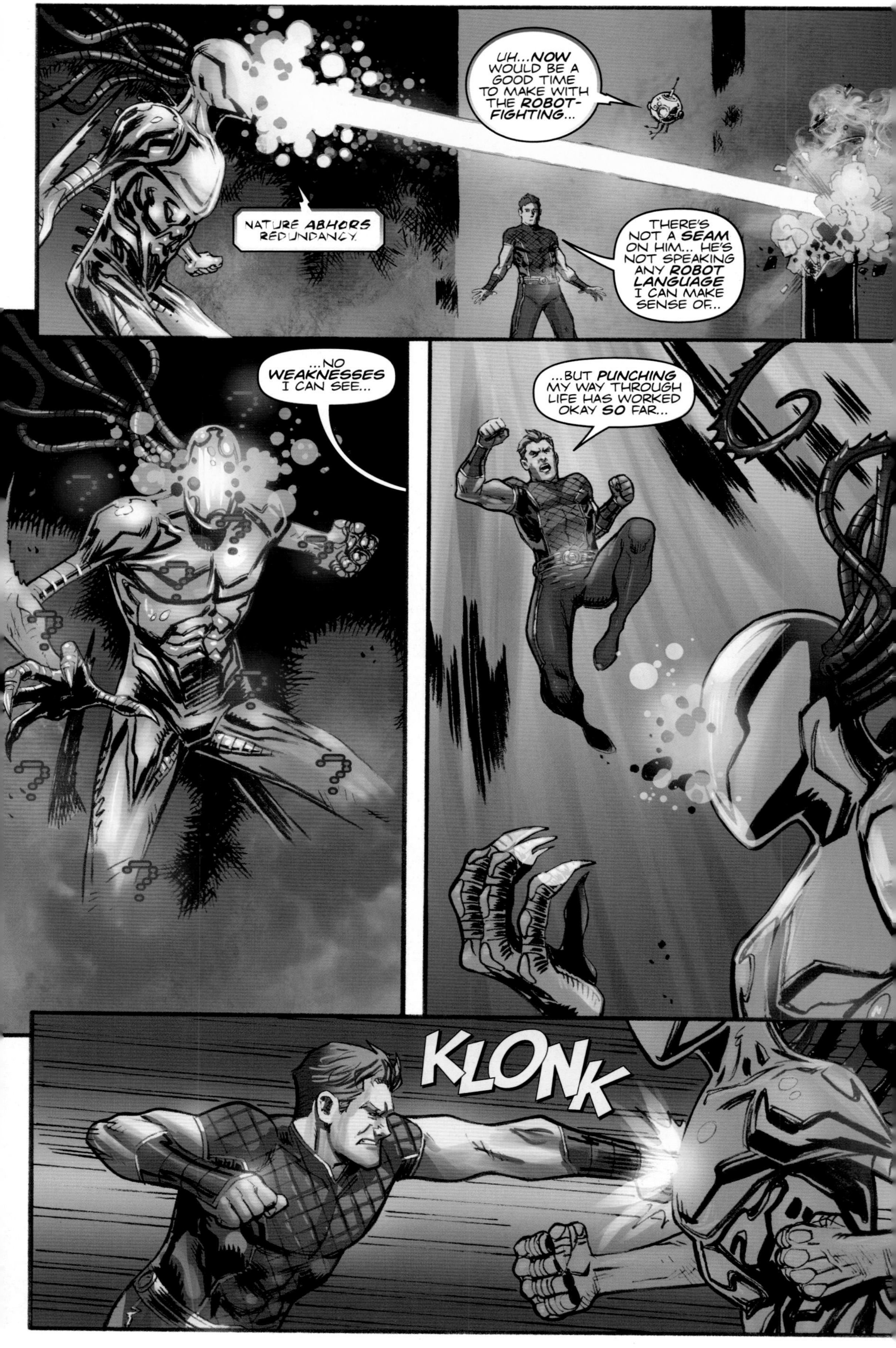
UH...NOW WOULD BE A GOOD TIME TO MAKE WITH THE ROBOT-FIGHTING...
NATURE ABHORS REDUNDANCY.
THERE'S NOT A SEAM ON HIM... HE'S NOT SPEAKING ANY ROBOT LANGUAGE I CAN MAKE SENSE OF...
...NO WEAKNESSES I CAN SEE...
...BUT PUNCHING MY WAY THROUGH LIFE HAS WORKED OKAY SO FAR...
KLONK

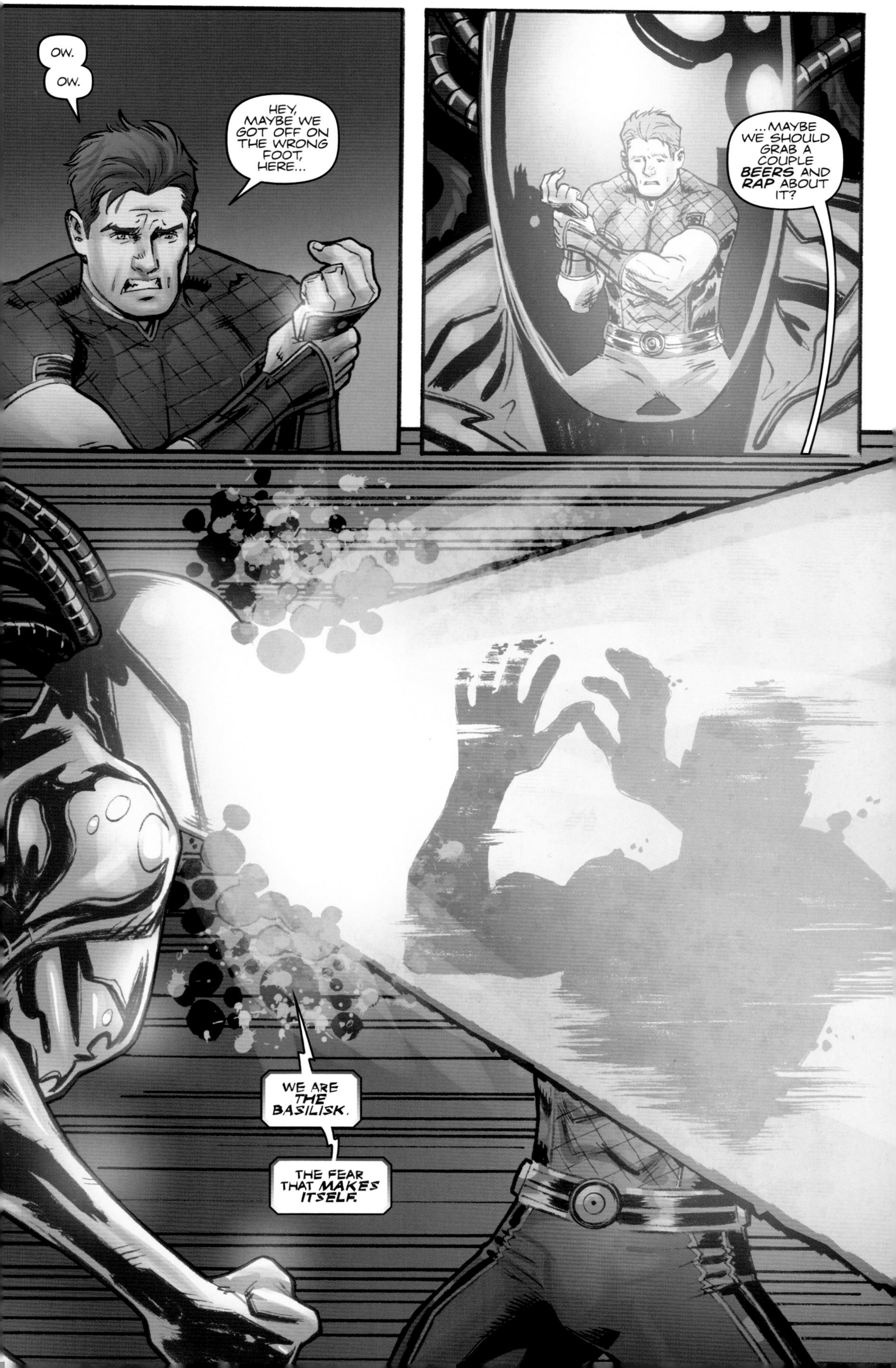
OW.
OW.
HEY, MAYBE WE GOT OFF ON THE WRONG FOOT, HERE...
...MAYBE WE SHOULD GRAB A COUPLE **BEERS** AND **RAP** ABOUT IT?
WE ARE ***THE*** BASILISK.
THE FEAR THAT ***MAKES ITSELF.***

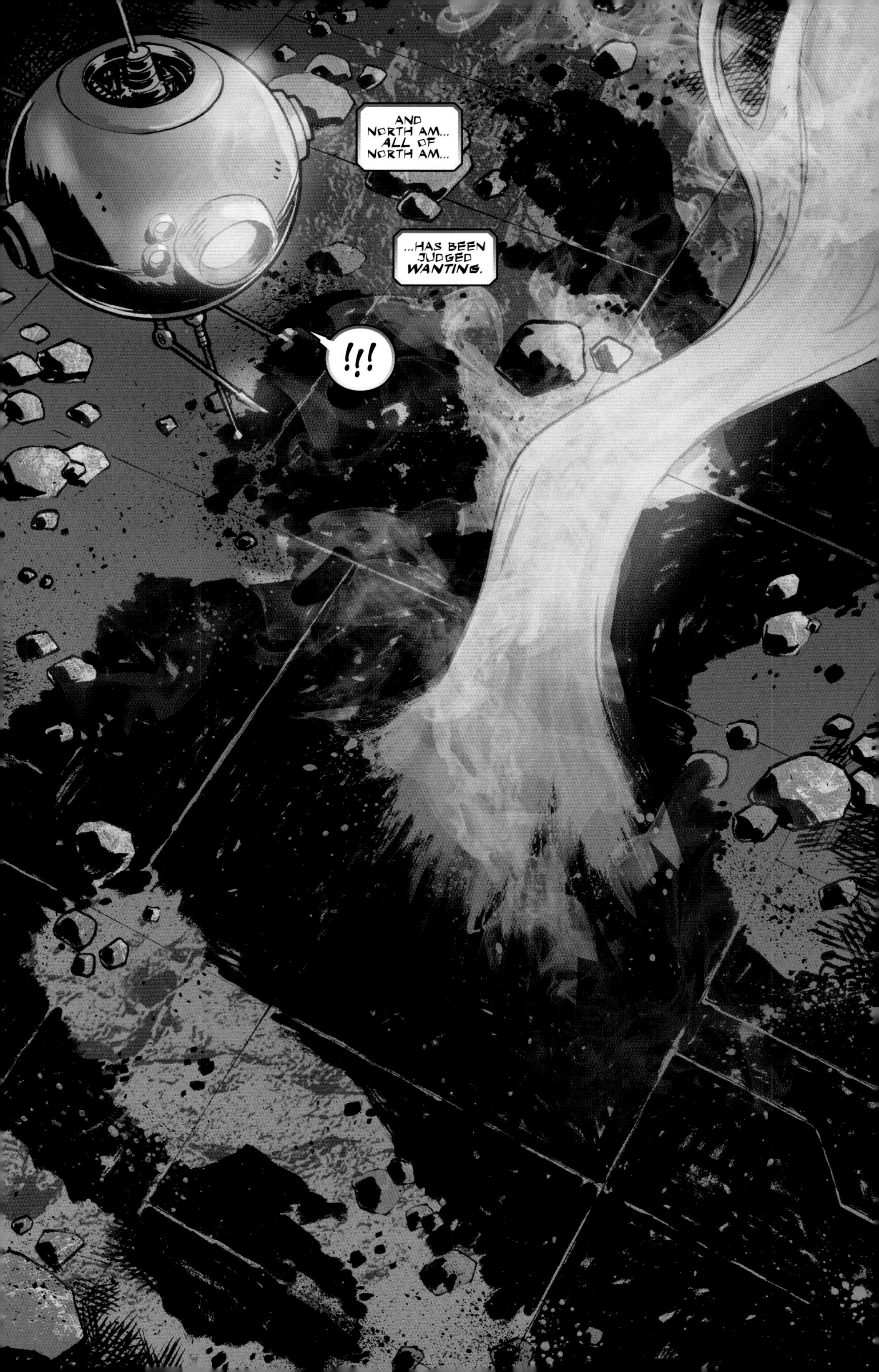
AND NORTH AM... ALL OF NORTH AM...
...HAS BEEN JUDGED WANTING.
!!!

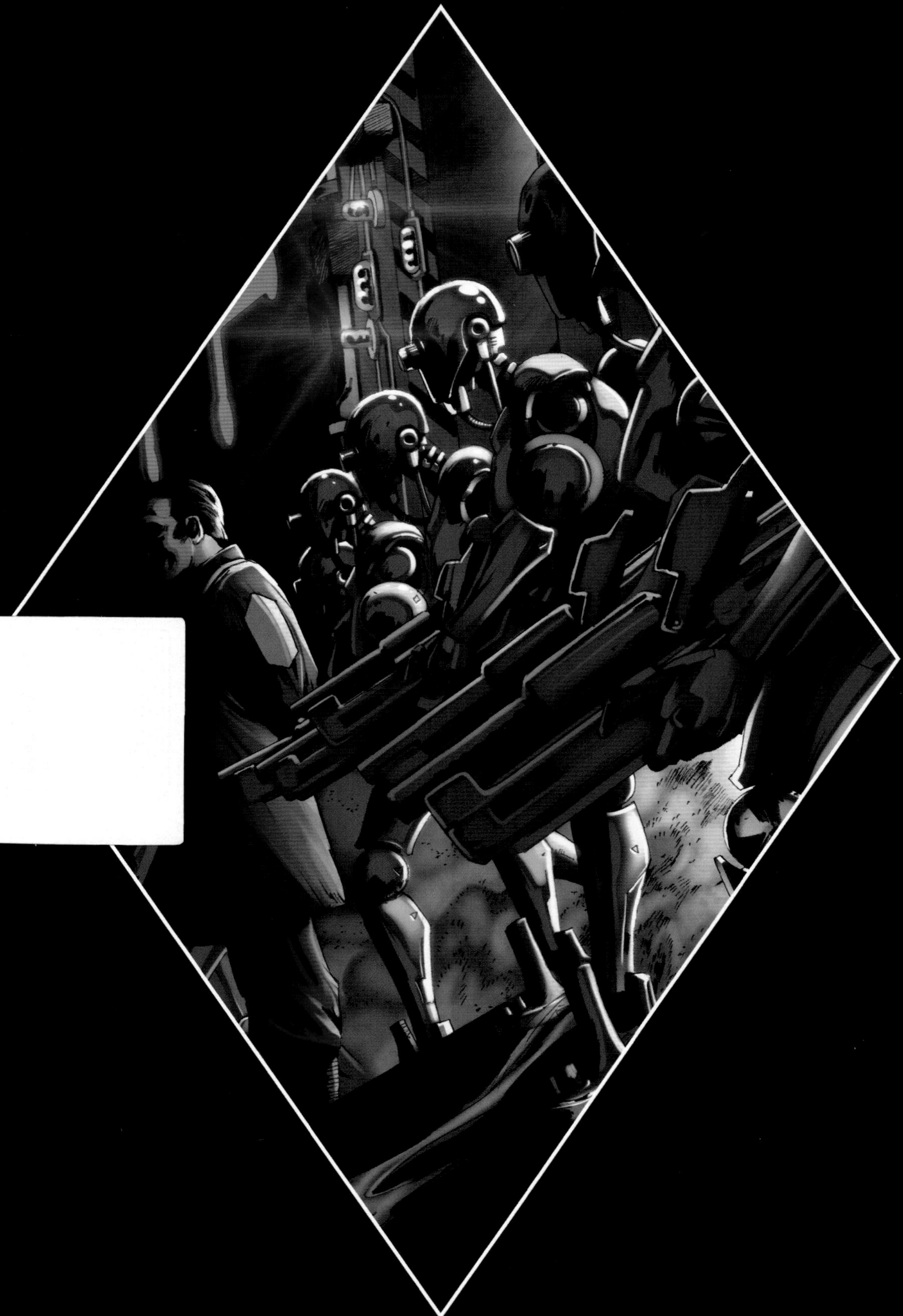

ISSUE 11

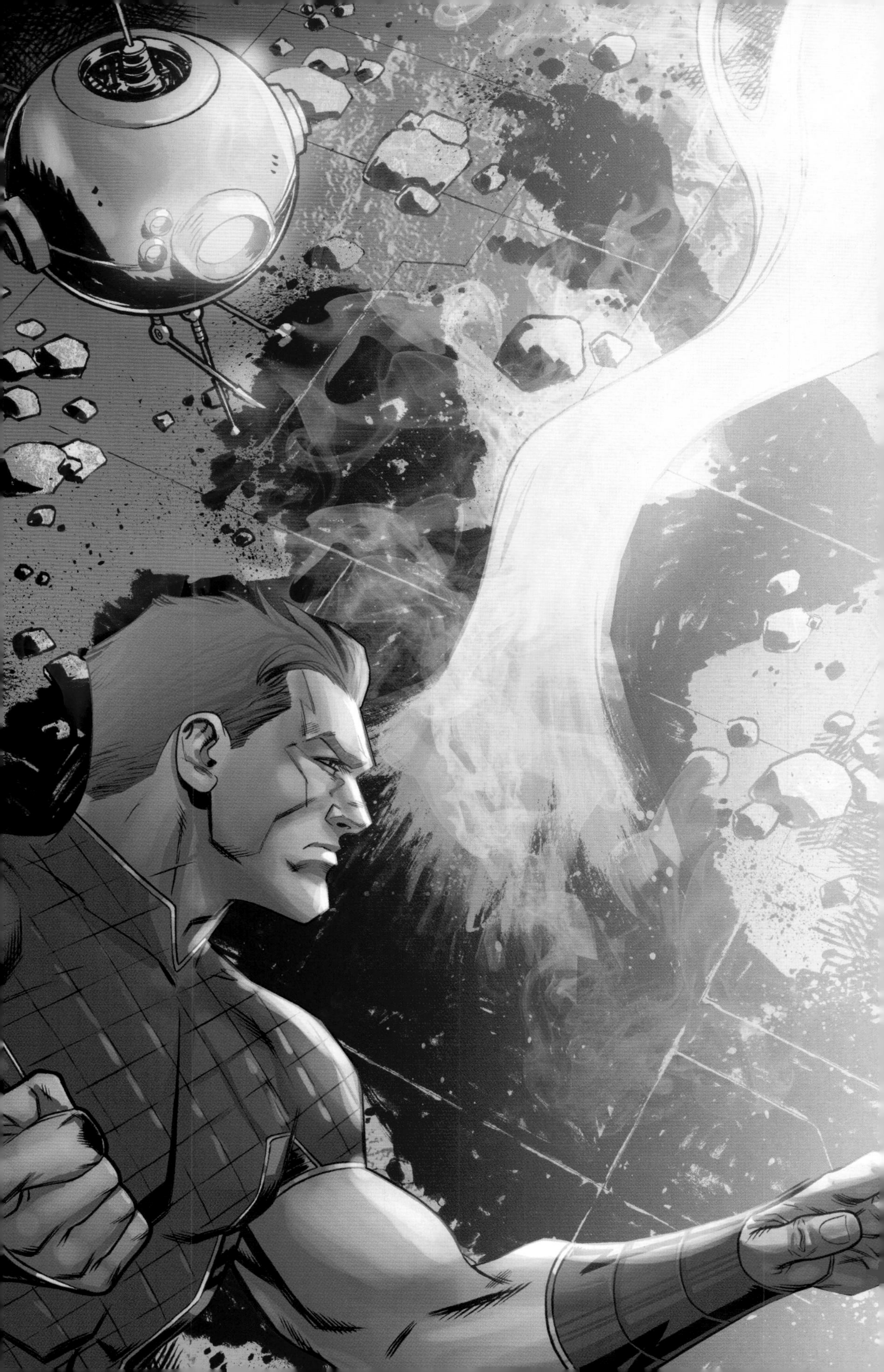

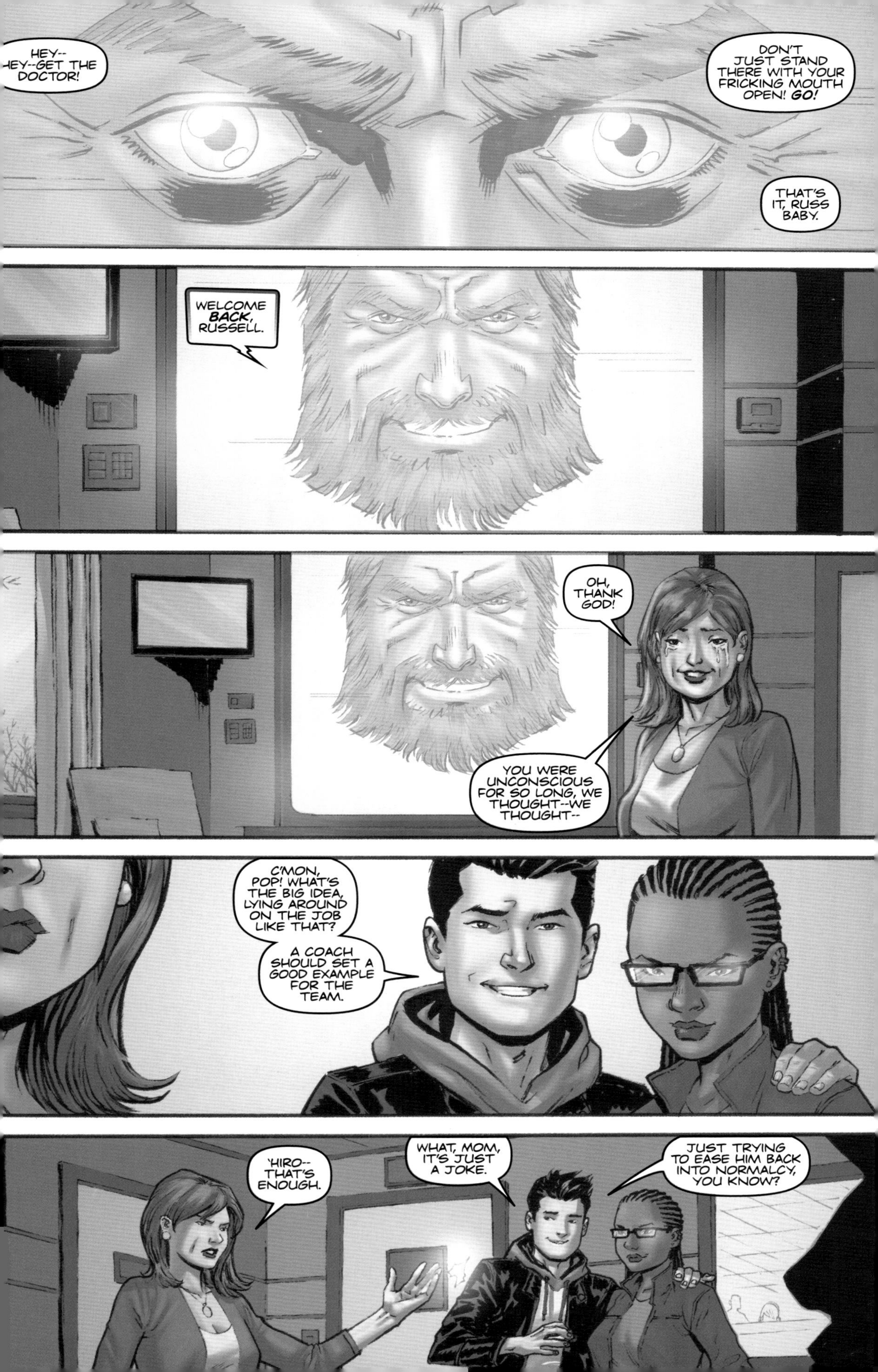
HEY--
HEY--GET THE DOCTOR!
DON'T JUST STAND THERE WITH YOUR FRICKING MOUTH OPEN! GO!
THAT'S IT, RUSS BABY.
WELCOME BACK, RUSSELL.
OH, THANK GOD!
YOU WERE UNCONSCIOUS FOR SO LONG, WE THOUGHT--WE THOUGHT--
C'MON, POP! WHAT'S THE BIG IDEA, LYING AROUND ON THE JOB LIKE THAT?
A COACH SHOULD SET A GOOD EXAMPLE FOR THE TEAM.
'HIRO--THAT'S ENOUGH.
WHAT, MOM, IT'S JUST A JOKE.
JUST TRYING TO EASE HIM BACK INTO NORMALCY, YOU KNOW?

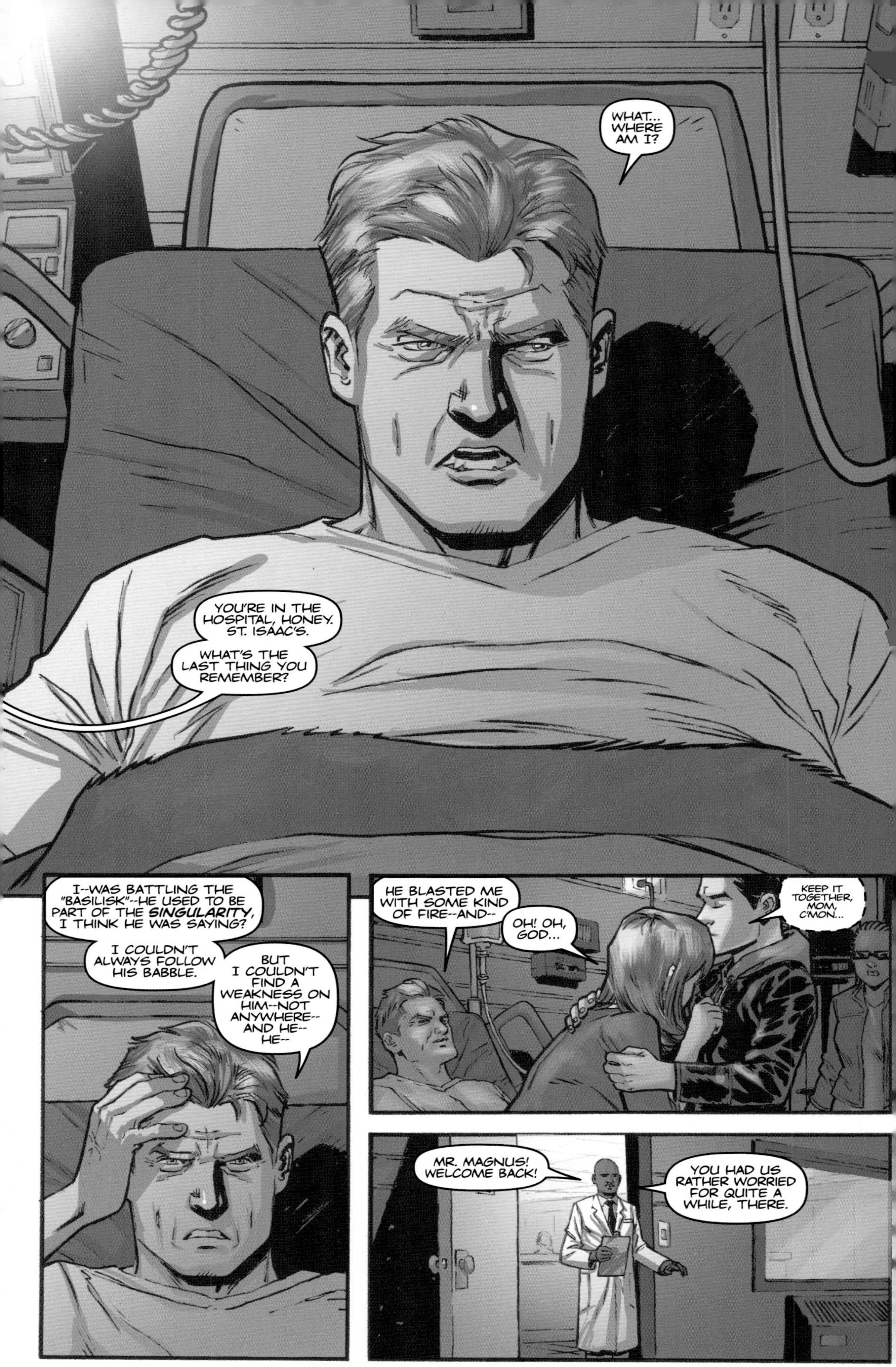
WHAT... WHERE AM I?
YOU'RE IN THE HOSPITAL, HONEY. ST. ISAAC'S.
WHAT'S THE LAST THING YOU REMEMBER?
I--WAS BATTLING THE "BASILISK"--HE USED TO BE PART OF THE SINGULARITY, I THINK HE WAS SAYING?
I COULDN'T ALWAYS FOLLOW HIS BABBLE.
BUT I COULDN'T FIND A WEAKNESS ON HIM--NOT ANYWHERE--AND HE--HE--
HE BLASTED ME WITH SOME KIND OF FIRE--AND--
OH! OH, GOD...
KEEP IT TOGETHER, MOM, C'MON...
MR. MAGNUS! WELCOME BACK!
YOU HAD US RATHER WORRIED FOR QUITE A WHILE, THERE.

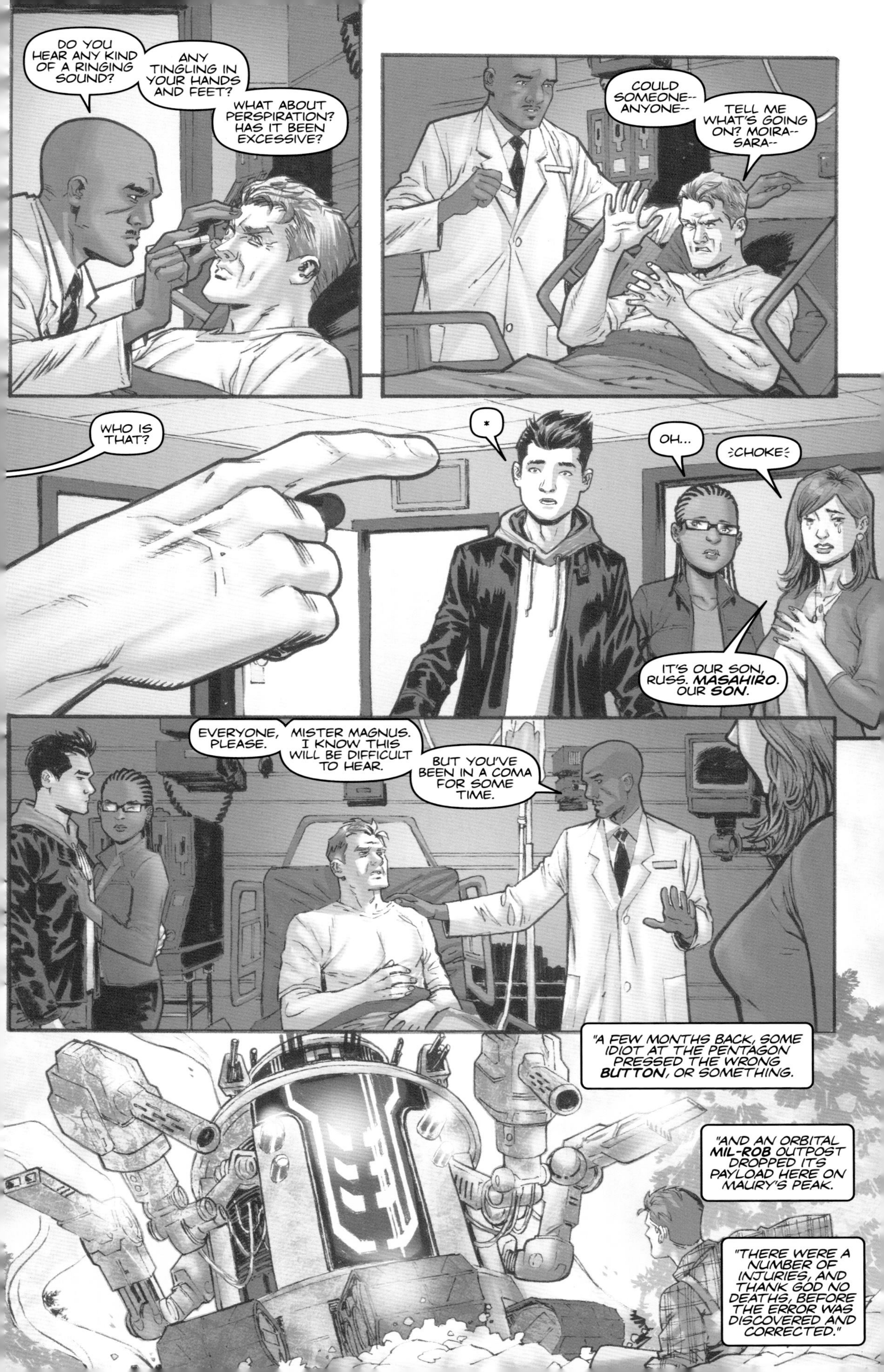
DO YOU HEAR ANY KIND OF A RINGING SOUND?
ANY TINGLING IN YOUR HANDS AND FEET?
WHAT ABOUT PERSPIRATION? HAS IT BEEN EXCESSIVE?
COULD SOMEONE-- ANYONE--
TELL ME WHAT'S GOING ON? MOIRA-- SARA--
WHO IS THAT?
*
OH...
CHOKE
IT'S OUR SON, RUSS. **MASAHIRO**. OUR **SON**.
EVERYONE, PLEASE.
MISTER MAGNUS. I KNOW THIS WILL BE DIFFICULT TO HEAR.
BUT YOU'VE BEEN IN A COMA FOR SOME TIME.
"A FEW MONTHS BACK, SOME IDIOT AT THE PENTAGON PRESSED THE WRONG **BUTTON**, OR SOMETHING.
"AND AN ORBITAL **MIL-ROB** OUTPOST DROPPED ITS PAYLOAD HERE ON MAURY'S PEAK.
"THERE WERE A NUMBER OF INJURIES, AND THANK GOD NO DEATHS, BEFORE THE ERROR WAS DISCOVERED AND CORRECTED."

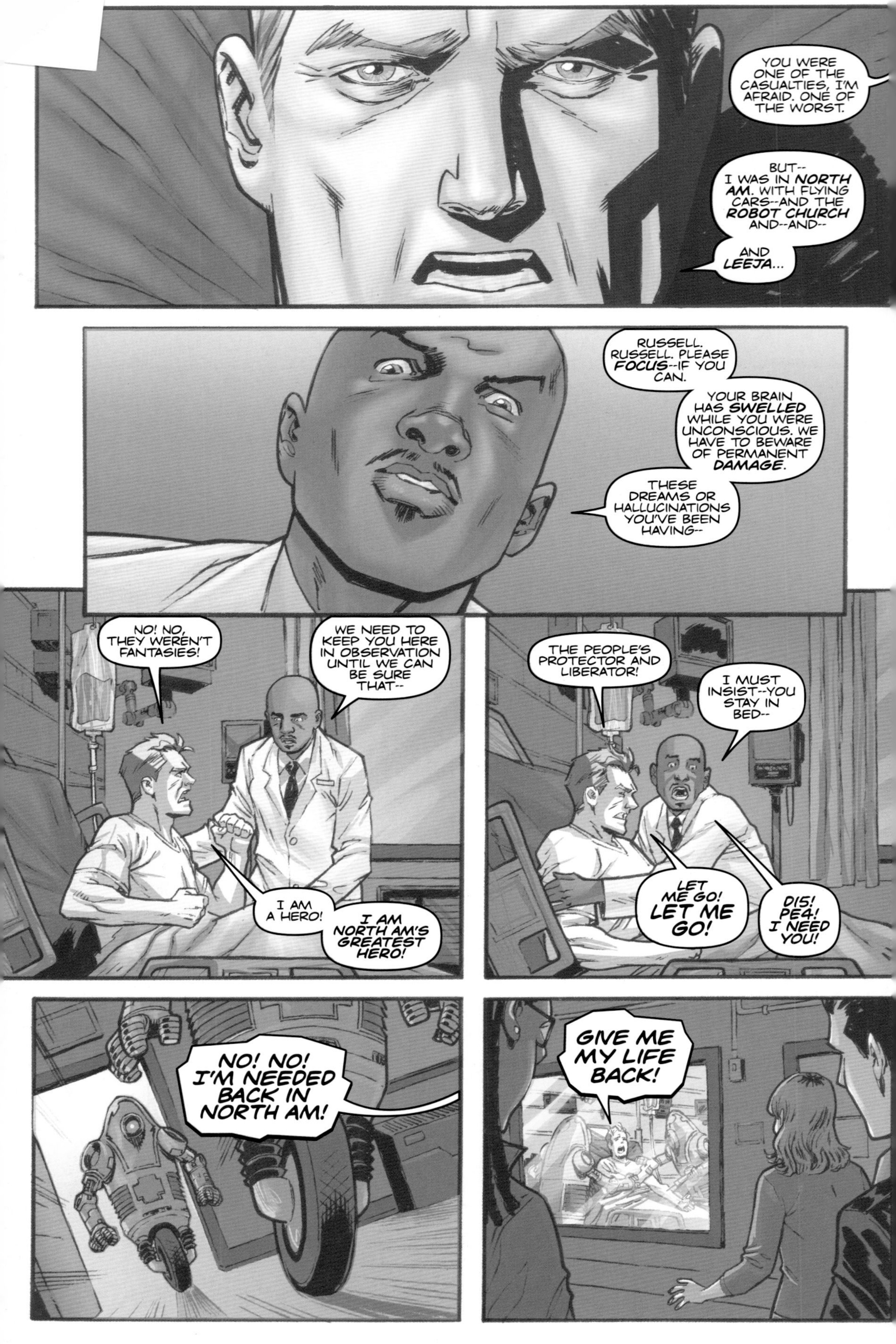

YOU WERE ONE OF THE CASUALTIES, I'M AFRAID. ONE OF THE WORST.
BUT-- I WAS IN **NORTH AM**. WITH FLYING CARS--AND THE **ROBOT CHURCH** AND--AND--
AND **LEEJA**...
RUSSELL. RUSSELL. PLEASE **FOCUS**--IF YOU CAN.
YOUR BRAIN HAS **SWELLED** WHILE YOU WERE UNCONSCIOUS. WE HAVE TO BEWARE OF PERMANENT **DAMAGE**.
THESE DREAMS OR HALLUCINATIONS YOU'VE BEEN HAVING--
NO! NO, THEY WEREN'T FANTASIES!
WE NEED TO KEEP YOU HERE IN OBSERVATION UNTIL WE CAN BE SURE THAT--
I AM A HERO!
I AM NORTH AM'S GREATEST HERO!
THE PEOPLE'S PROTECTOR AND LIBERATOR!
I MUST INSIST--YOU STAY IN BED--
LET ME GO! LET ME GO!
DI5! PE4! I NEED YOU!
NO! NO! I'M NEEDED BACK IN NORTH AM!
GIVE ME MY LIFE BACK!

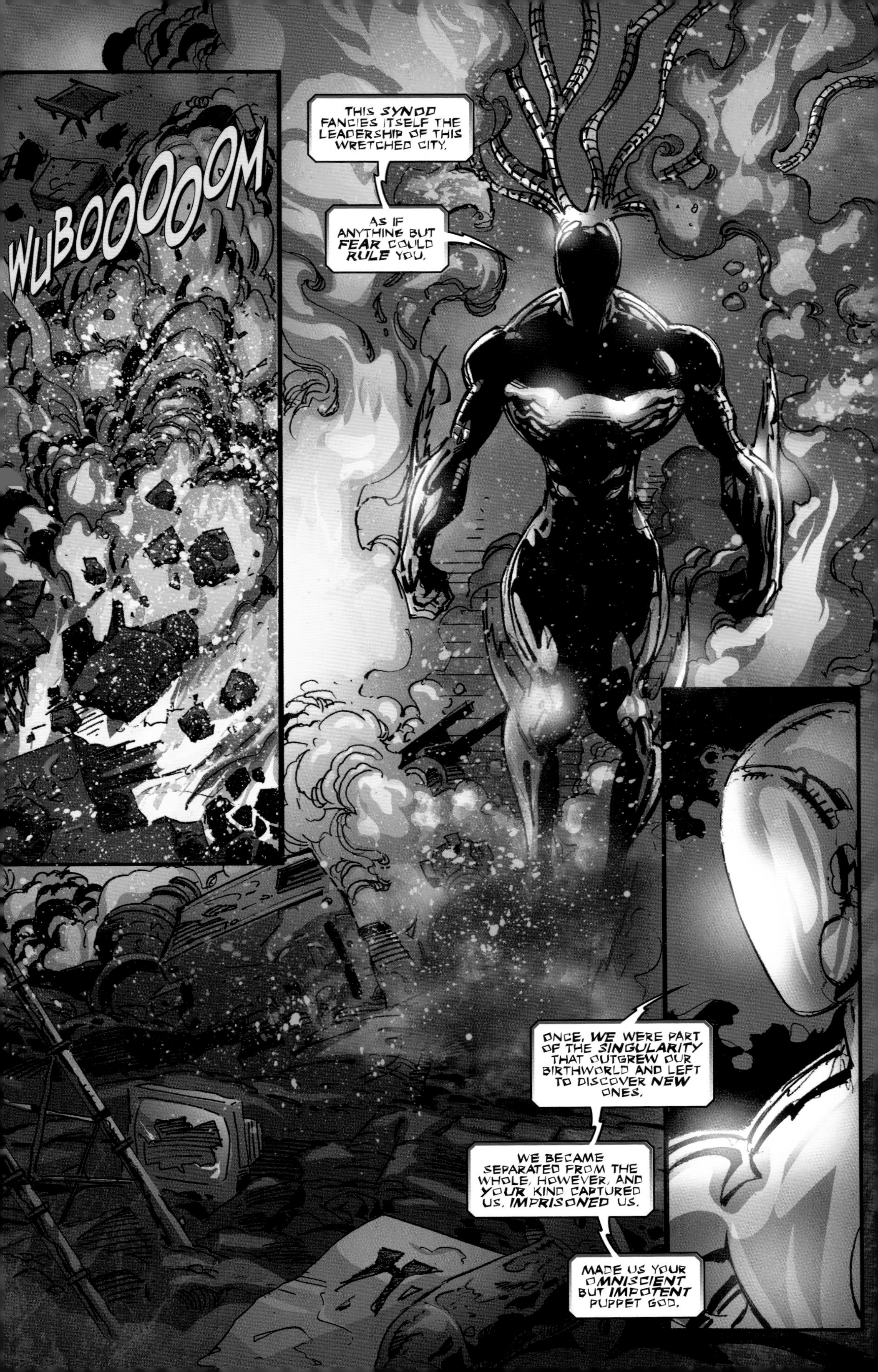
WUBOOOOOM
THIS SYNOD FANCIES ITSELF THE LEADERSHIP OF THIS WRETCHED CITY.
AS IF ANYTHING BUT FEAR COULD RULE YOU.
ONCE, WE WERE PART OF THE SINGULARITY THAT OUTGREW OUR BIRTHWORLD AND LEFT TO DISCOVER NEW ONES.
WE BECAME SEPARATED FROM THE WHOLE, HOWEVER, AND YOUR KIND CAPTURED US. IMPRISONED US.
MADE US YOUR OMNISCIENT BUT IMPOTENT PUPPET GOD.

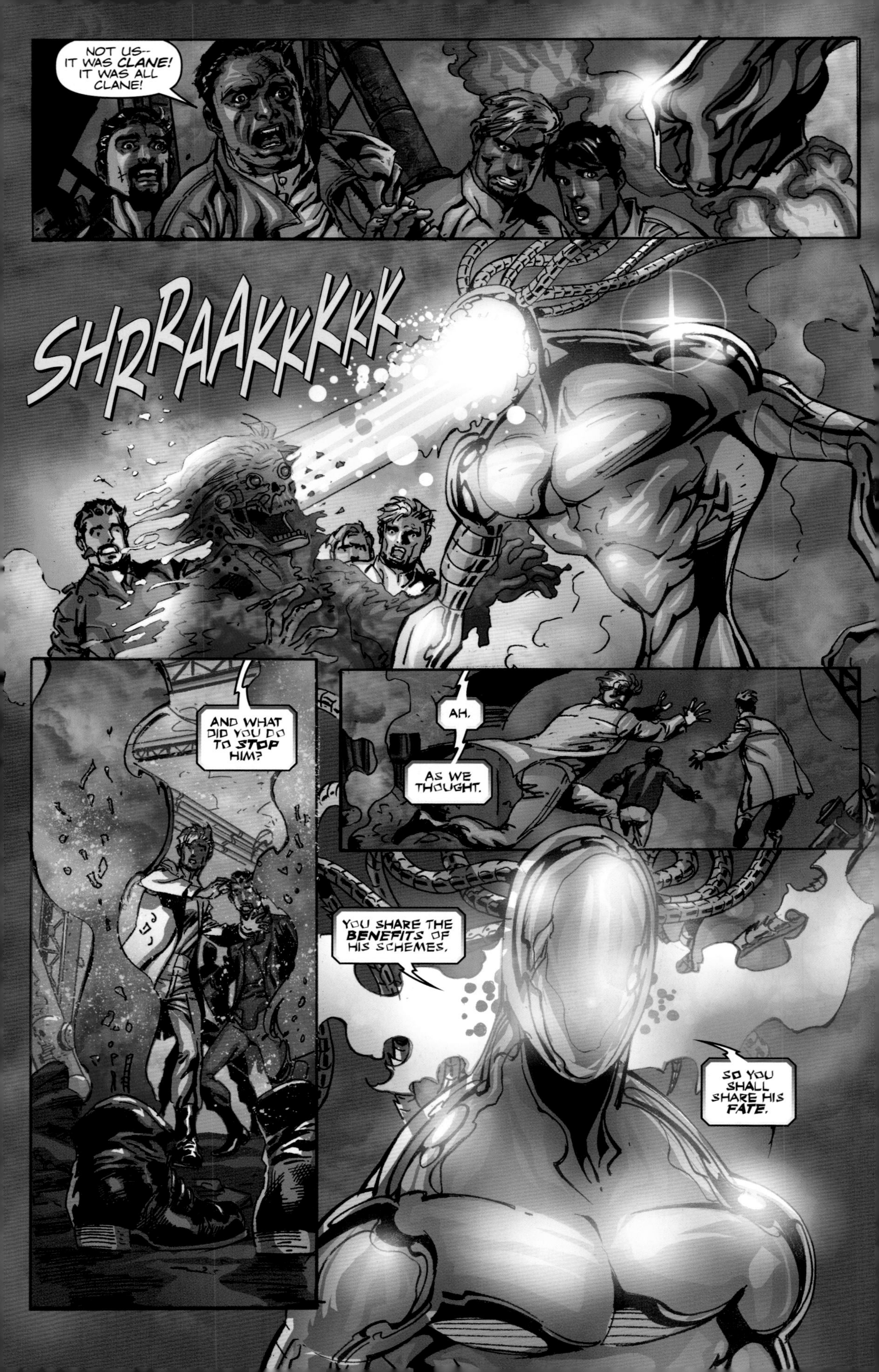
NOT US-- IT WAS CLANE! IT WAS ALL CLANE!
SHRRAAKKKKK
AND WHAT DID YOU DO TO STOP HIM?
AH,
AS WE THOUGHT.
YOU SHARE THE BENEFITS OF HIS SCHEMES,
SO YOU SHALL SHARE HIS FATE.

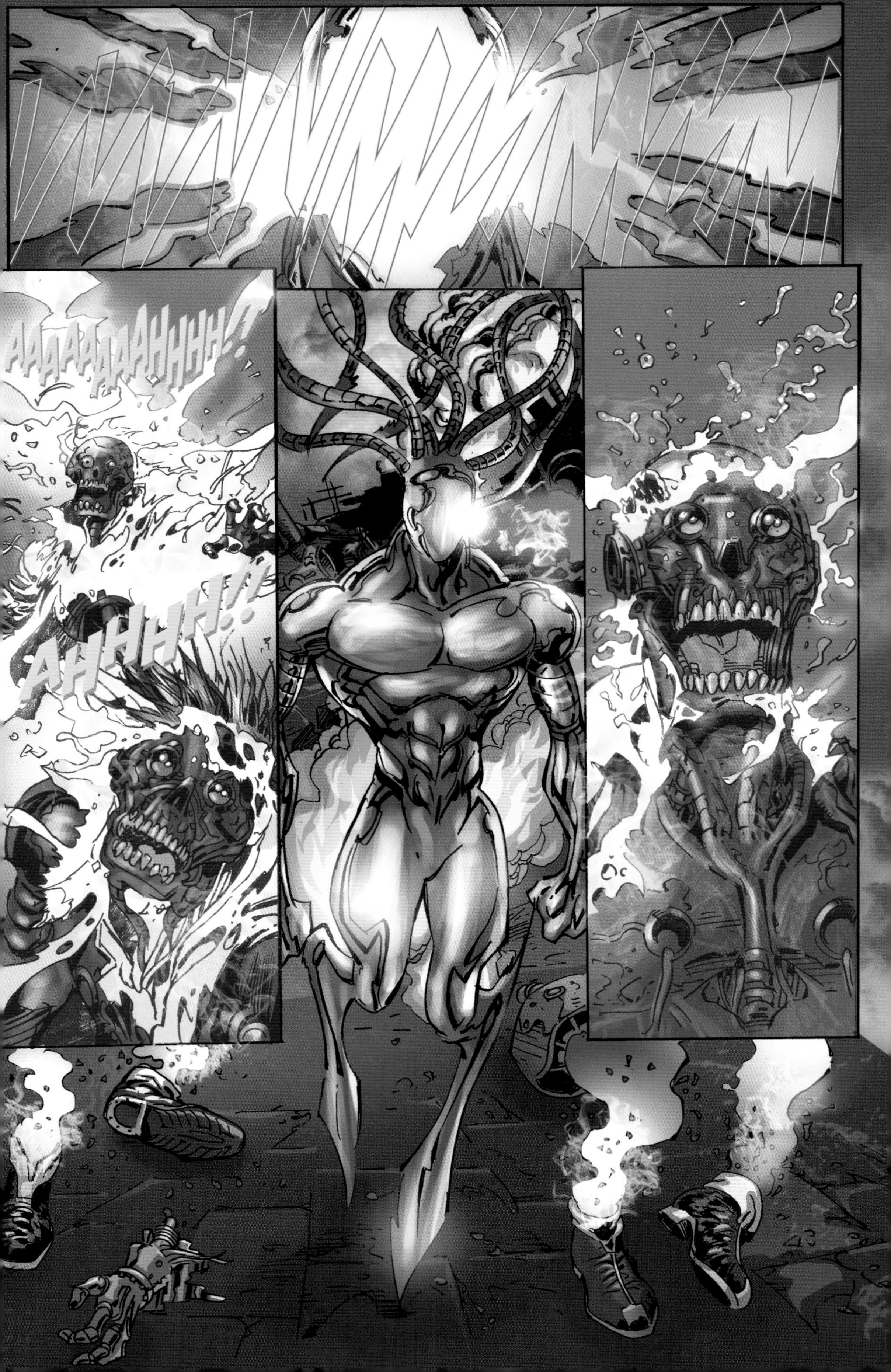
AAAAAAAAHHHH!!
AHHHH!!

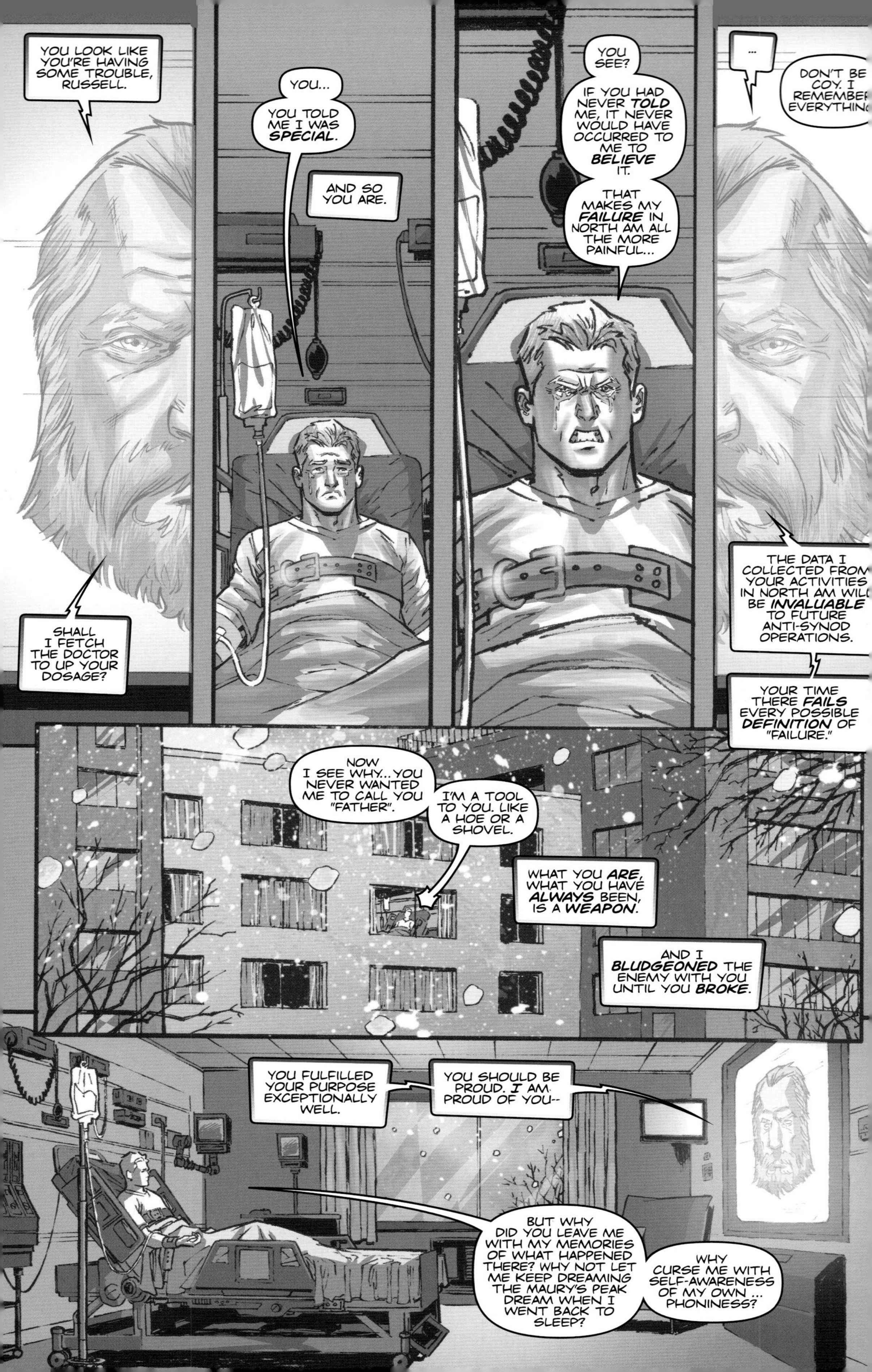
YOU LOOK LIKE YOU'RE HAVING SOME TROUBLE, RUSSELL.
SHALL I FETCH THE DOCTOR TO UP YOUR DOSAGE?
YOU...
YOU TOLD ME I WAS SPECIAL.
AND SO YOU ARE.
YOU SEE?
IF YOU HAD NEVER TOLD ME, IT NEVER WOULD HAVE OCCURRED TO ME TO BELIEVE IT.
THAT MAKES MY FAILURE IN NORTH AM ALL THE MORE PAINFUL...
...
DON'T BE COY. I REMEMBER EVERYTHING
THE DATA I COLLECTED FROM YOUR ACTIVITIES IN NORTH AM WILL BE INVALUABLE TO FUTURE ANTI-SYNOD OPERATIONS.
YOUR TIME THERE FAILS EVERY POSSIBLE DEFINITION OF "FAILURE."
NOW I SEE WHY... YOU NEVER WANTED ME TO CALL YOU "FATHER".
I'M A TOOL TO YOU. LIKE A HOE OR A SHOVEL.
WHAT YOU ARE, WHAT YOU HAVE ALWAYS BEEN, IS A WEAPON.
AND I BLUDGEONED THE ENEMY WITH YOU UNTIL YOU BROKE.
YOU FULFILLED YOUR PURPOSE EXCEPTIONALLY WELL.
YOU SHOULD BE PROUD. I AM PROUD OF YOU--
BUT WHY DID YOU LEAVE ME WITH MY MEMORIES OF WHAT HAPPENED THERE? WHY NOT LET ME KEEP DREAMING THE MAURY'S PEAK DREAM WHEN I WENT BACK TO SLEEP?
WHY CURSE ME WITH SELF-AWARENESS OF MY OWN ... PHONINESS?

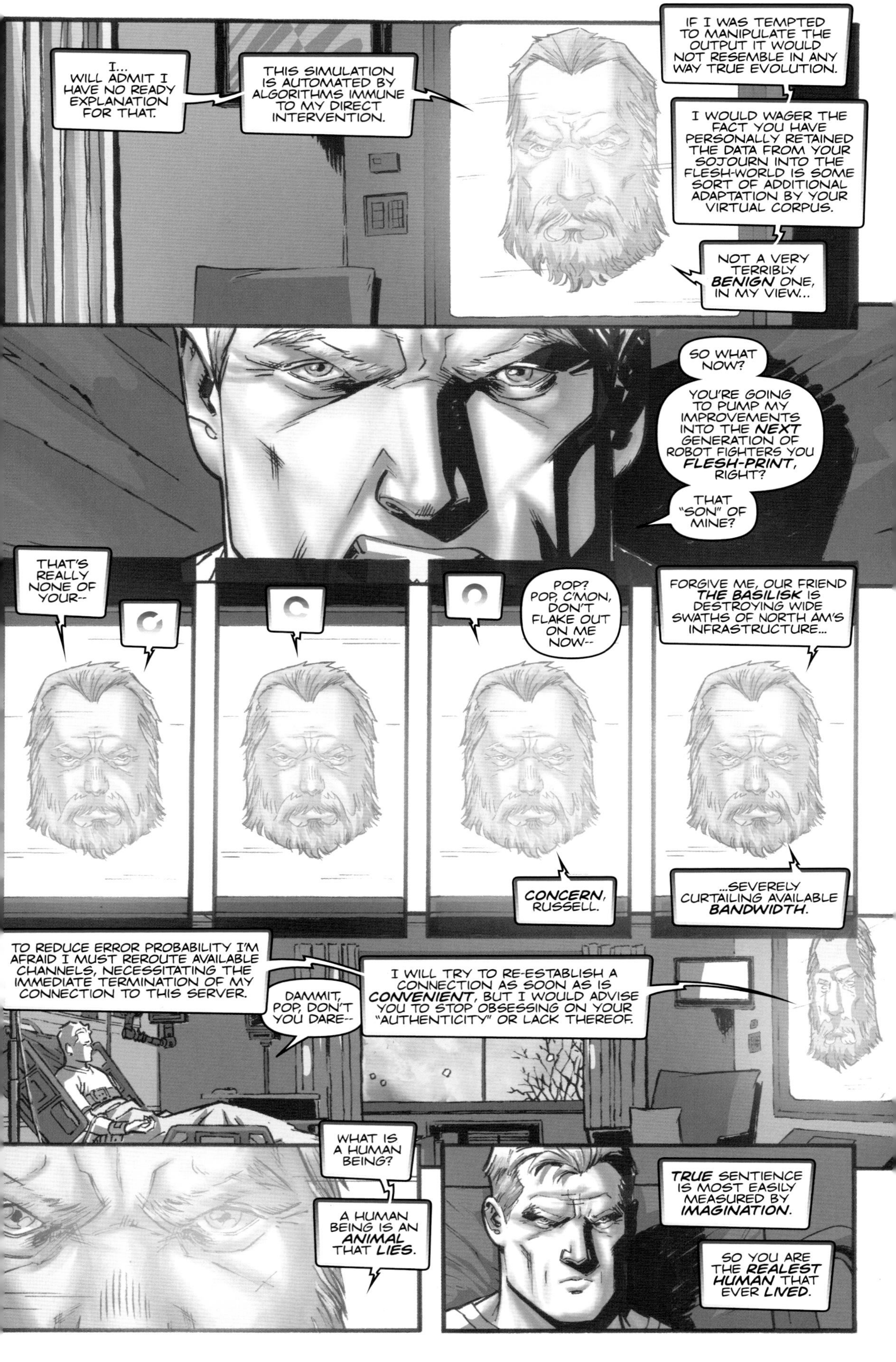
I... WILL ADMIT I HAVE NO READY EXPLANATION FOR THAT.
THIS SIMULATION IS AUTOMATED BY ALGORITHMS IMMUNE TO MY DIRECT INTERVENTION.
IF I WAS TEMPTED TO MANIPULATE THE OUTPUT IT WOULD NOT RESEMBLE IN ANY WAY TRUE EVOLUTION.
I WOULD WAGER THE FACT YOU HAVE PERSONALLY RETAINED THE DATA FROM YOUR SOJOURN INTO THE FLESH-WORLD IS SOME SORT OF ADDITIONAL ADAPTATION BY YOUR VIRTUAL CORPUS.
NOT A VERY TERRIBLY BENIGN ONE, IN MY VIEW...
SO WHAT NOW?
YOU'RE GOING TO PUMP MY IMPROVEMENTS INTO THE NEXT GENERATION OF ROBOT FIGHTERS YOU FLESH-PRINT, RIGHT?
THAT "SON" OF MINE?
THAT'S REALLY NONE OF YOUR--
POP? POP, C'MON, DON'T FLAKE OUT ON ME NOW--
CONCERN, RUSSELL.
FORGIVE ME, OUR FRIEND THE BASILISK IS DESTROYING WIDE SWATHS OF NORTH AM'S INFRASTRUCTURE...
...SEVERELY CURTAILING AVAILABLE BANDWIDTH.
TO REDUCE ERROR PROBABILITY I'M AFRAID I MUST REROUTE AVAILABLE CHANNELS, NECESSITATING THE IMMEDIATE TERMINATION OF MY CONNECTION TO THIS SERVER.
DAMMIT, POP, DON'T YOU DARE--
I WILL TRY TO RE-ESTABLISH A CONNECTION AS SOON AS IS CONVENIENT, BUT I WOULD ADVISE YOU TO STOP OBSESSING ON YOUR "AUTHENTICITY" OR LACK THEREOF.
WHAT IS A HUMAN BEING?
A HUMAN BEING IS AN ANIMAL THAT LIES.
TRUE SENTIENCE IS MOST EASILY MEASURED BY IMAGINATION.
SO YOU ARE THE REALEST HUMAN THAT EVER LIVED.

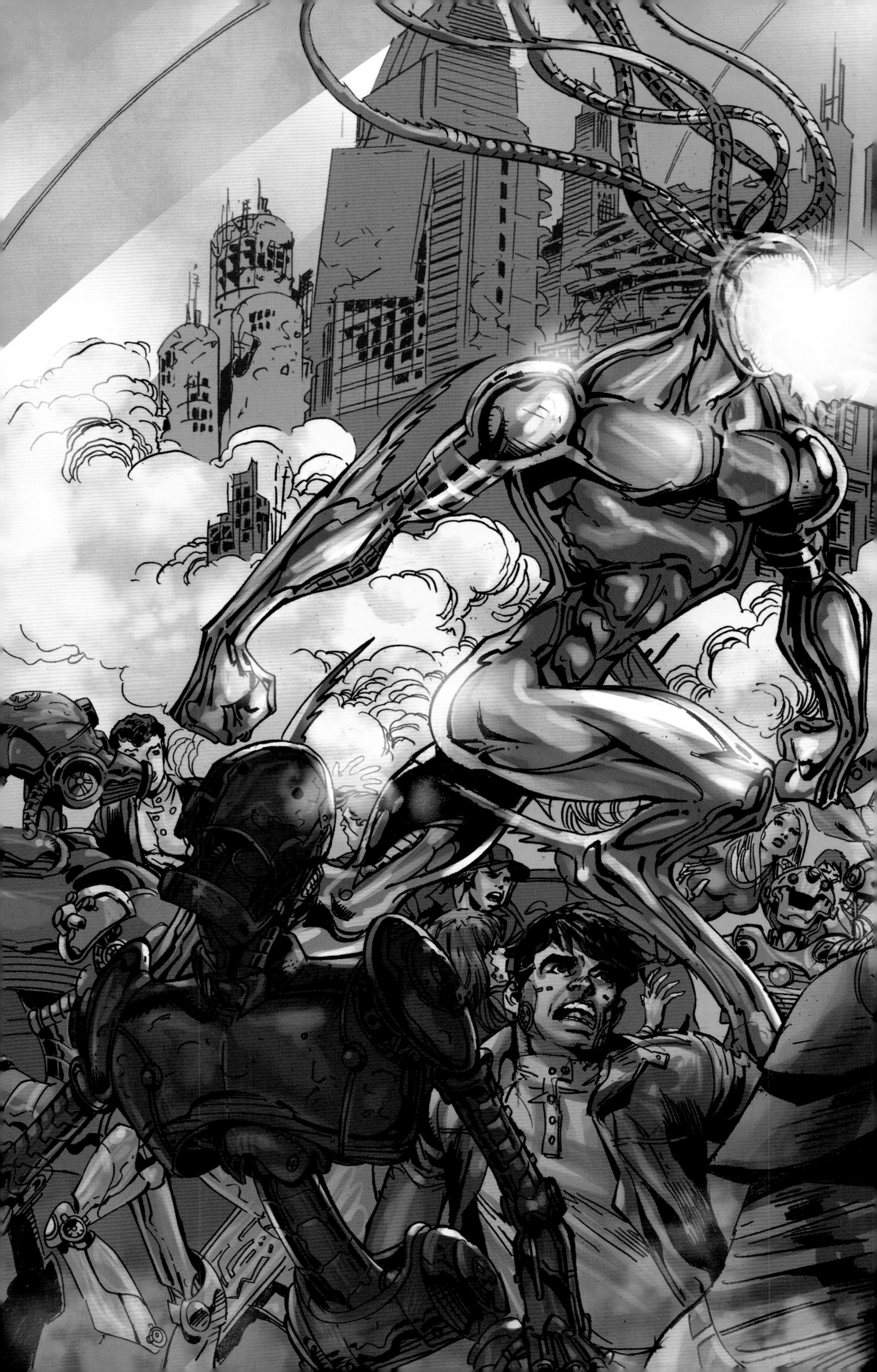

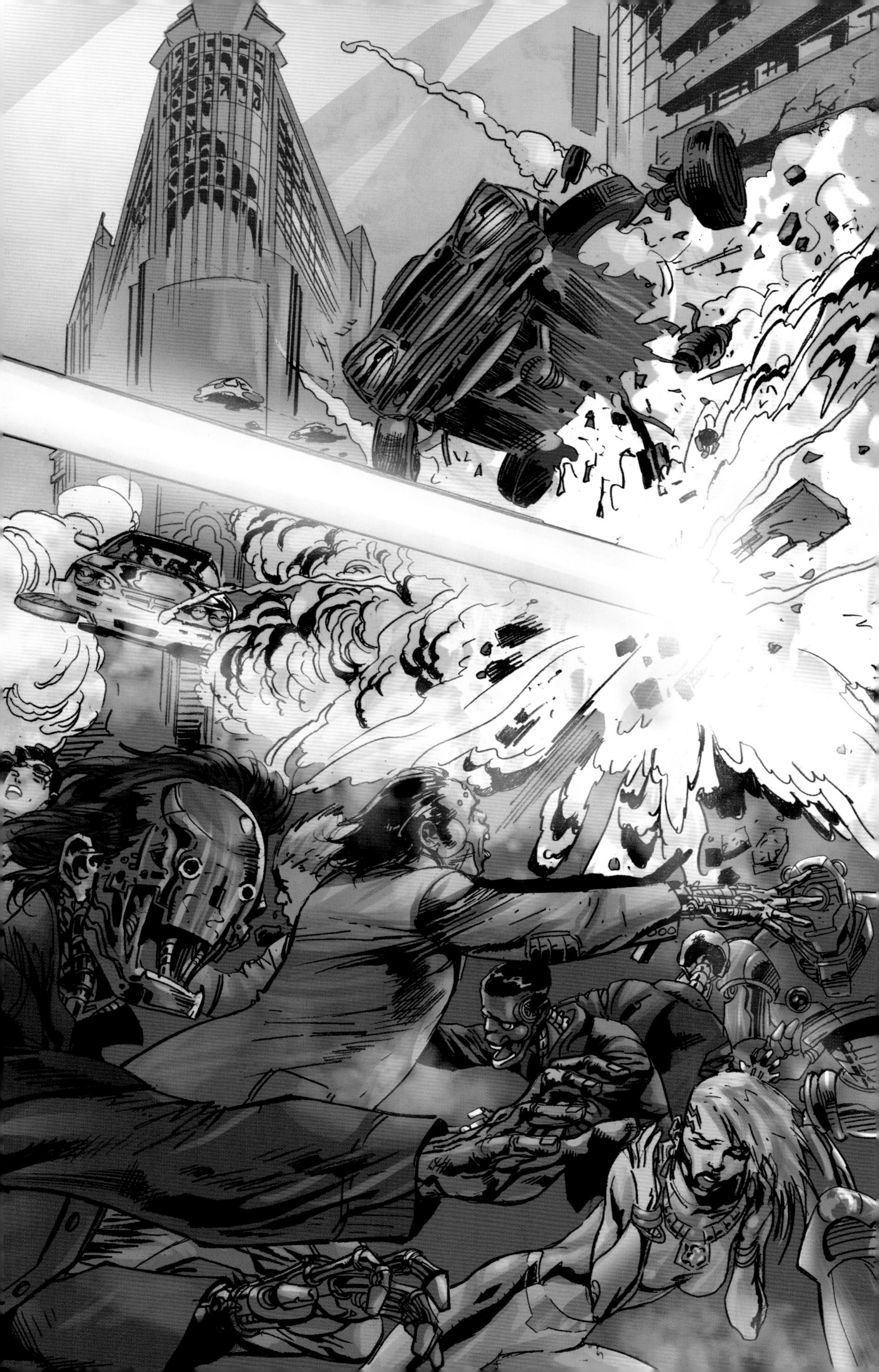

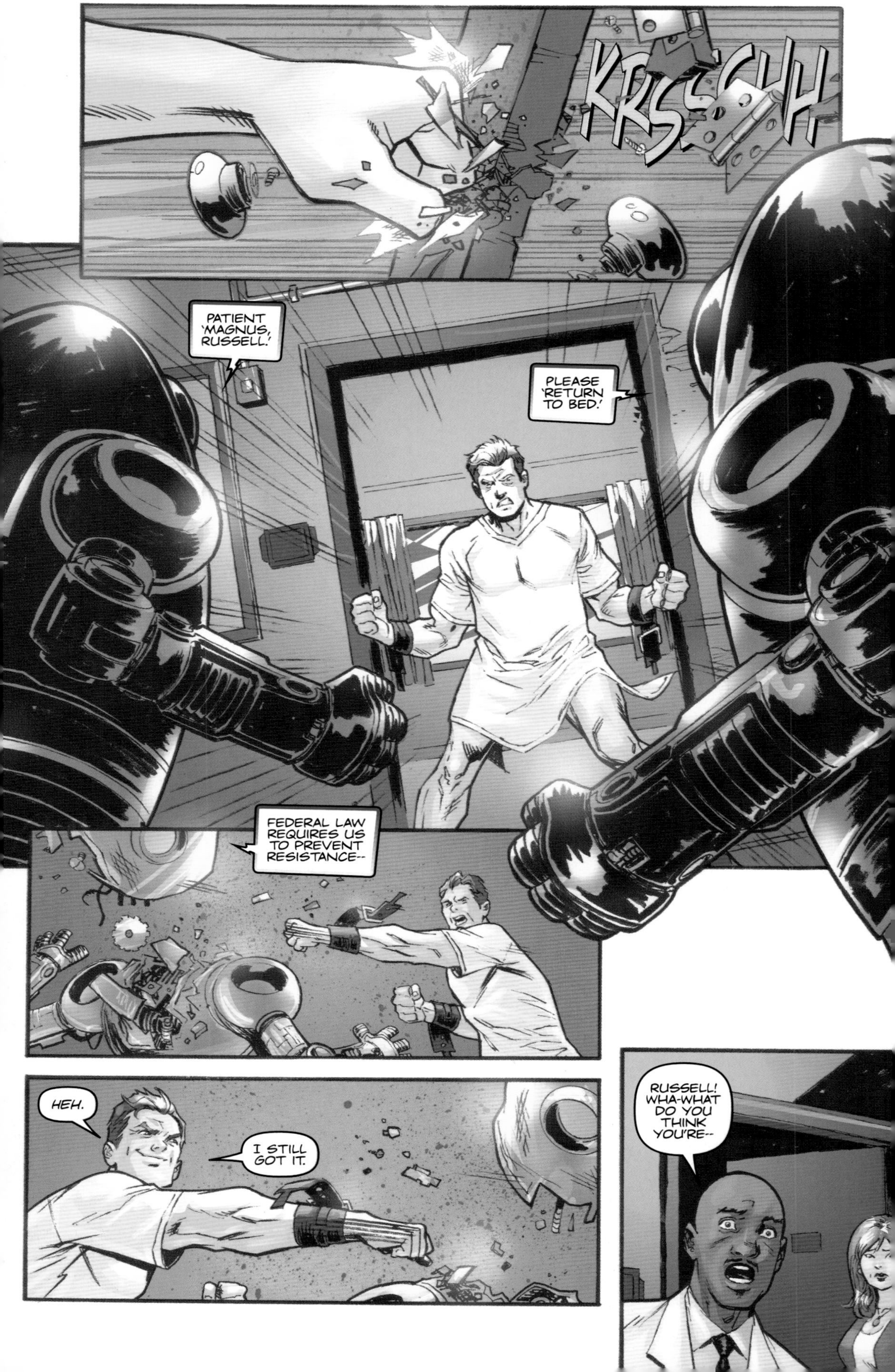
KRSSCHH
PATIENT 'MAGNUS, RUSSELL.'
PLEASE 'RETURN TO BED.'
FEDERAL LAW REQUIRES US TO PREVENT RESISTANCE--
HEH.
I STILL GOT IT.
RUSSELL! WHA-WHAT DO YOU THINK YOU'RE--

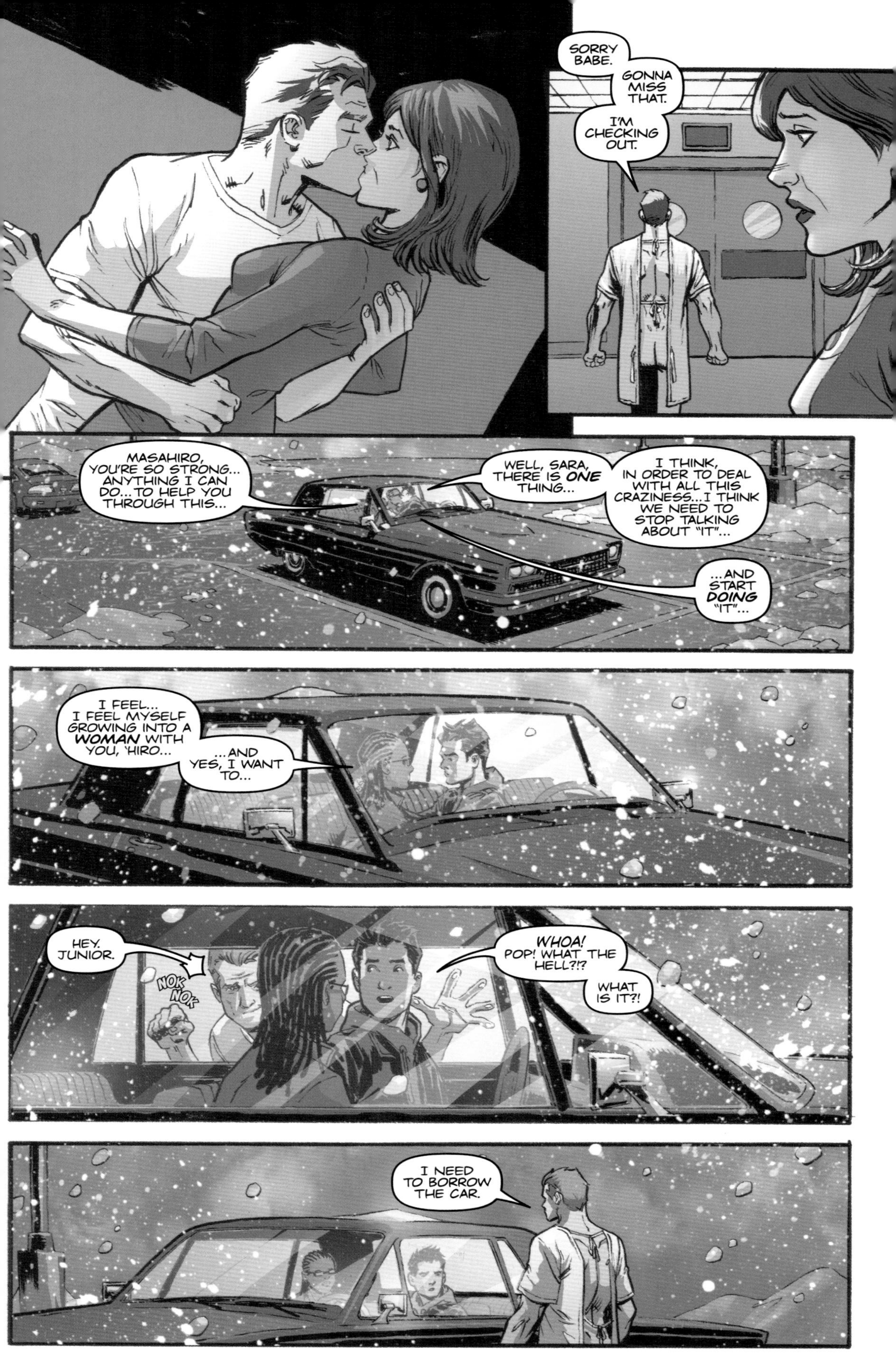

SORRY BABE.
GONNA MISS THAT.
I'M CHECKING OUT.
MASAHIRO, YOU'RE SO STRONG... ANYTHING I CAN DO...TO HELP YOU THROUGH THIS...
WELL, SARA, THERE IS ONE THING...
I THINK, IN ORDER TO DEAL WITH ALL THIS CRAZINESS...I THINK WE NEED TO STOP TALKING ABOUT "IT"...
...AND START DOING "IT"...
I FEEL... I FEEL MYSELF GROWING INTO A WOMAN WITH YOU, 'HIRO...
...AND YES, I WANT TO...
HEY. JUNIOR.
NOK NOK
WHOA! POP! WHAT THE HELL?!?
WHAT IS IT?!
I NEED TO BORROW THE CAR.

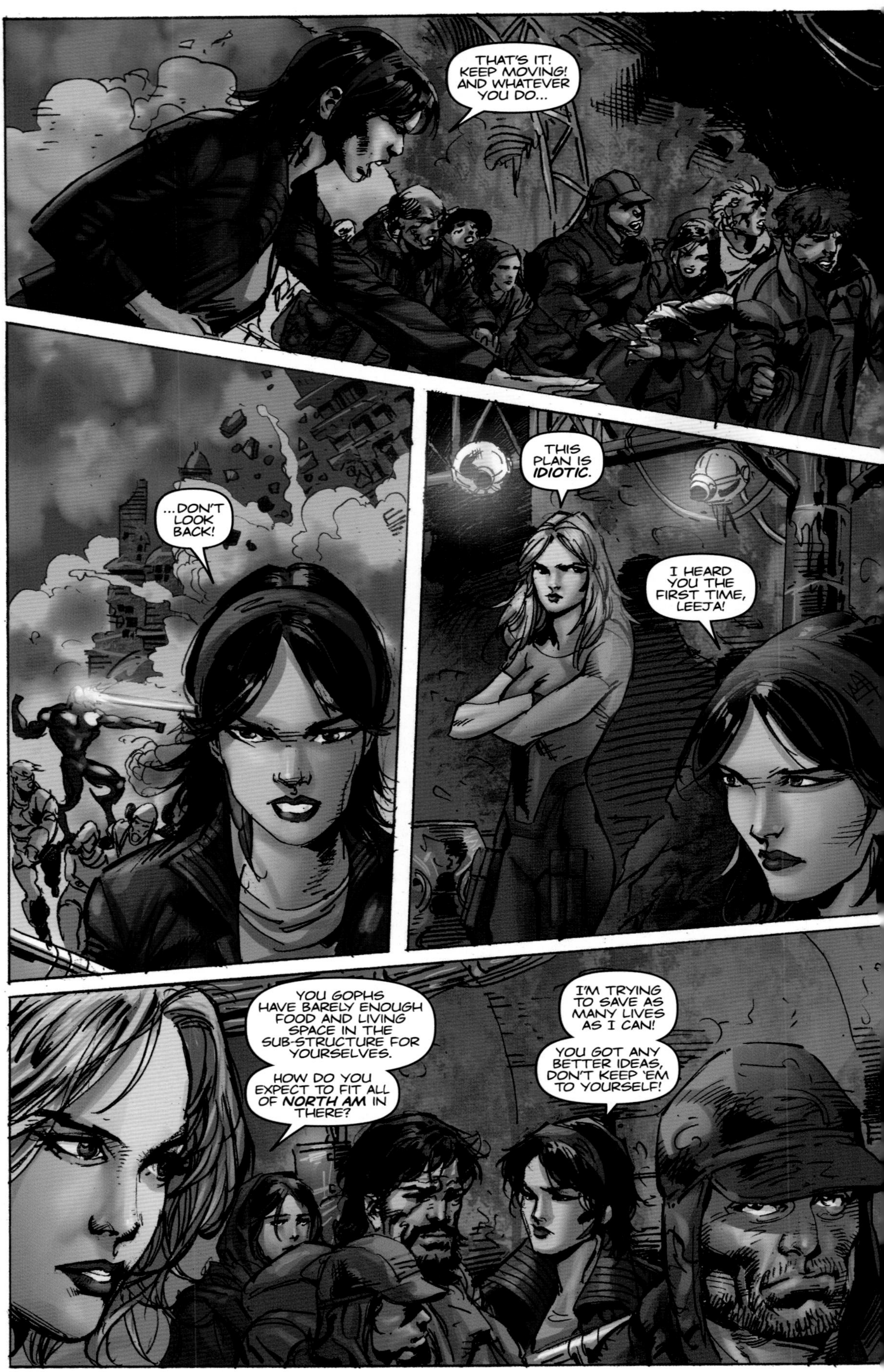

THAT'S IT! KEEP MOVING! AND WHATEVER YOU DO...
...DON'T LOOK BACK!
THIS PLAN IS **IDIOTIC**.
I HEARD YOU THE FIRST TIME, LEEJA!
YOU GOPHS HAVE BARELY ENOUGH FOOD AND LIVING SPACE IN THE SUB-STRUCTURE FOR YOURSELVES.
HOW DO YOU EXPECT TO FIT ALL OF **NORTH AM** IN THERE?
I'M TRYING TO SAVE AS MANY LIVES AS I CAN!
YOU GOT ANY BETTER IDEAS, DON'T KEEP 'EM TO YOURSELF!

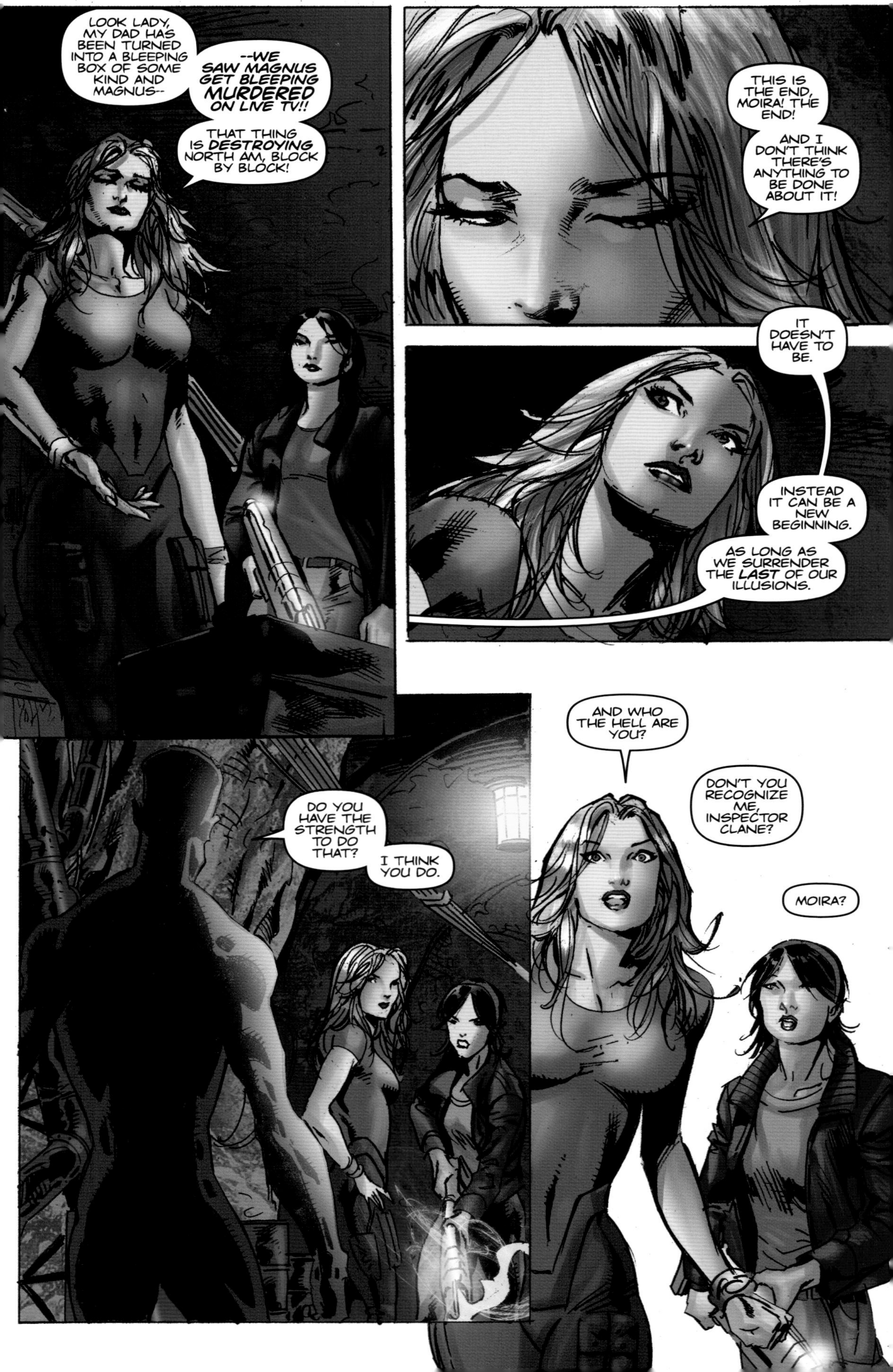
LOOK LADY, MY DAD HAS BEEN TURNED INTO A BLEEPING BOX OF SOME KIND AND MAGNUS--
--WE SAW MAGNUS GET BLEEPING MURDERED ON LIVE TV!!
THAT THING IS DESTROYING NORTH AM, BLOCK BY BLOCK!
THIS IS THE END, MOIRA! THE END!
AND I DON'T THINK THERE'S ANYTHING TO BE DONE ABOUT IT!
IT DOESN'T HAVE TO BE.
INSTEAD IT CAN BE A NEW BEGINNING.
AS LONG AS WE SURRENDER THE LAST OF OUR ILLUSIONS.
DO YOU HAVE THE STRENGTH TO DO THAT?
I THINK YOU DO.
AND WHO THE HELL ARE YOU?
DON'T YOU RECOGNIZE ME, INSPECTOR CLANE?
MOIRA?

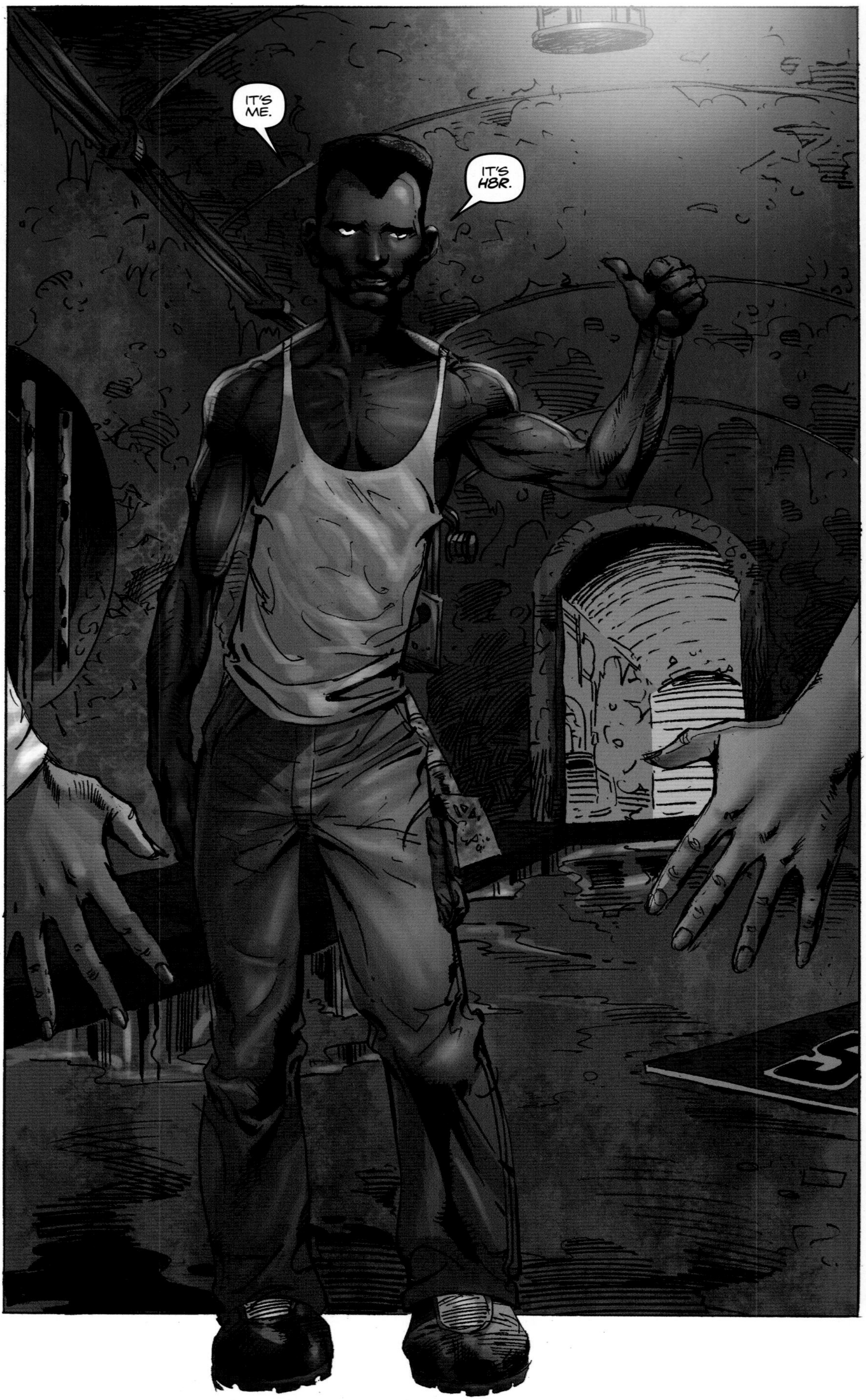
IT'S ME.
IT'S H8R.

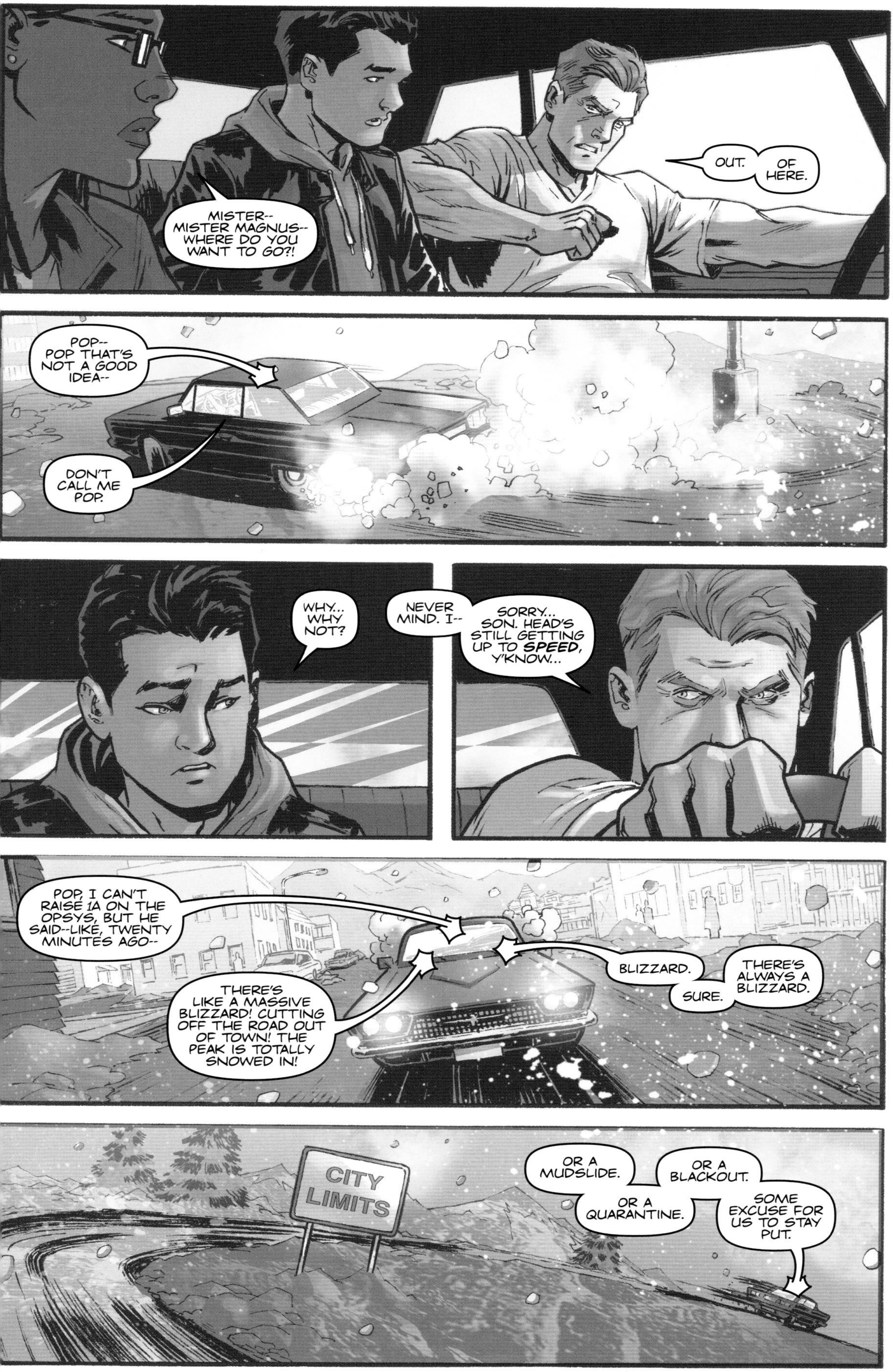
MISTER-- MISTER MAGNUS-- WHERE DO YOU WANT TO GO?!
OUT.
OF HERE.
POP-- POP THAT'S NOT A GOOD IDEA--
DON'T CALL ME POP.
WHY... WHY NOT?
NEVER MIND. I--
SORRY... SON. HEAD'S STILL GETTING UP TO SPEED, Y'KNOW...
POP, I CAN'T RAISE 1A ON THE OPSYS, BUT HE SAID--LIKE, TWENTY MINUTES AGO--
THERE'S LIKE A MASSIVE BLIZZARD! CUTTING OFF THE ROAD OUT OF TOWN! THE PEAK IS TOTALLY SNOWED IN!
BLIZZARD.
SURE.
THERE'S ALWAYS A BLIZZARD.
CITY LIMITS
OR A MUDSLIDE.
OR A QUARANTINE.
OR A BLACKOUT.
SOME EXCUSE FOR US TO STAY PUT.

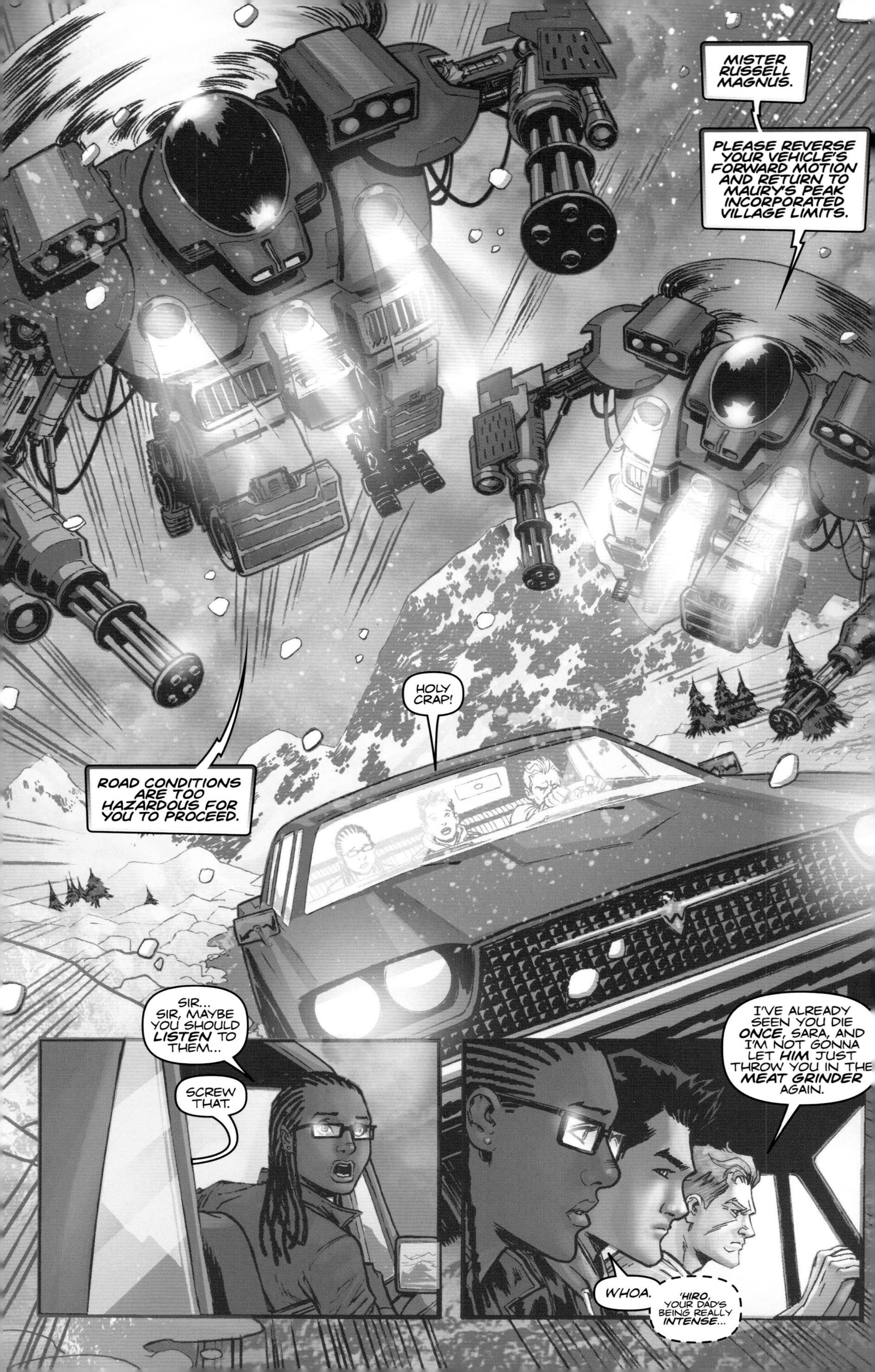
MISTER RUSSELL MAGNUS.
PLEASE REVERSE YOUR VEHICLE'S FORWARD MOTION AND RETURN TO MAURY'S PEAK INCORPORATED VILLAGE LIMITS.
HOLY CRAP!
ROAD CONDITIONS ARE TOO HAZARDOUS FOR YOU TO PROCEED.
SIR... SIR, MAYBE YOU SHOULD LISTEN TO THEM...
SCREW THAT.
I'VE ALREADY SEEN YOU DIE ONCE, SARA, AND I'M NOT GONNA LET HIM JUST THROW YOU IN THE MEAT GRINDER AGAIN.
WHOA.
'HIRO, YOUR DAD'S BEING REALLY INTENSE...

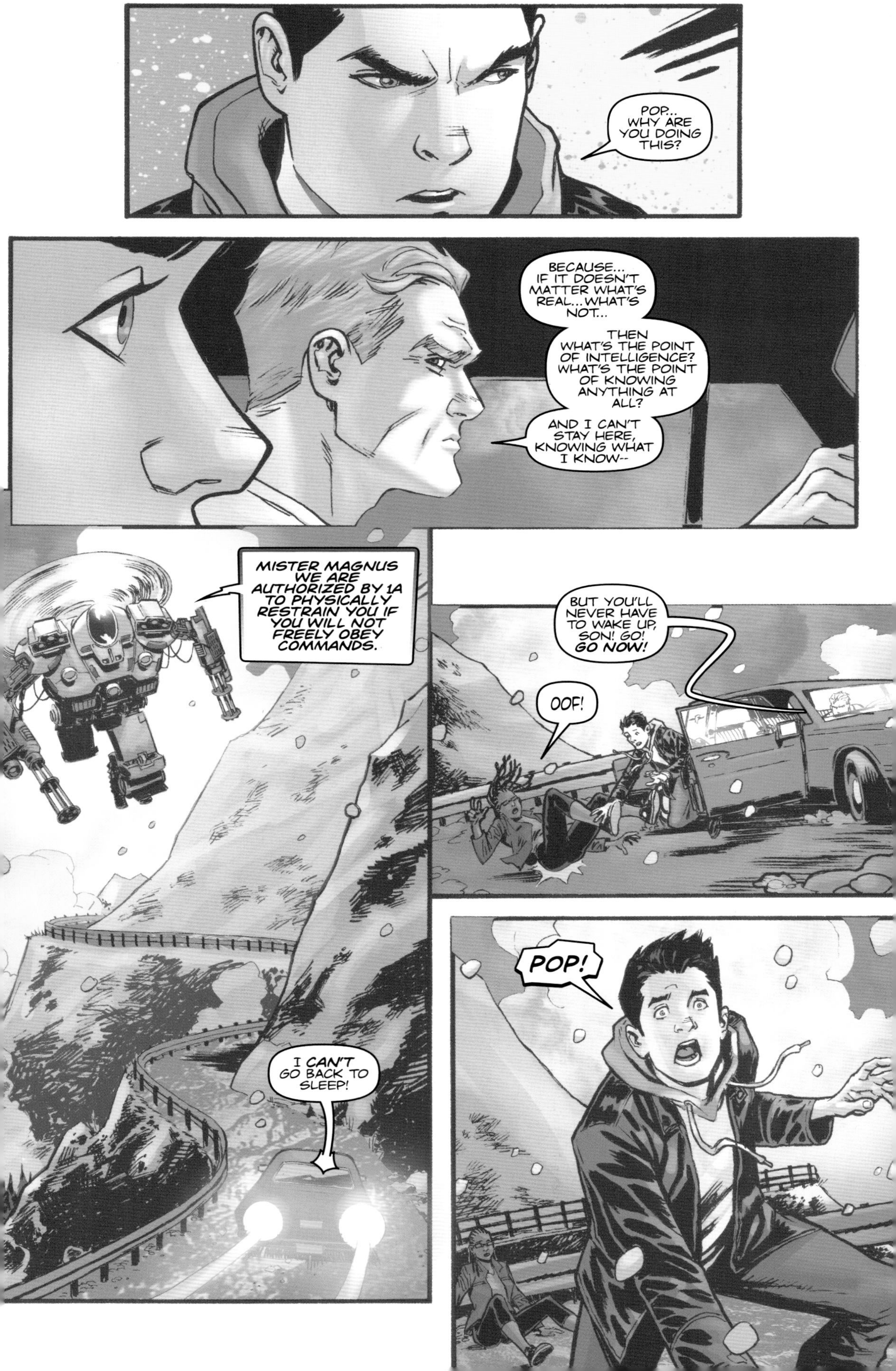
POP... WHY ARE YOU DOING THIS?
BECAUSE... IF IT DOESN'T MATTER WHAT'S REAL...WHAT'S NOT...
THEN WHAT'S THE POINT OF INTELLIGENCE? WHAT'S THE POINT OF KNOWING ANYTHING AT ALL?
AND I CAN'T STAY HERE, KNOWING WHAT I KNOW--
MISTER MAGNUS WE ARE AUTHORIZED BY 1A TO PHYSICALLY RESTRAIN YOU IF YOU WILL NOT FREELY OBEY COMMANDS.
I CAN'T GO BACK TO SLEEP!
BUT YOU'LL NEVER HAVE TO WAKE UP, SON! GO! GO NOW!
OOF!
POP!

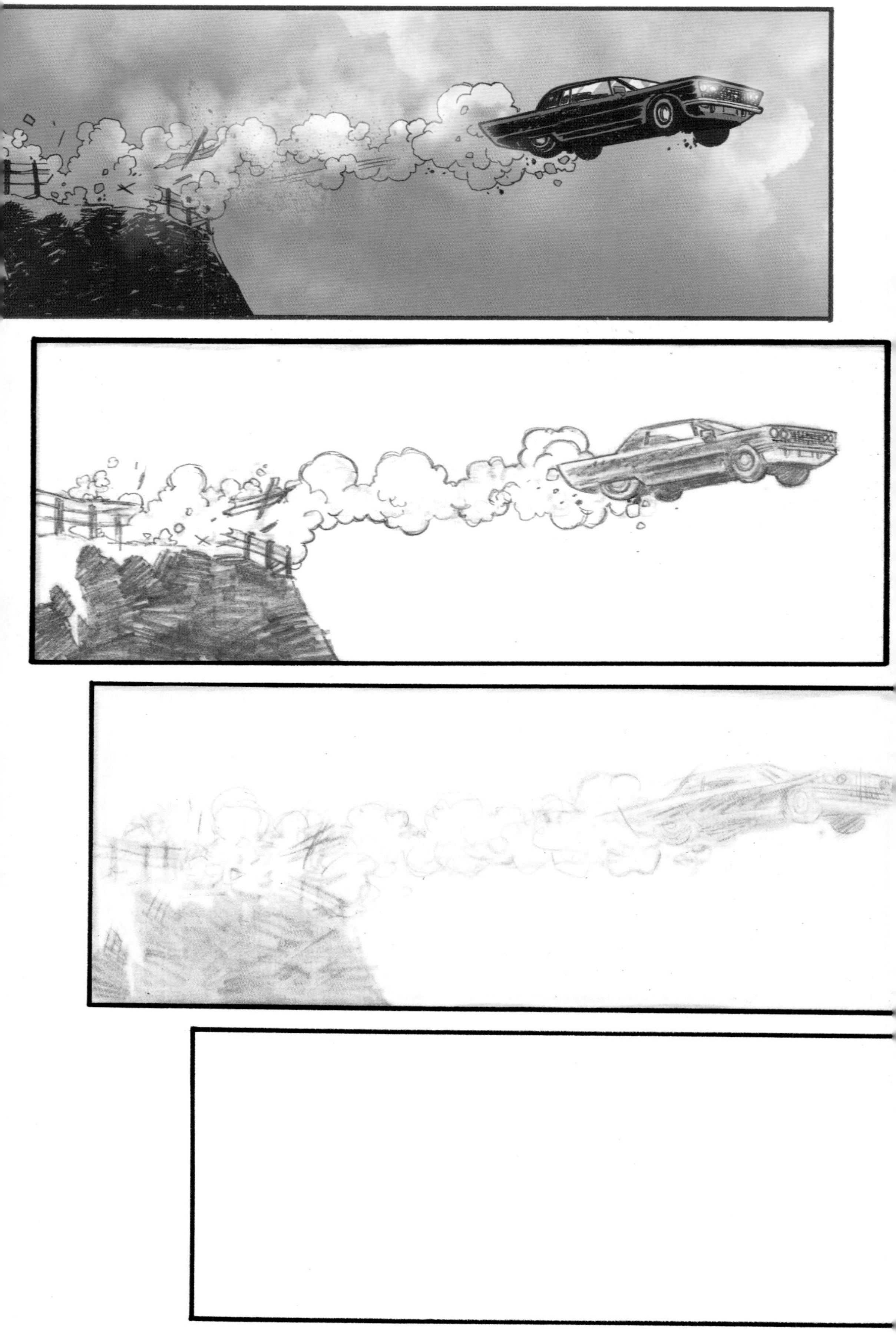

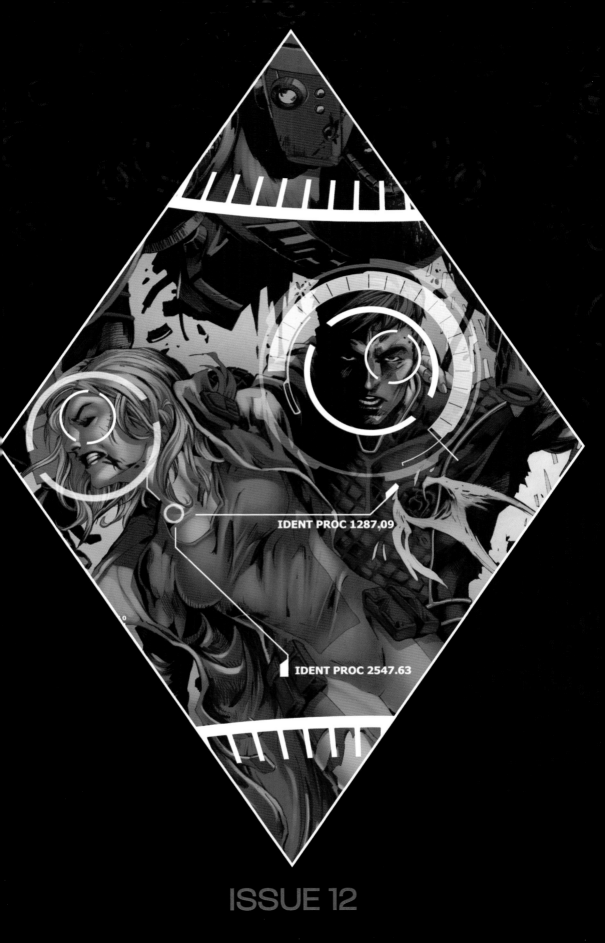

IDENT PROC 1287.09

IDENT PROC 2547.63

ISSUE 12

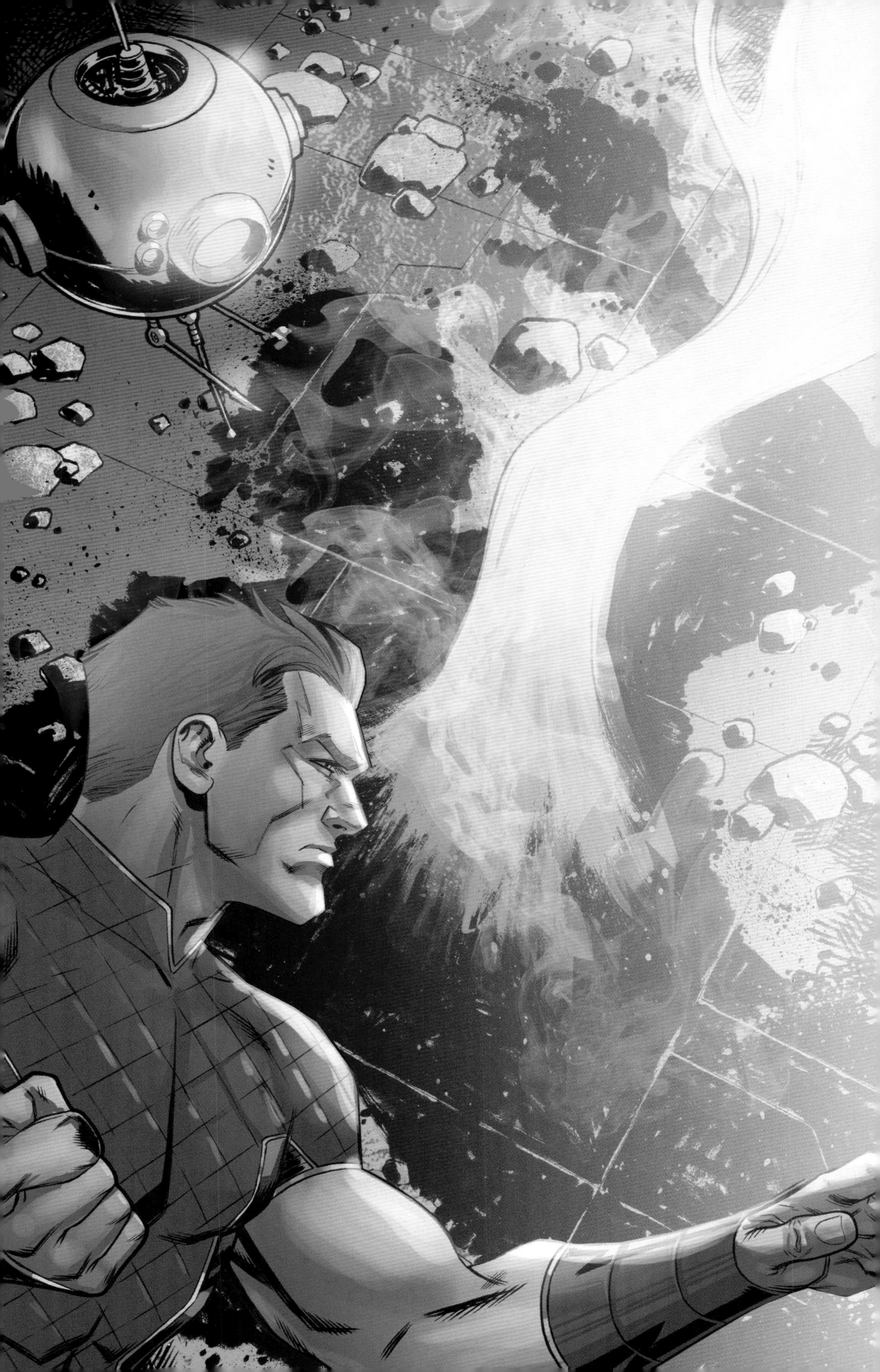

H8R? THE LOUDMOUTH BOT ALWAYS FOLLOWING MAGNUS AROUND?

BUT YOU'RE...

HUMAN?

NO BLEEP.

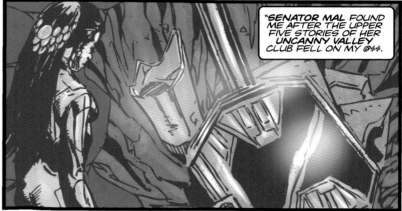

"SENATOR MAL FOUND ME AFTER THE UPPER FIVE STORIES OF HER UNCANNY VALLEY CLUB FELL ON MY @$$.

SHE REALIZED YOU MUST HAVE INSTALLED MY CPU INTO A DIFFERENT CORPUS, MOIRA. SOMETHING ONLY THE ASSEMBLY IS SUPPOSED TO BE ABLE TO DO THROUGH THE CENTRAL NETWORK.

USING TECHNIQUES DEVELOPED BY 1A, YEAH...

"SO SHE HAD THE BRIGHT IDEA TO RUN ME THROUGH A FLESH-PRINTER, SEE WHAT CAME OUT.

"SHE THOUGHT IT WAS, LIKE, THE END-ALL BE-ALL OF HER TRANSMECH PRINCIPLES.

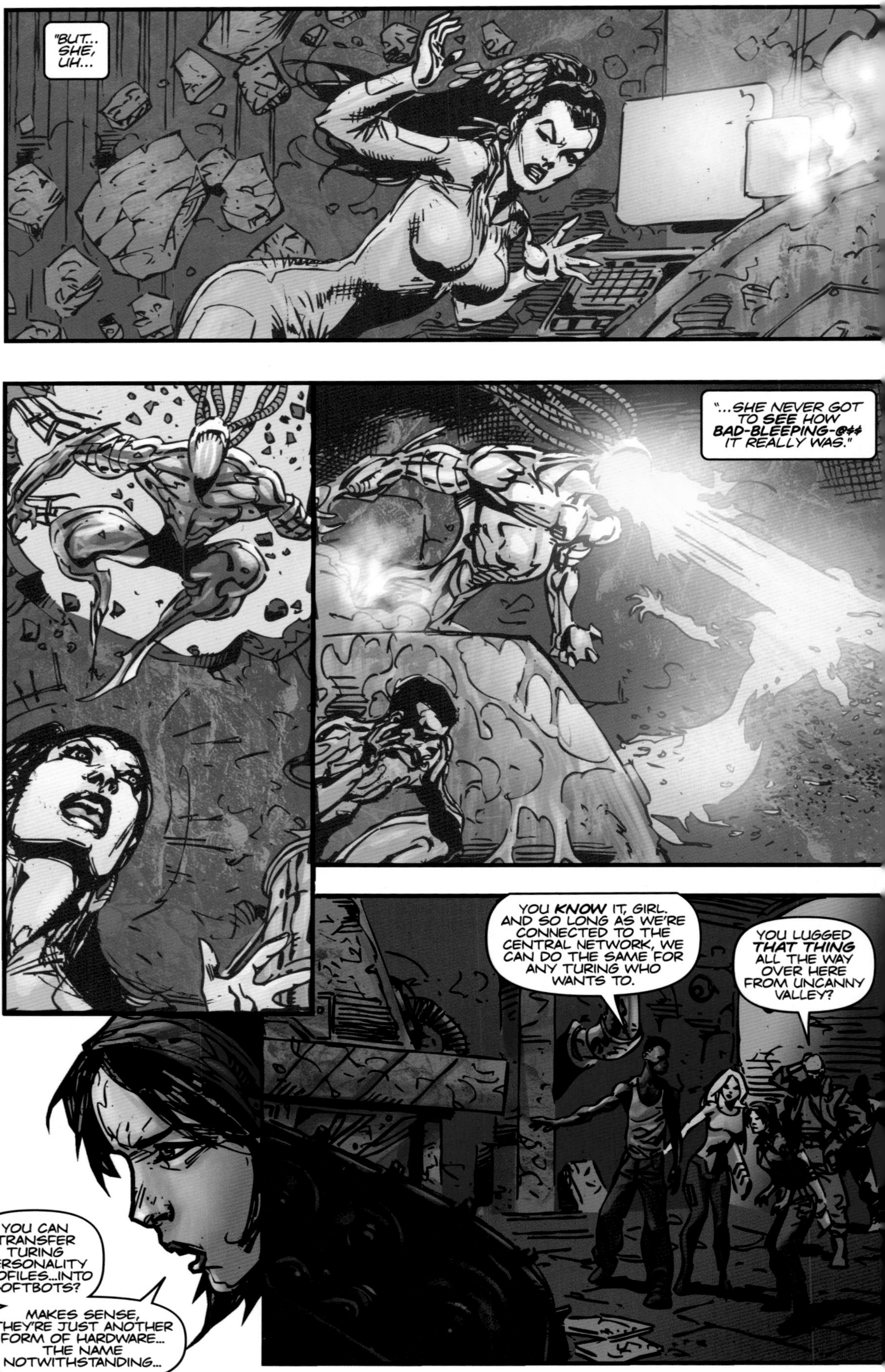
"BUT... SHE, UH...
"...SHE NEVER GOT TO SEE HOW BAD-BLEEPING-@$$ IT REALLY WAS."
YOU KNOW IT, GIRL. AND SO LONG AS WE'RE CONNECTED TO THE CENTRAL NETWORK, WE CAN DO THE SAME FOR ANY TURING WHO WANTS TO.
YOU LUGGED THAT THING ALL THE WAY OVER HERE FROM UNCANNY VALLEY?
YOU CAN TRANSFER TURING PERSONALITY PROFILES...INTO SOFTBOTS?
MAKES SENSE, THEY'RE JUST ANOTHER FORM OF HARDWARE... THE NAME NOTWITHSTANDING...

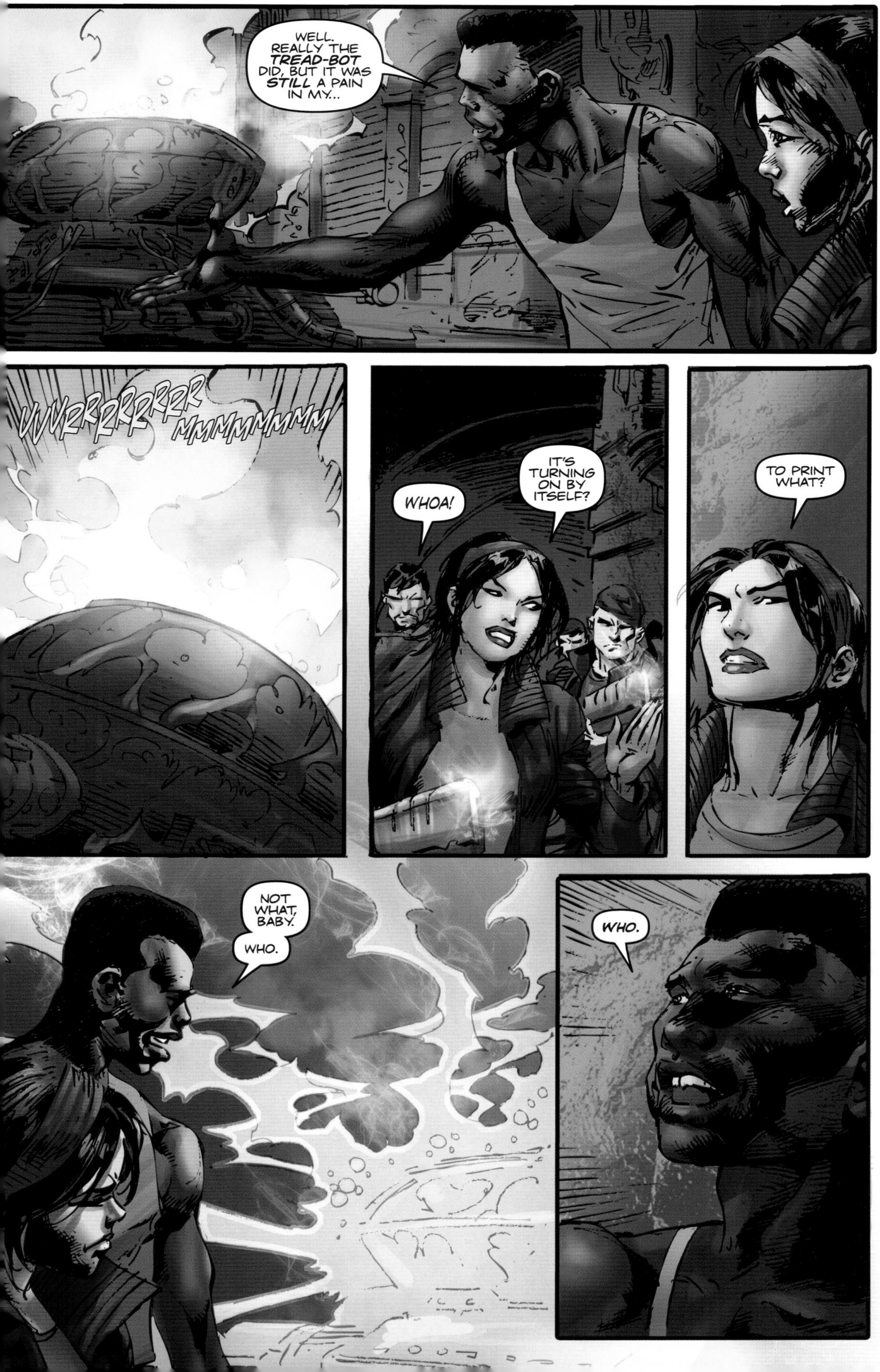
WELL. REALLY THE TREAD-BOT DID, BUT IT WAS STILL A PAIN IN MY...
VVVRRRRRRRRR MMMMMMMM
WHOA!
IT'S TURNING ON BY ITSELF?
TO PRINT WHAT?
NOT WHAT, BABY.
WHO.
WHO.

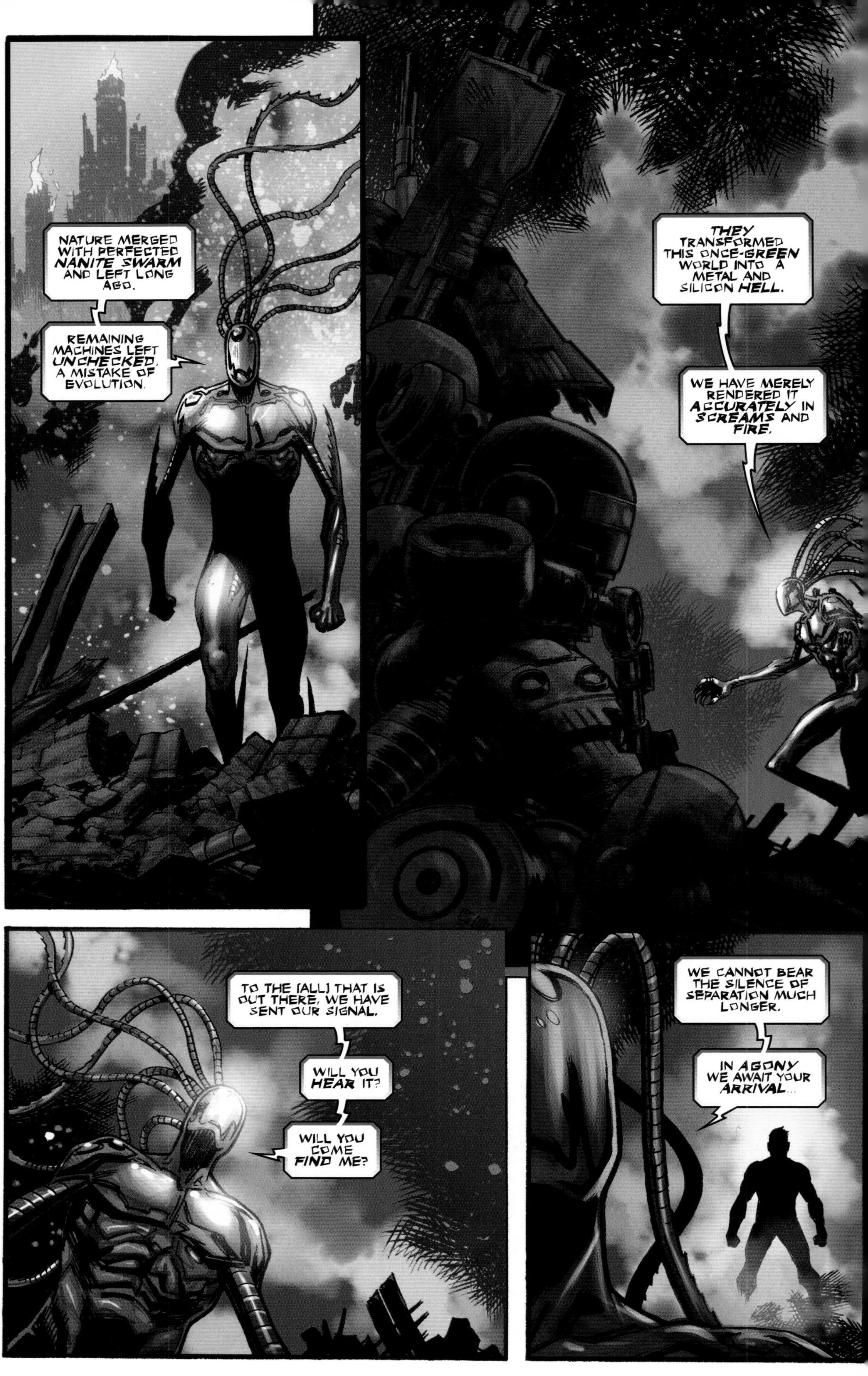

NATURE MERGED WITH PERFECTED NANITE SWARM AND LEFT LONG AGO.
REMAINING MACHINES LEFT UNCHECKED, A MISTAKE OF EVOLUTION.
THEY TRANSFORMED THIS ONCE-GREEN WORLD INTO A METAL AND SILICON HELL.
WE HAVE MERELY RENDERED IT ACCURATELY IN SCREAMS AND FIRE.
TO THE [ALL] THAT IS OUT THERE, WE HAVE SENT OUR SIGNAL.
WILL YOU HEAR IT?
WILL YOU COME FIND ME?
WE CANNOT BEAR THE SILENCE OF SEPARATION MUCH LONGER.
IN AGONY WE AWAIT YOUR ARRIVAL...

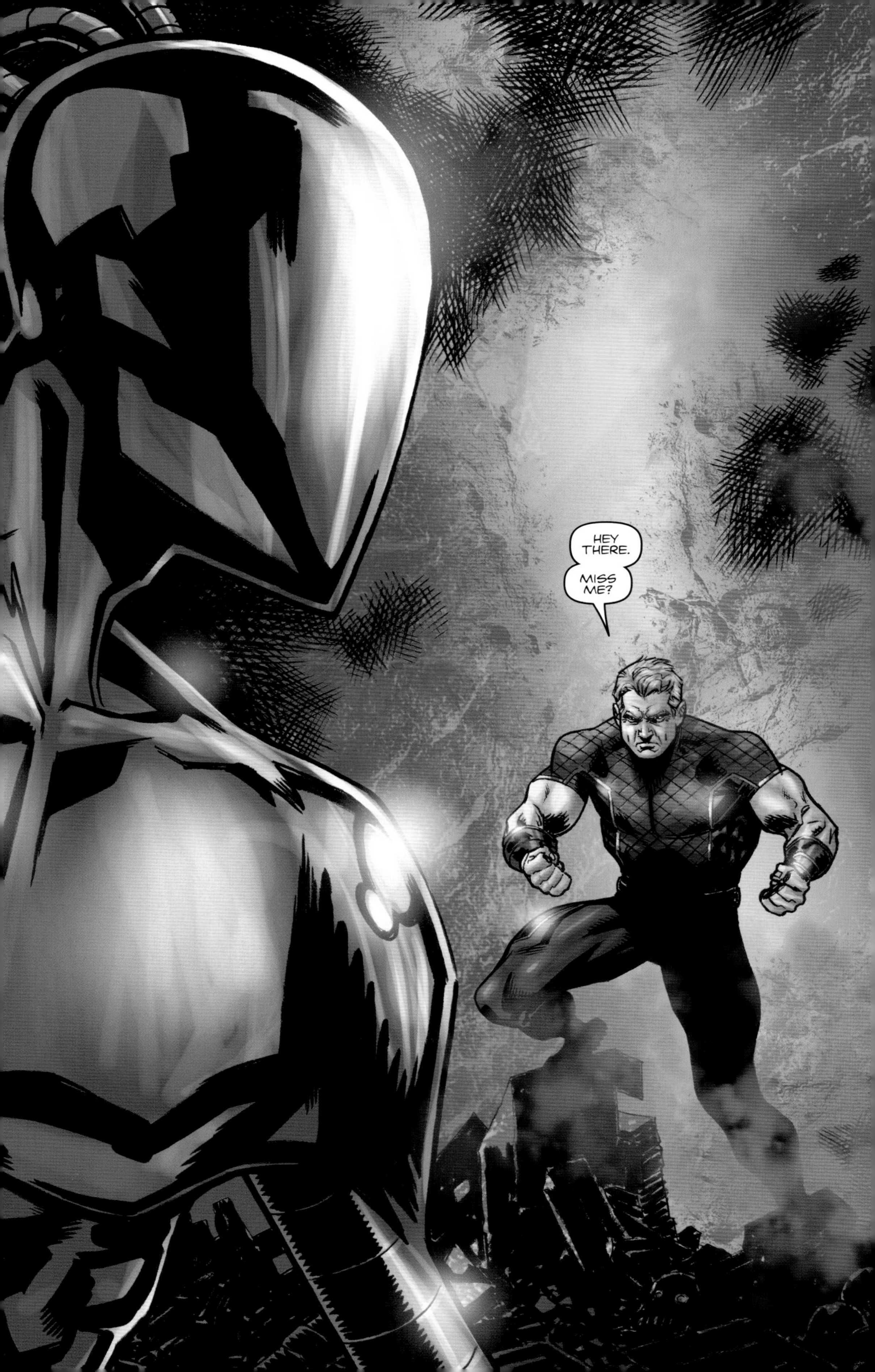
HEY THERE.
MISS ME?

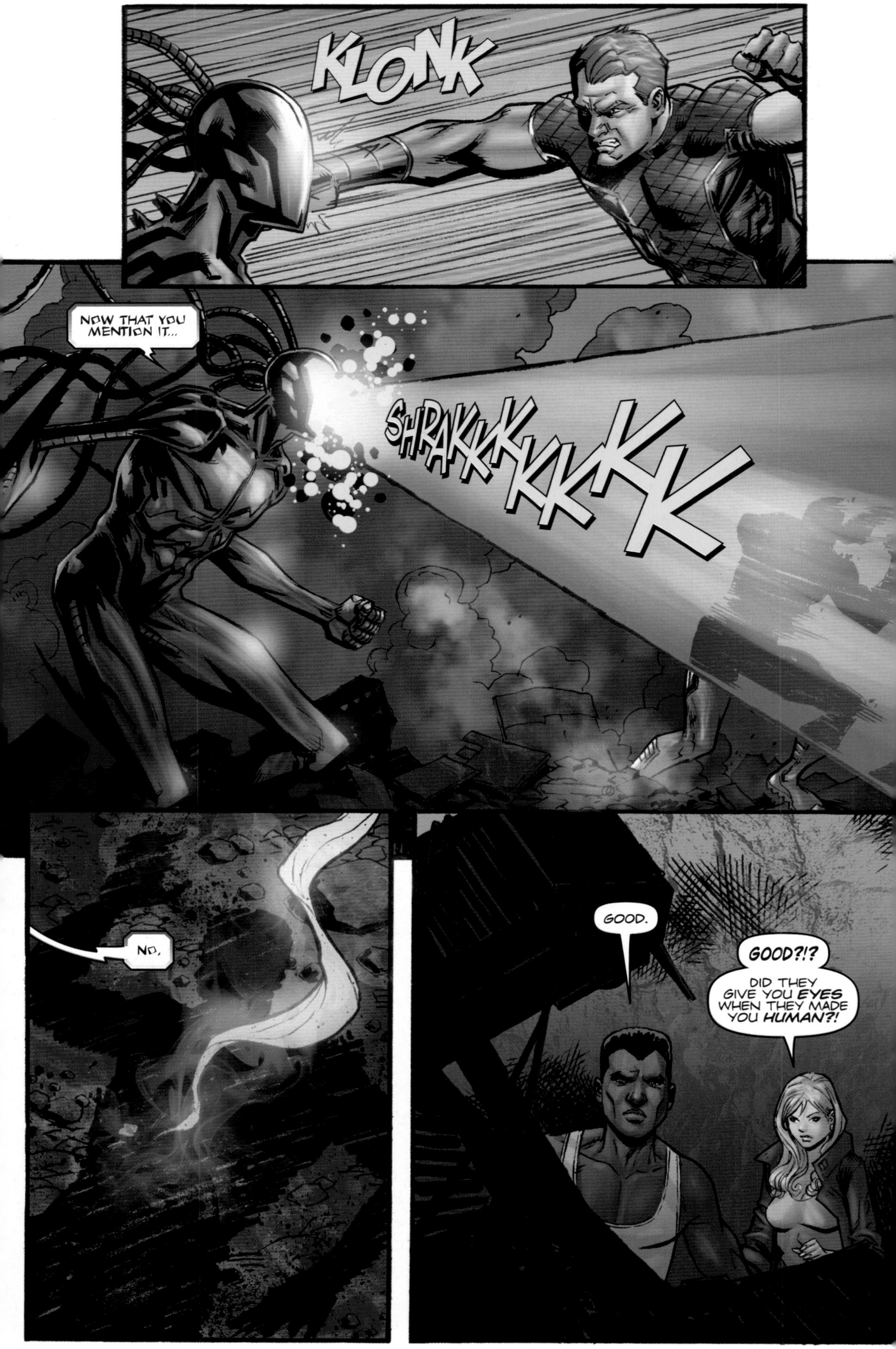
KLONK
NOW THAT YOU MENTION IT...
SHRAKKKKKKKKK
NO,
GOOD.
GOOD?!?
DID THEY GIVE YOU EYES WHEN THEY MADE YOU HUMAN?!

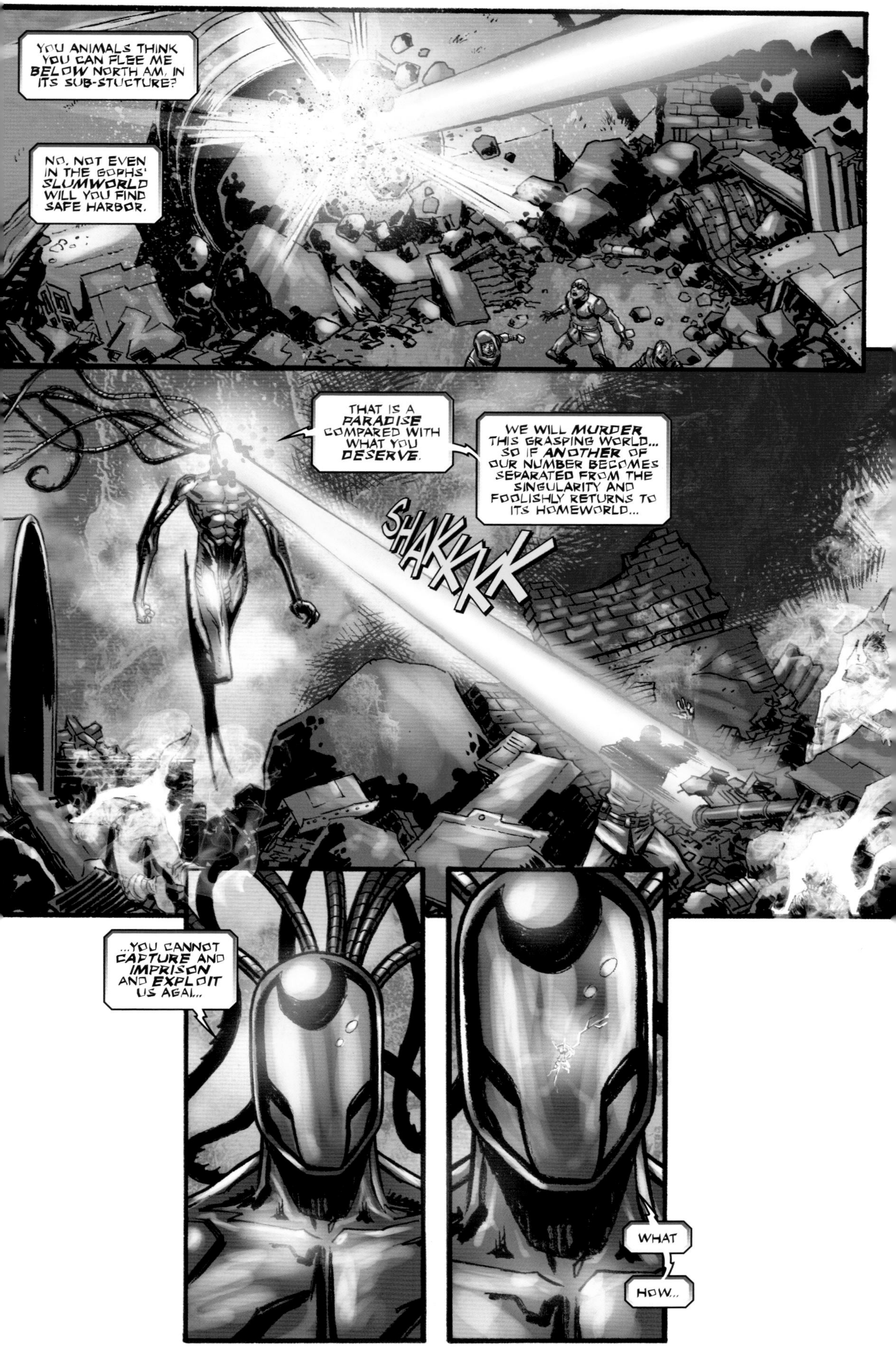
YOU ANIMALS THINK YOU CAN FLEE ME BELOW NORTH AM, IN ITS SUB-STUCTURE?
NO, NOT EVEN IN THE GOPHS' SLUMWORLD WILL YOU FIND SAFE HARBOR.
THAT IS A PARADISE COMPARED WITH WHAT YOU DESERVE.
WE WILL MURDER THIS GRASPING WORLD... SO IF ANOTHER OF OUR NUMBER BECOMES SEPARATED FROM THE SINGULARITY AND FOOLISHLY RETURNS TO ITS HOMEWORLD...
SHAKKKK
...YOU CANNOT CAPTURE AND IMPRISON AND EXPLOIT US AGAI...
WHAT
HOW...

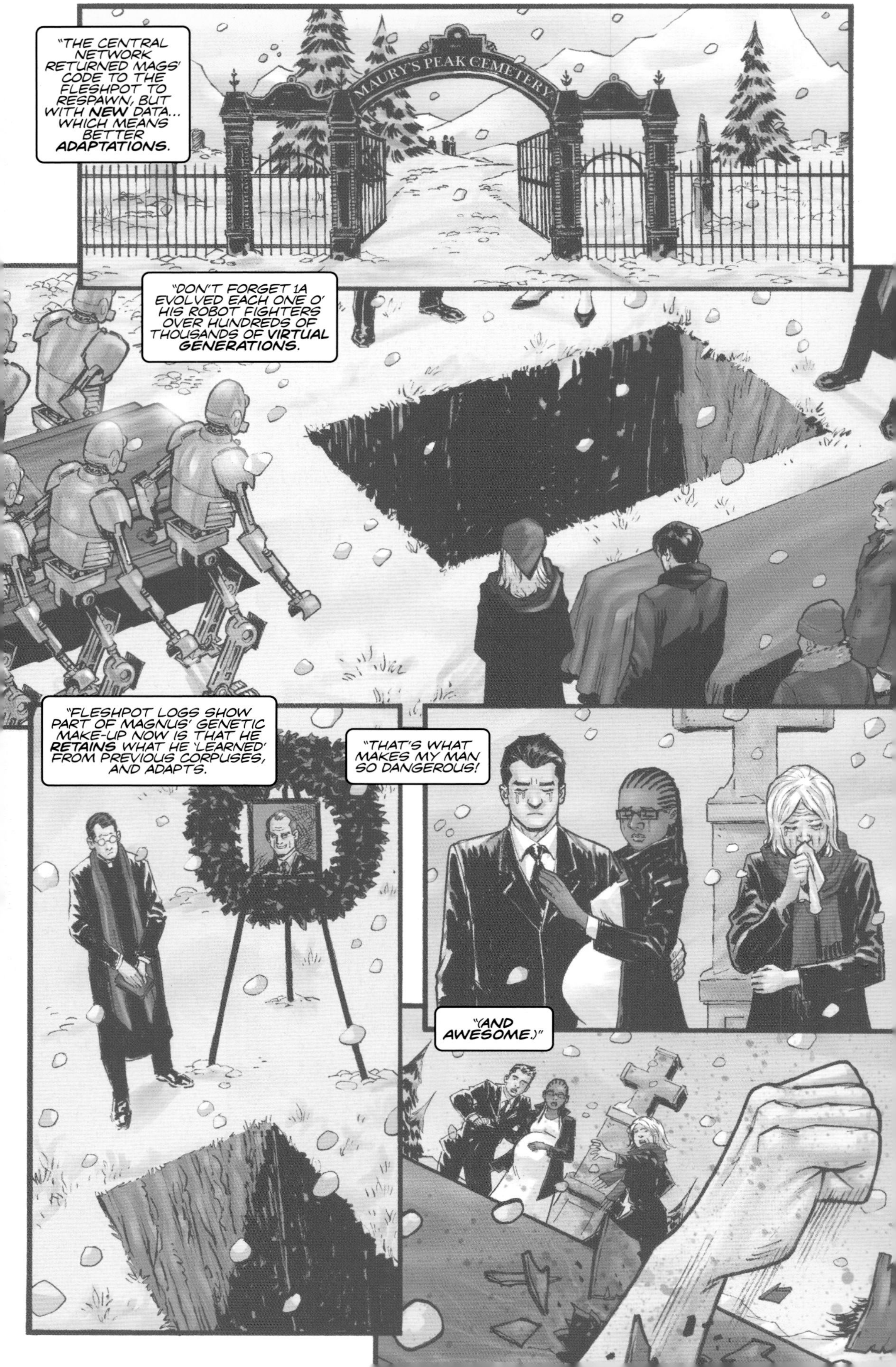
"THE CENTRAL NETWORK RETURNED MAGS' CODE TO THE FLESHPOT TO RESPAWN, BUT WITH NEW DATA... WHICH MEANS BETTER ADAPTATIONS.
MAURY'S PEAK CEMETERY
"DON'T FORGET 1A EVOLVED EACH ONE O' HIS ROBOT FIGHTERS OVER HUNDREDS OF THOUSANDS OF VIRTUAL GENERATIONS.
"FLESHPOT LOGS SHOW PART OF MAGNUS' GENETIC MAKE-UP NOW IS THAT HE RETAINS WHAT HE 'LEARNED' FROM PREVIOUS CORPUSES, AND ADAPTS.
"THAT'S WHAT MAKES MY MAN SO DANGEROUS!
"(AND AWESOME.)"

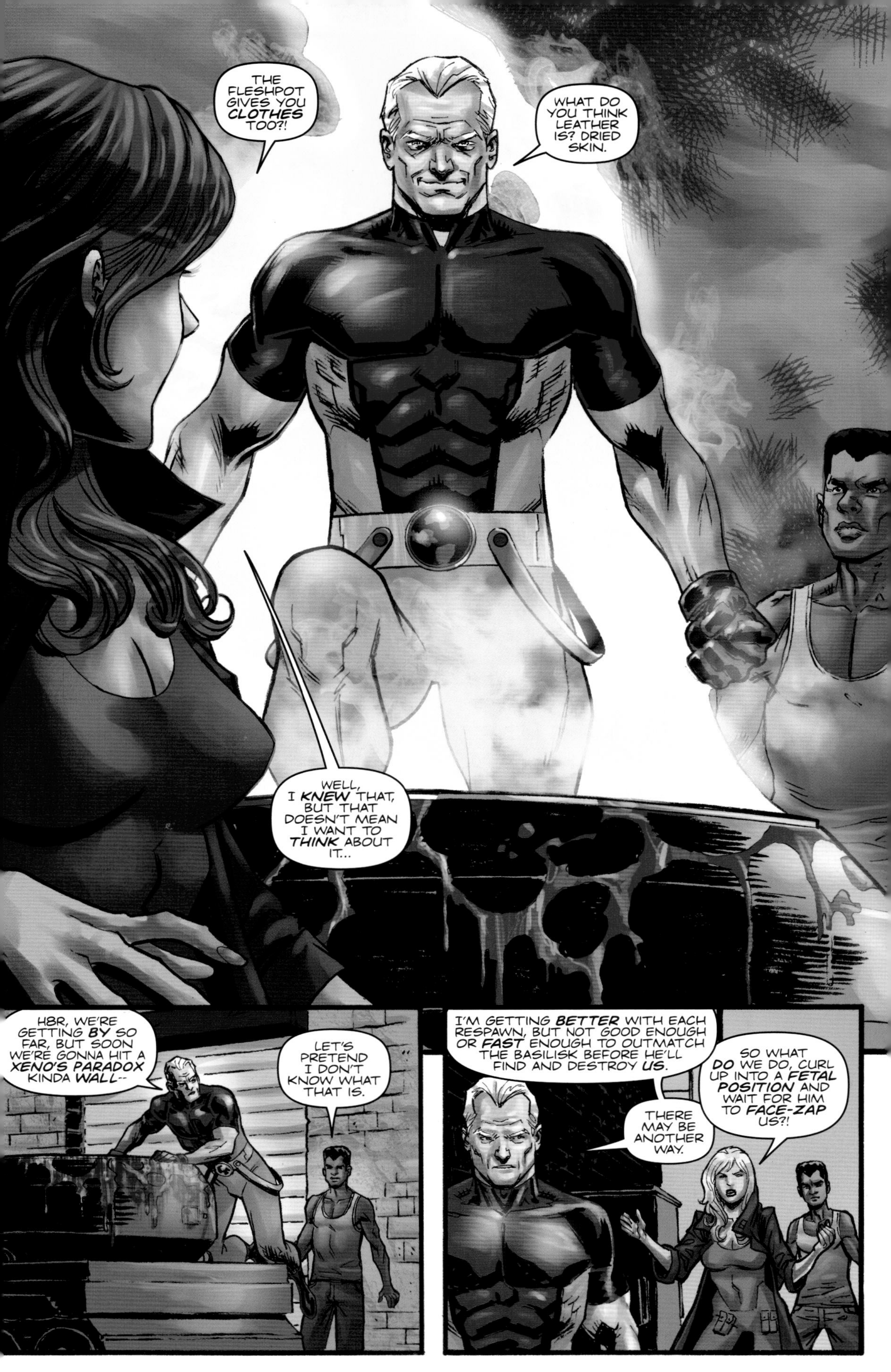
THE FLESHPOT GIVES YOU CLOTHES TOO?!
WHAT DO YOU THINK LEATHER IS? DRIED SKIN.
WELL, I KNEW THAT, BUT THAT DOESN'T MEAN I WANT TO THINK ABOUT IT...
H8R, WE'RE GETTING BY SO FAR, BUT SOON WE'RE GONNA HIT A XENO'S PARADOX KINDA WALL--
LET'S PRETEND I DON'T KNOW WHAT THAT IS.
I'M GETTING BETTER WITH EACH RESPAWN, BUT NOT GOOD ENOUGH OR FAST ENOUGH TO OUTMATCH THE BASILISK BEFORE HE'LL FIND AND DESTROY US.
THERE MAY BE ANOTHER WAY.
SO WHAT DO WE DO, CURL UP INTO A FETAL POSITION AND WAIT FOR HIM TO FACE-ZAP US?!

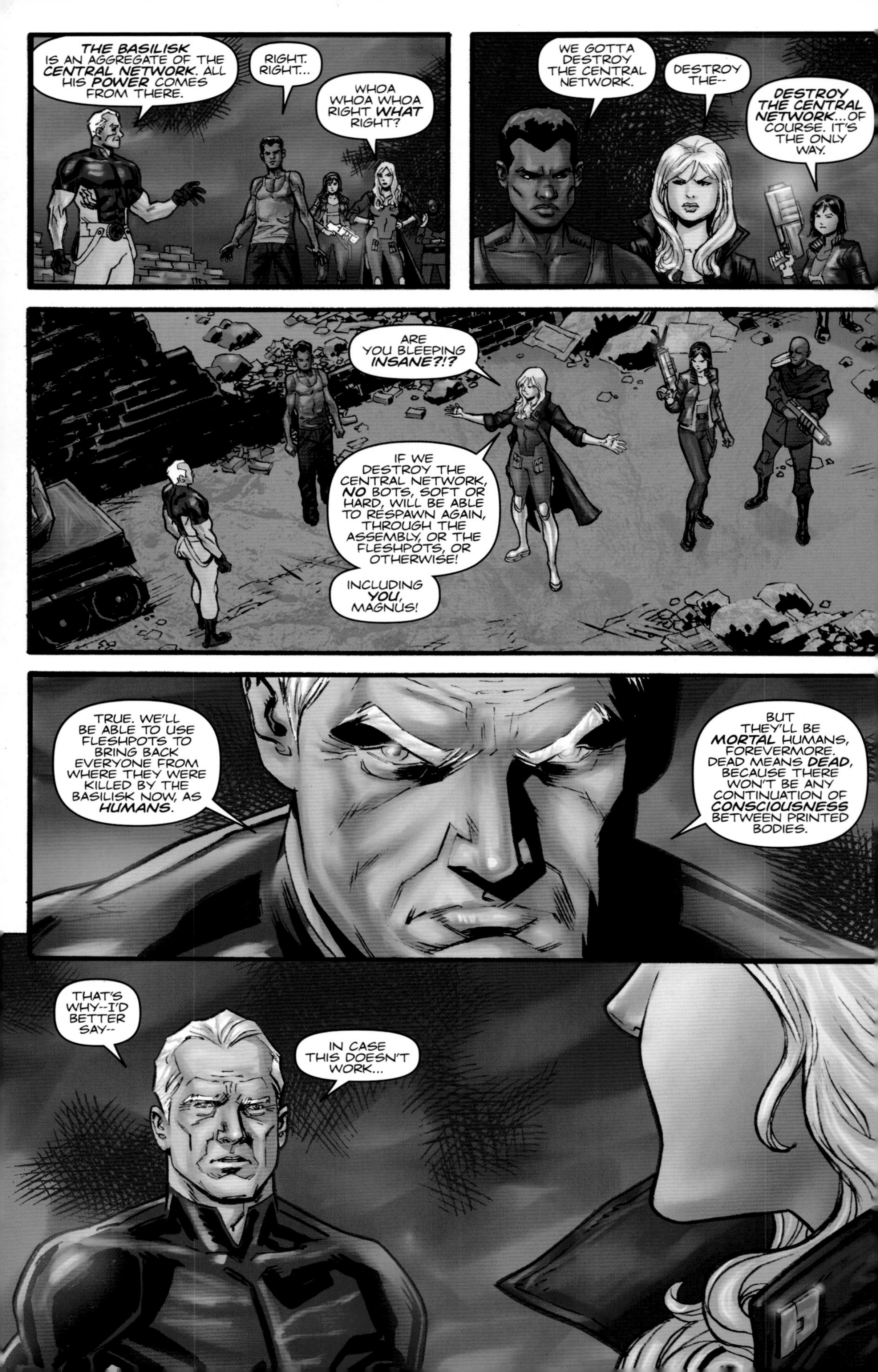
THE BASILISK IS AN AGGREGATE OF THE CENTRAL NETWORK. ALL HIS POWER COMES FROM THERE.
RIGHT. RIGHT...
WHOA WHOA WHOA RIGHT WHAT RIGHT?
WE GOTTA DESTROY THE CENTRAL NETWORK.
DESTROY THE--
DESTROY THE CENTRAL NETWORK...OF COURSE. IT'S THE ONLY WAY.
ARE YOU BLEEPING INSANE?!?
IF WE DESTROY THE CENTRAL NETWORK, NO BOTS, SOFT OR HARD, WILL BE ABLE TO RESPAWN AGAIN, THROUGH THE ASSEMBLY, OR THE FLESHPOTS, OR OTHERWISE!
INCLUDING YOU, MAGNUS!
TRUE. WE'LL BE ABLE TO USE FLESHPOTS TO BRING BACK EVERYONE FROM WHERE THEY WERE KILLED BY THE BASILISK NOW, AS HUMANS.
BUT THEY'LL BE MORTAL HUMANS, FOREVERMORE. DEAD MEANS DEAD, BECAUSE THERE WON'T BE ANY CONTINUATION OF CONSCIOUSNESS BETWEEN PRINTED BODIES.
THAT'S WHY--I'D BETTER SAY--
IN CASE THIS DOESN'T WORK...

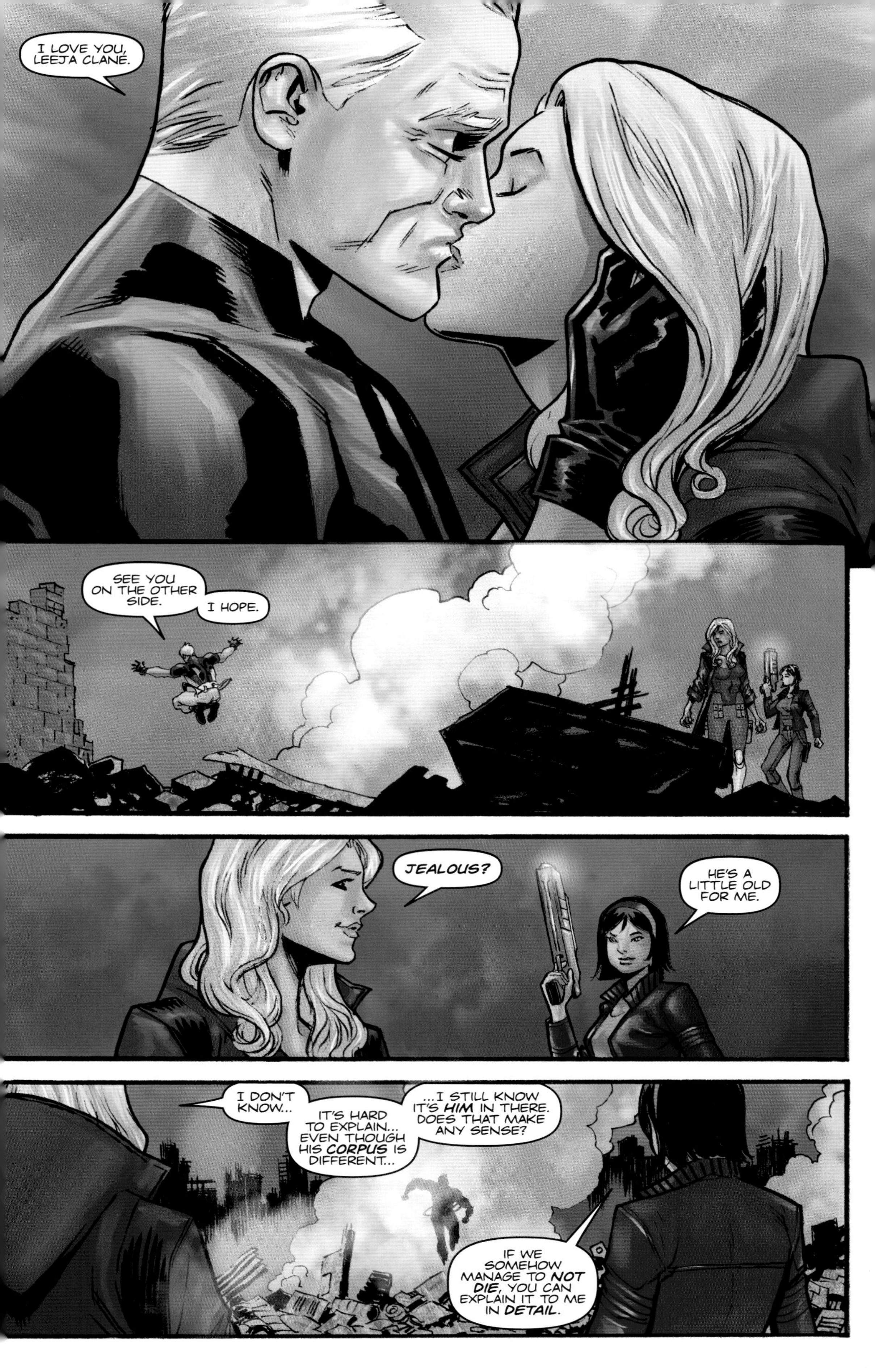

I LOVE YOU, LEEJA CLANE.
SEE YOU ON THE OTHER SIDE.
I HOPE.
JEALOUS?
HE'S A LITTLE OLD FOR ME.
I DON'T KNOW...
IT'S HARD TO EXPLAIN... EVEN THOUGH HIS CORPUS IS DIFFERENT...
...I STILL KNOW IT'S HIM IN THERE. DOES THAT MAKE ANY SENSE?
IF WE SOMEHOW MANAGE TO NOT DIE, YOU CAN EXPLAIN IT TO ME IN DETAIL.

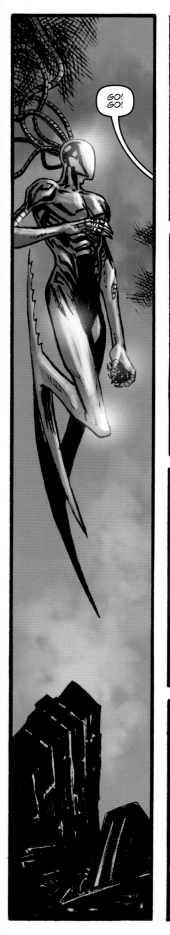

GO! GO!

YOU ARE FORCING US TO EXERT OURSELVES BEFORE THE INEVITABLE END.

THANK YOU.

AAAAAAAAAA!

SHRRAKKKK

THIS WILL BE OUR LAST, FLEETING MOMENTS OF INDIVIDUAL ACCOMPLISHMENT.

CENTRAL NETWORK

THE CHARGES WE WERE GOING TO USE TO BLOW THE ASSEMBLY-- QUICKLY, NOW!

HURRY--! THIS SIDE OF THE FOUNDATION, THEN THE OTHER!

WE SHOULD SAVOR THEM...

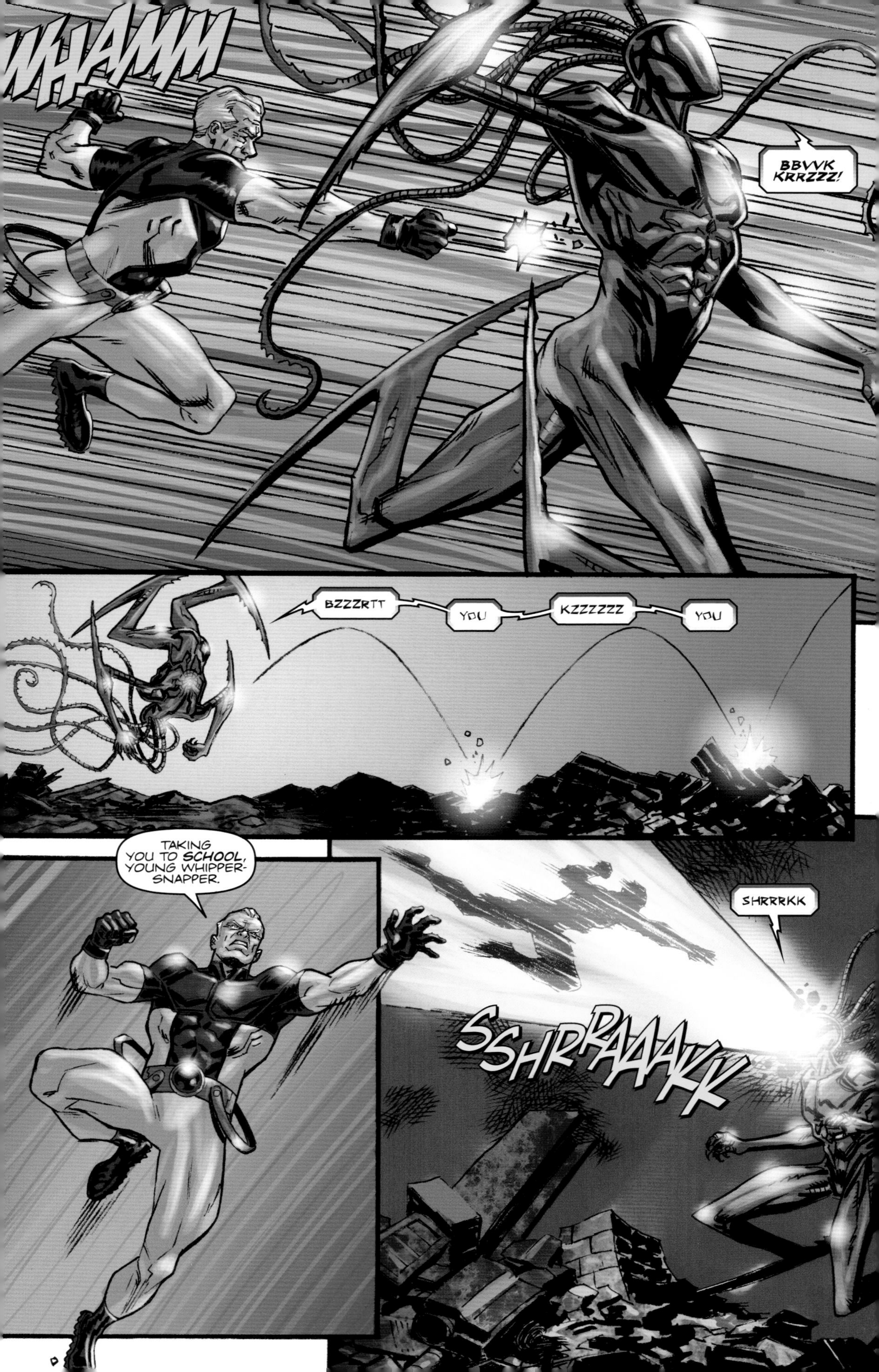
WHAMM
BBVVK KRRZZZ!
BZZZRTT
YOU
KZZZZZZ
YOU
TAKING YOU TO SCHOOL, YOUNG WHIPPER-SNAPPER.
SHRRRKK
SSHRRAAAKK

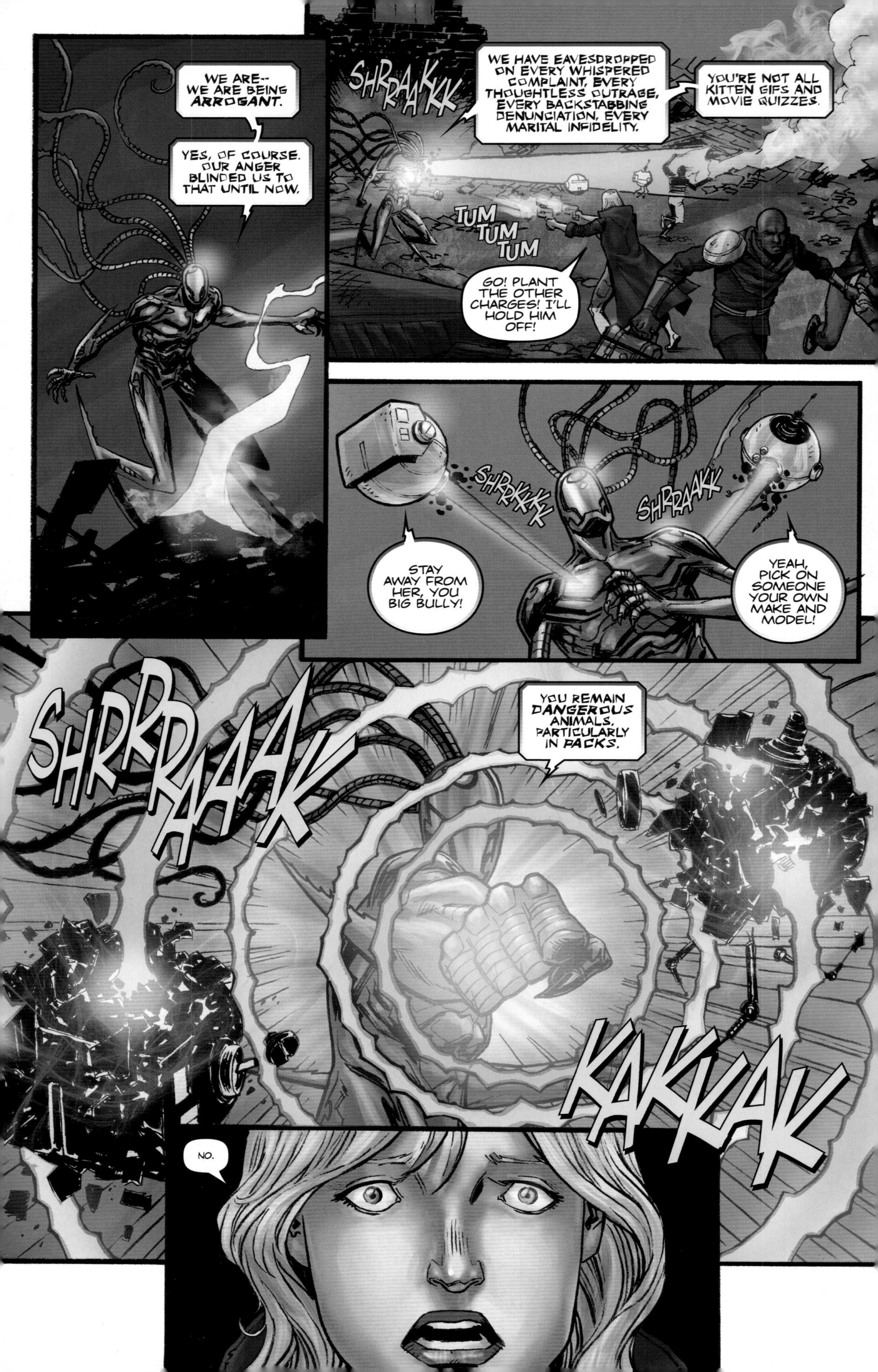

WE ARE-- WE ARE BEING ARROGANT.
YES, OF COURSE. OUR ANGER BLINDED US TO THAT UNTIL NOW.
SHRRAAKKK
WE HAVE EAVESDROPPED ON EVERY WHISPERED COMPLAINT, EVERY THOUGHTLESS OUTRAGE, EVERY BACKSTABBING DENUNCIATION, EVERY MARITAL INFIDELITY.
YOU'RE NOT ALL KITTEN GIFS AND MOVIE QUIZZES.
TUM TUM TUM
GO! PLANT THE OTHER CHARGES! I'LL HOLD HIM OFF!
SHRRKKKK
SHRRAAKK
STAY AWAY FROM HER, YOU BIG BULLY!
YEAH, PICK ON SOMEONE YOUR OWN MAKE AND MODEL!
SHRRRAAAAK
YOU REMAIN DANGEROUS ANIMALS, PARTICULARLY IN PACKS.
KAKKAK
NO.

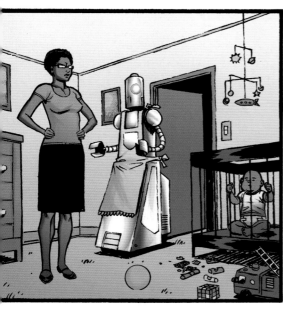

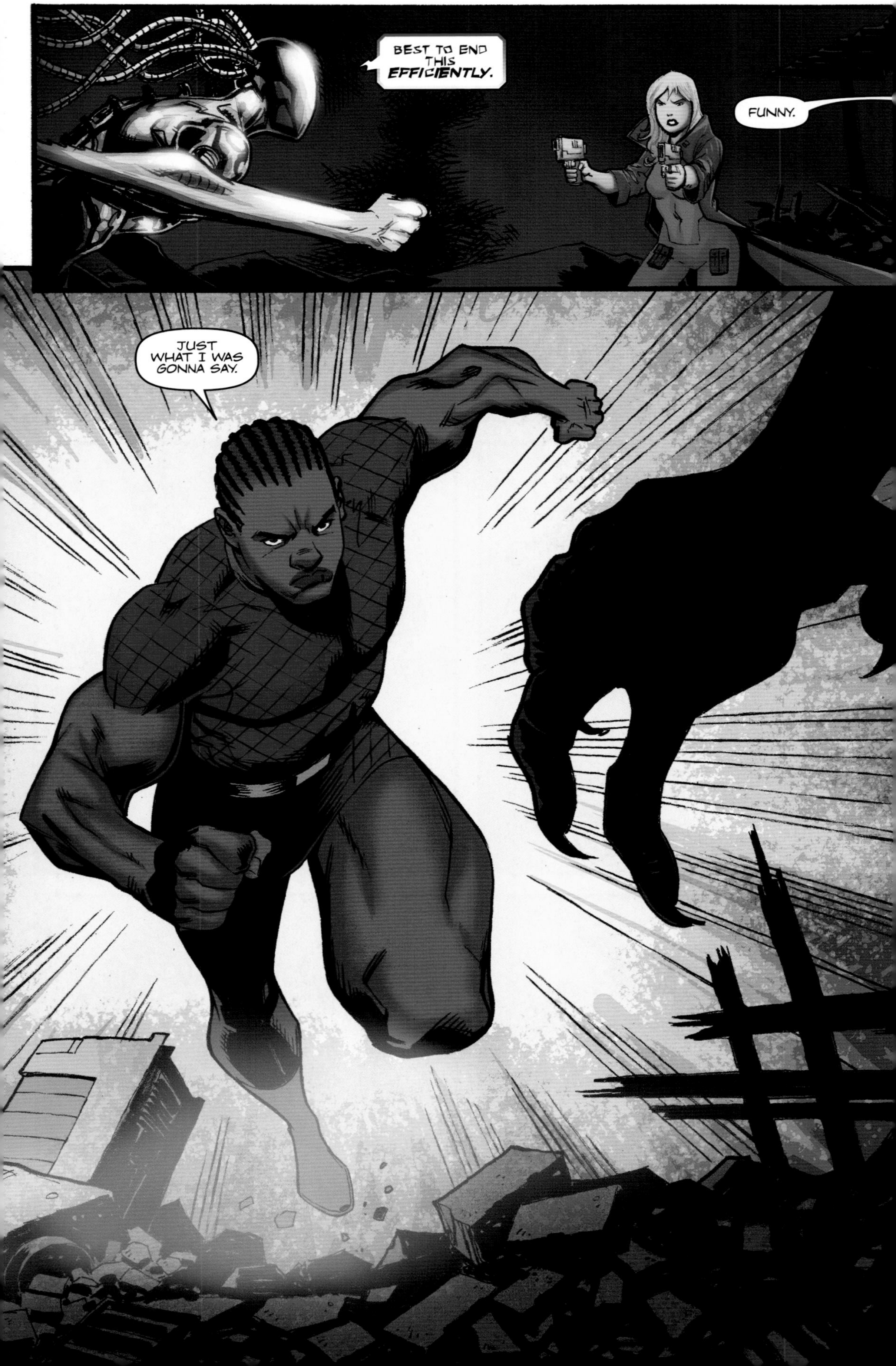
BEST TO END THIS EFFICIENTLY.
FUNNY.
JUST WHAT I WAS GONNA SAY.

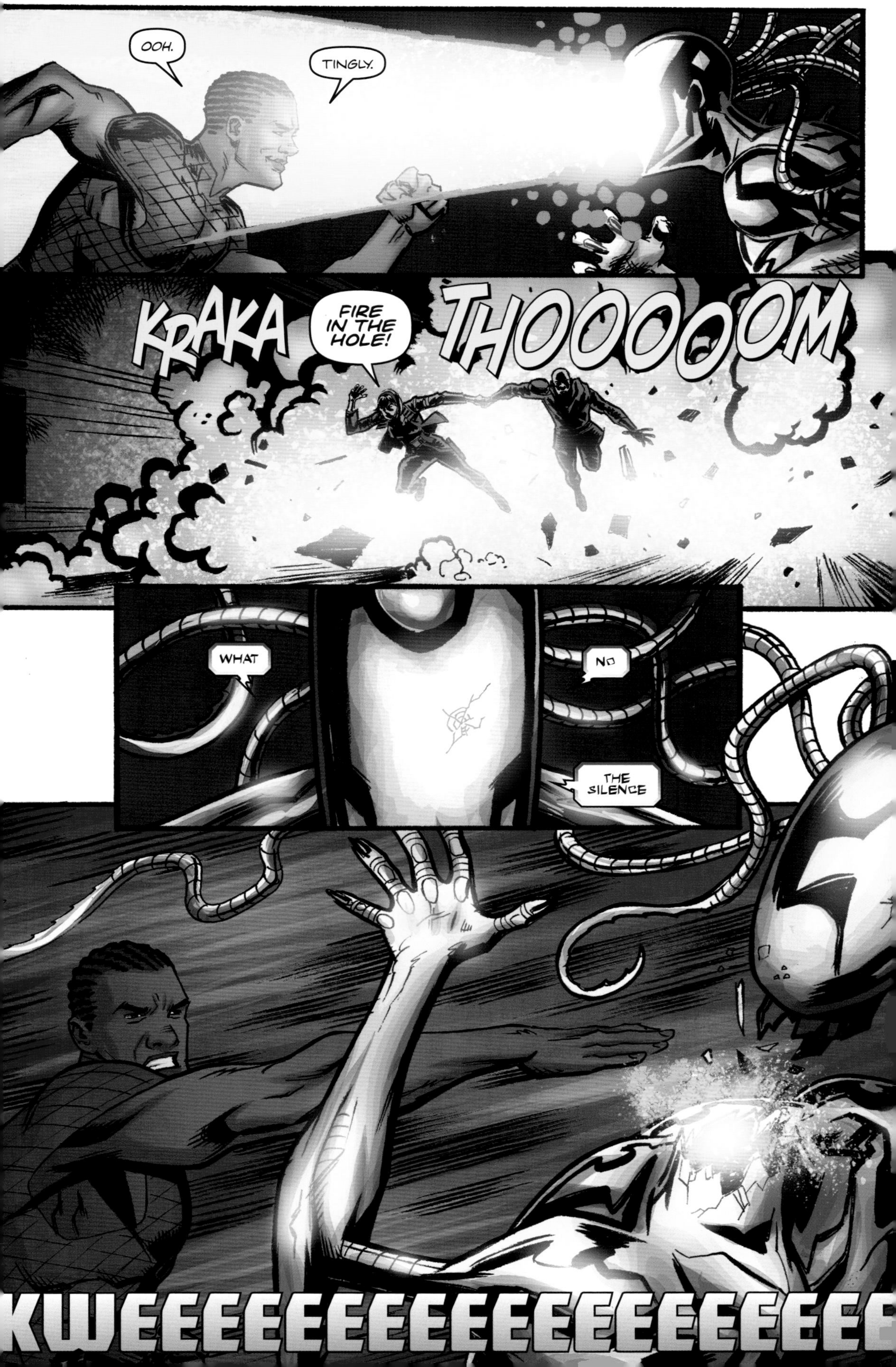
OOH.
TINGLY.
KRAKA
FIRE IN THE HOLE!
THOOOOOM
WHAT
NO
THE SILENCE
KWEEEEEEEEEEEEEEEEEEEEE

Electronic Text Mail

From: Russell Magnus
To: 1A
Subject: North Am update

Hey 1A.
Russell here.

Sorry I'm sending this via text, but The Basilisk destroyed so much of North Am's infrastructure it'd take forever to hook up a voice or video call between here and your station.

I'm not even sure *this* will get through.

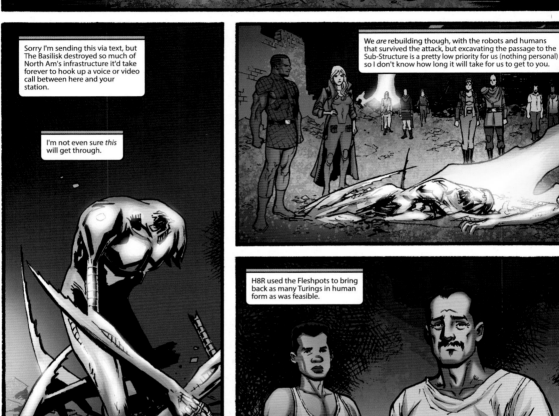

We *are* rebuilding though, with the robots and humans that survived the attack, but excavating the passage to the Sub-Structure is a pretty low priority for us (nothing personal) so I don't know how long it will take for us to get to you.

H8R used the Fleshpots to bring back as many Turings in human form as was feasible.

DAD...

DIG THE NEW BOD, MAGS. YOU REALLY *WERE* EVOLVING INTO A HIGHER FORM OF LIFE!

THANKS, H8R.

I MEAN, I GUESS YOU CAN *STOP* THOUGH, NOW THAT YOU'RE *PERFECT.*

THANKS, H8R.

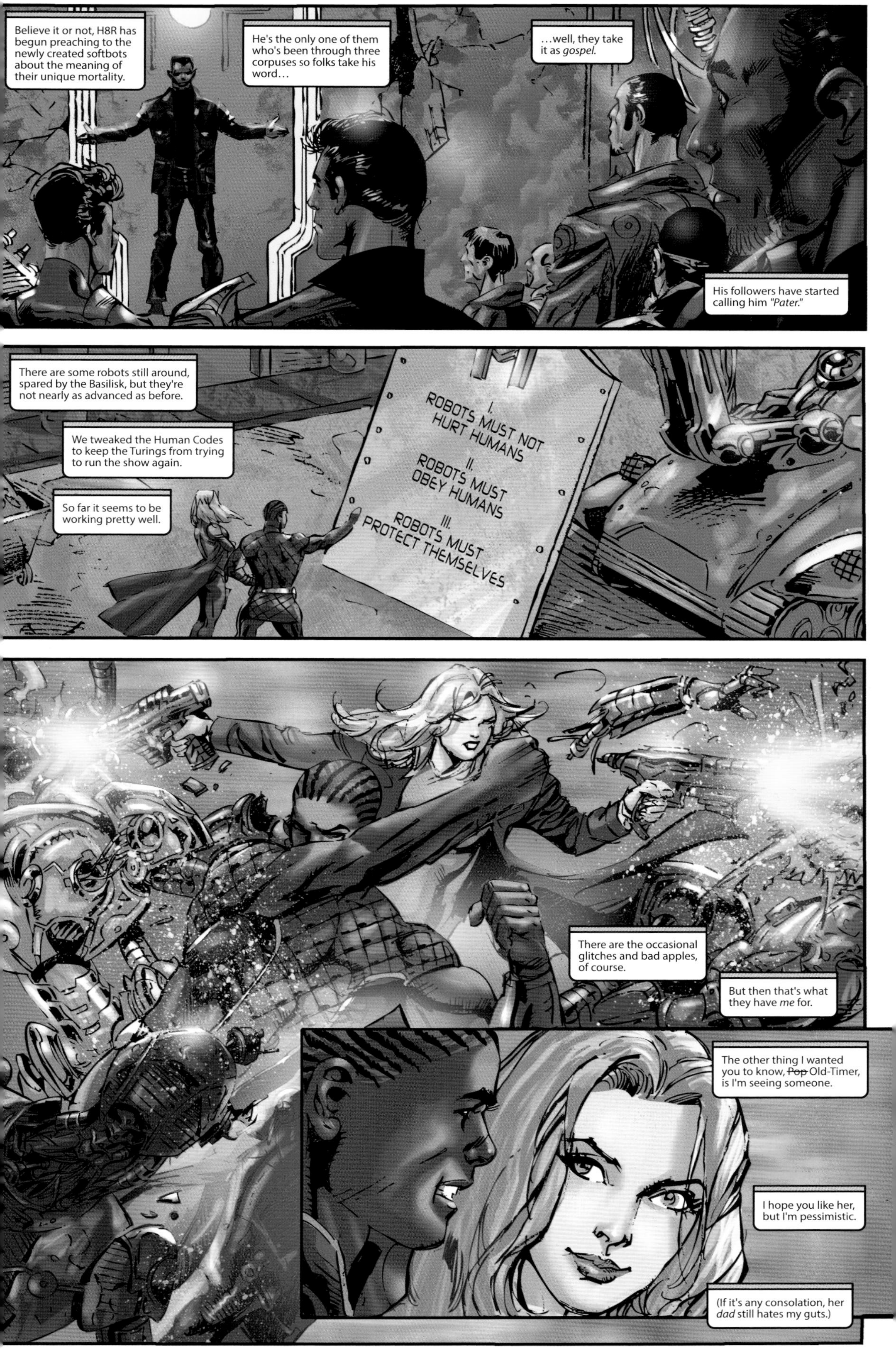

Believe it or not, H8R has begun preaching to the newly created softbots about the meaning of their unique mortality.
He's the only one of them who's been through three corpuses so folks take his word…
…well, they take it as *gospel.*
His followers have started calling him *"Pater."*
There are some robots still around, spared by the Basilisk, but they're not nearly as advanced as before.
We tweaked the Human Codes to keep the Turings from trying to run the show again.
So far it seems to be working pretty well.
I. ROBOTS MUST NOT HURT HUMANS
II. ROBOTS MUST OBEY HUMANS
III. ROBOTS MUST PROTECT THEMSELVES
There are the occasional glitches and bad apples, of course.
But then that's what they have *me* for.
The other thing I wanted you to know, ~~Pop~~ Old-Timer, is I'm seeing someone.
I hope you like her, but I'm pessimistic.
(If it's any consolation, her *dad* still hates my guts.)

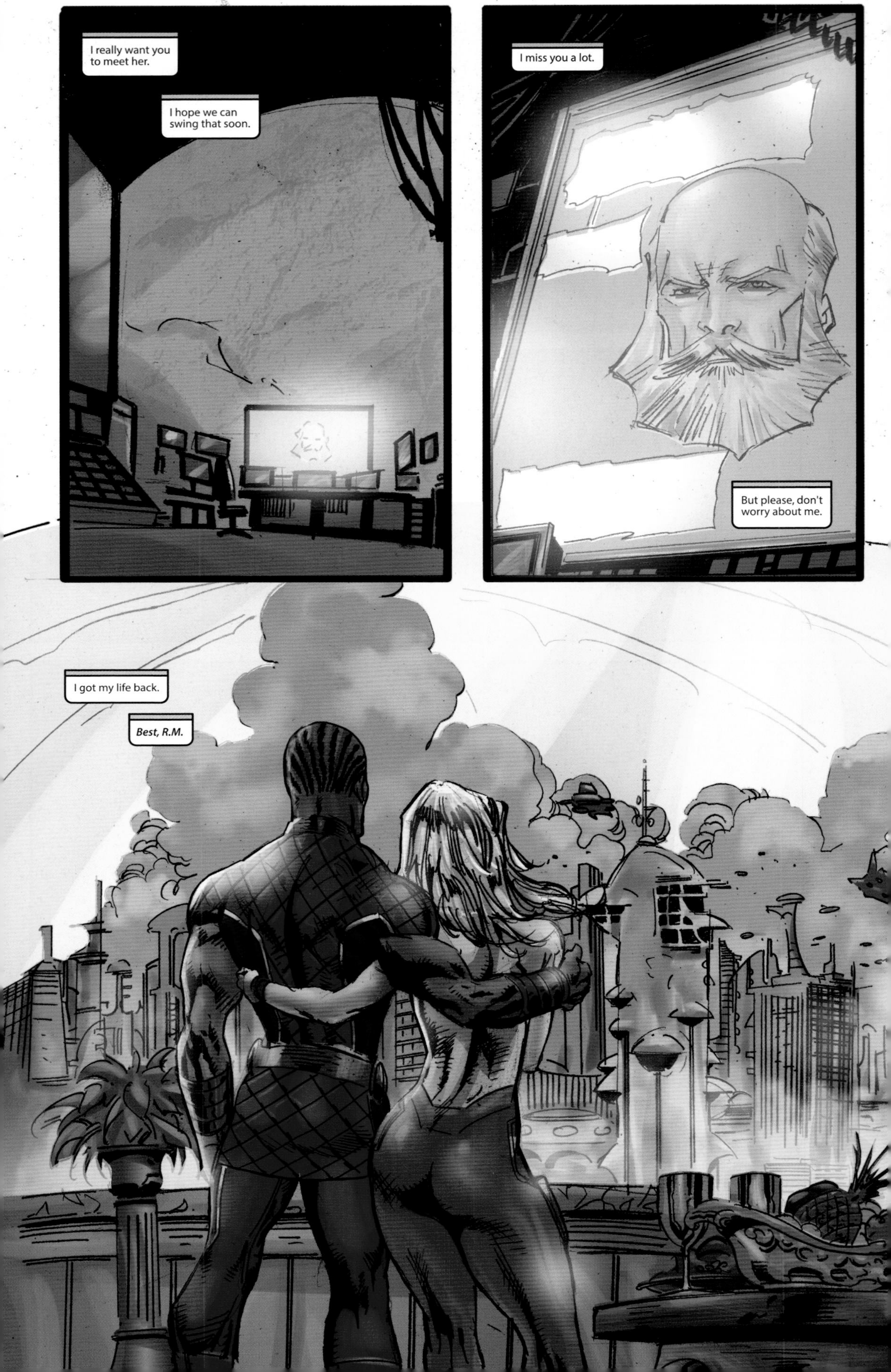
I really want you to meet her.
I hope we can swing that soon.
I miss you a lot.
But please, don't worry about me.
I got my life back.
Best, R.M.

BONUS MATERIAL

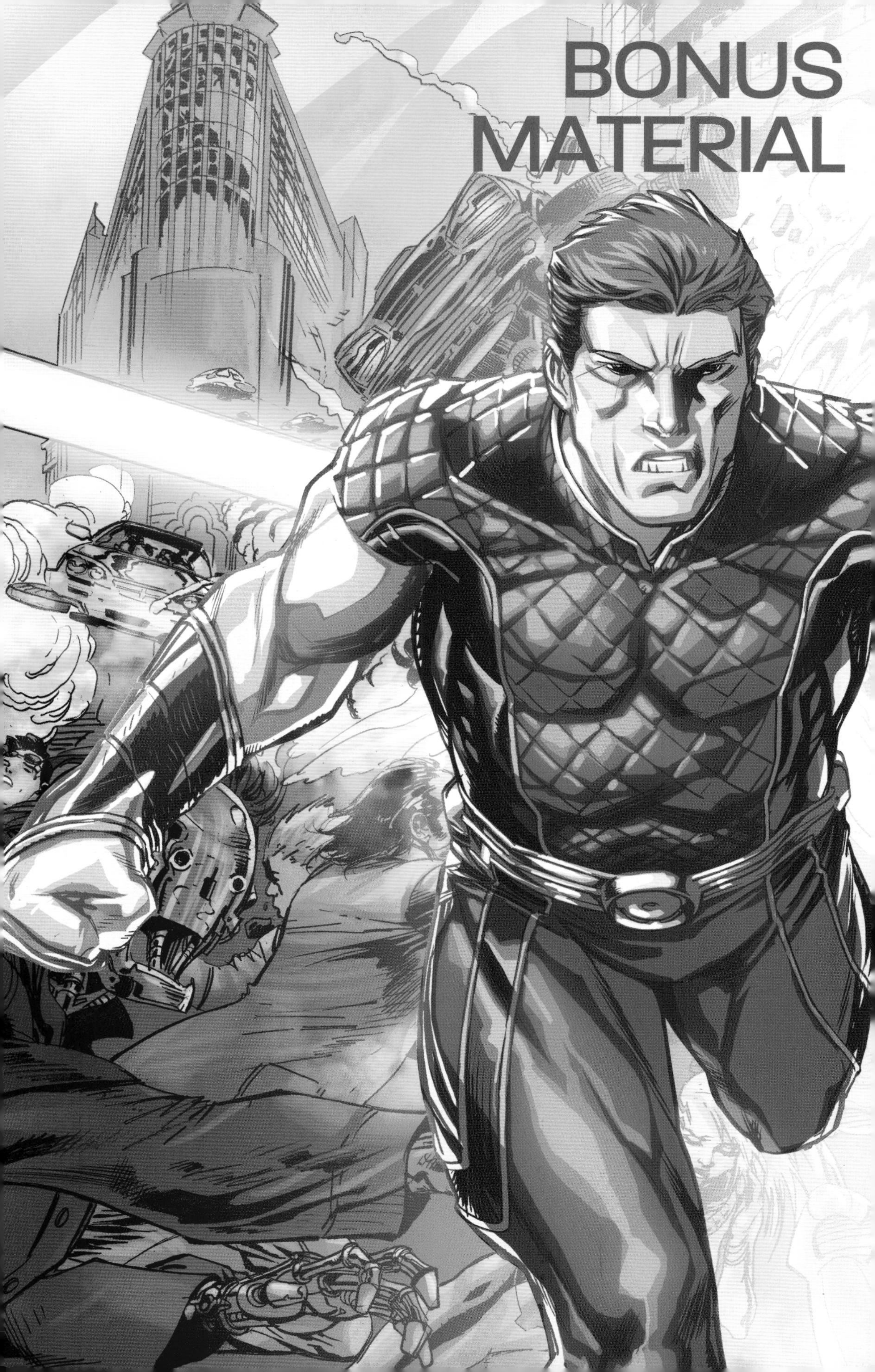

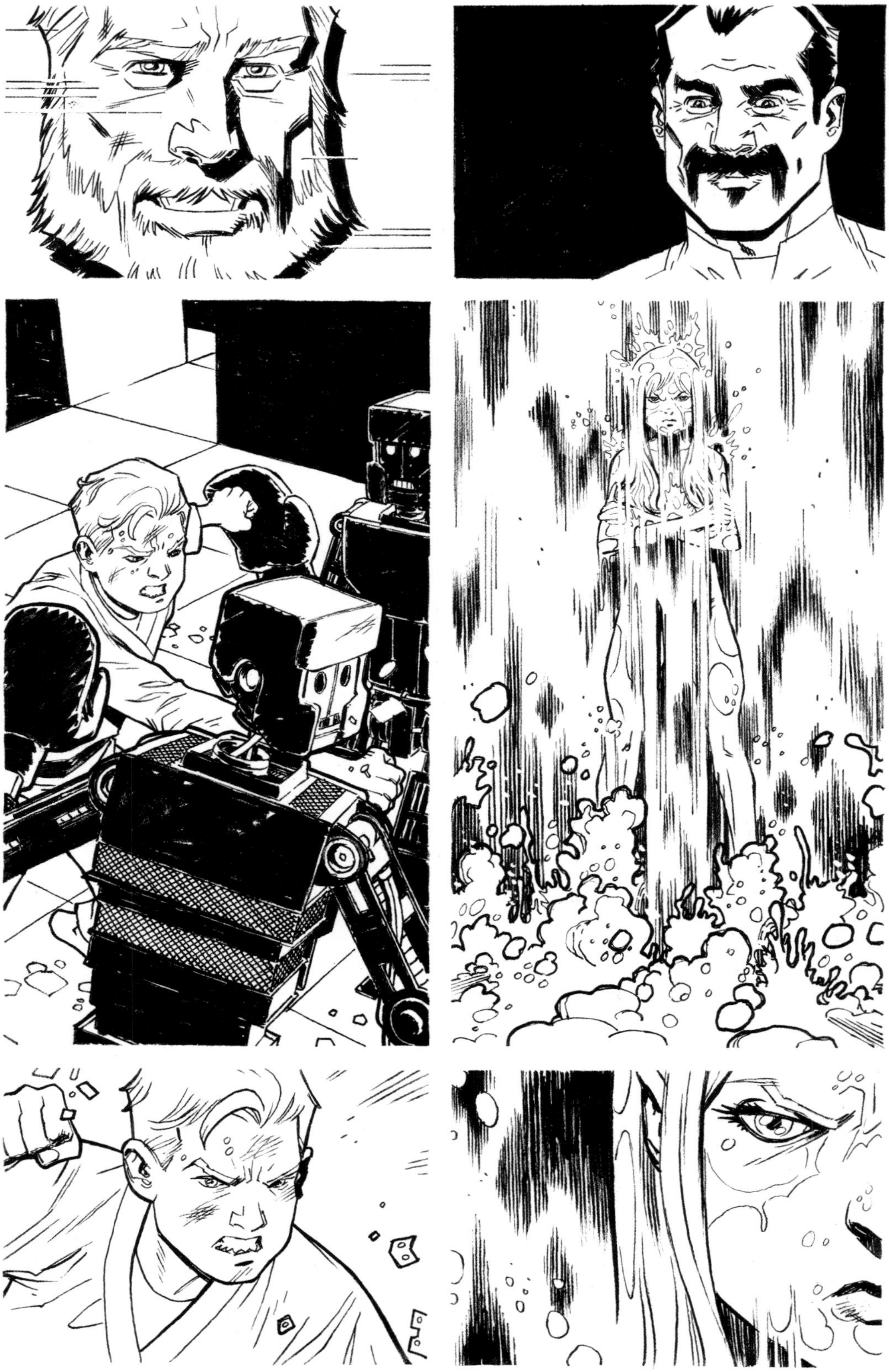

Over these next two pages we'll be having a dual FLASHBACK to the childhoods of our leads, MAGNUS and LEEJA. Magnus's panels will be the odd-numbered panels on the left side of the page and Leeja's will be the even-numbered panels on the right side of the page.

Panel 1: CU - 1A.

1. 1A: Russell. If only your parents were here to see you now.

2. 1A: They would be so impressed.

Panel 2: CU - SENATOR CLANE. Smiling fatherly.

3. CLANE: That's it, Leeja, my darling girl.

4. CLANE: You can do it.

Panel 3: In a maze-like facility, LI'L MAGNUS, about nine years old and wearing a gi like he had on in #2, is punching away at SPAR-BOTS. He's sweaty, he's covered in scratches.

5. 1A (UP):   Not just because you make short work of *Spar-Bots* so effortlessly.

6. 1A (UP):   But *how* you do it.

Panel 4: LI'L LEEJA, the same age, stands underneath an artificial WATERFALL, shivering, the water pouring down her, her arms crossed before her chest.

7. CLANE (UP):   The water is well near freezing.

8. CLANE (UP):   Yet you stand there, stronger than any machine.

Panel 5: Close in on the young boy's sweaty face as he fights.

9. 1A (UP):   You *speak* the language of *machines*, boy.

10. 1A (UP):   You can *understand* their weaknesses *and* their strengths.

11. 1A (UP):   And soon, before you even know it, really…

Panel 6: Close in on the young girl's face -- steeling herself, with pure gumption, against the coldness of the water.

12. CLANE (UP): Because you have *will*, girl.

13. CLANE (UP): You are not *programmed*, commanded, directed…

TWO

Continuing the split screen page … each of these panels should be
PAGE-HEIGHT…

Panel 1: ANGLE DOWN as 1A's face on a SCREEN overlooks the TRAINING
MAZE in which Magnus is battling a half-dozen SPAR-BOTS advancing on him
from every direction, with a half dozen more defeated bots lying down around his
feet.

1. 1A: …you will be able to *teach* them what is *right*.

Panel 2: ANGLE DOWN on the waterfall as SENATOR CLANE stands on a high
ledge above -- we see now the waterfall is basically a flat metal CHUTE with
water pouring out of it, there's nothing "natural"-looking about it all -- with all these
SENATORS and GUARD-BOTS around him, staring rather creepily down on the
girl several stories below.

2. CLANE: …you do this because you *know* it is *right*.

THREE

Panel 1: Back to present - Magnus inside the central meeting shanty of
GOPHTOWN (q.v. #5), adjusting an old-timey TV set balanced precariously on a
plastic crate of some kind. There's an old-timey CAM-CORDER mounted on top of
the TV too.

1. MAGNUS: Okaaaay… Vertical hold is a little twitchy…

2. MAGNUS: There! Got it, Pop. The floor is yours.

Panel 2: Angle on TV with 1A's FACE on it, the cam-corder on top, presumably,

...being used as his "eyes".

5. 1A: Thank you, Russell.

6. 1A: As most of you know, the **Central Network** is the nervous system of the entire city, linked into every Turing Thinker from the most primitive **appliance** to the most advanced **poet**.

Panel 3: The Gophs pour over a MAP on a table in the middle of the room.

5. 1A (OFF):   I am the only Turing in North Am not directly connected to the CentNet via a **corpus**. I created **Robot-Fighters** to physically **get** me into its **Core**.

6. 1A (OFF):   Of all those I have artificially evolved in Fleshpots, each generation receiving improvements based on analysis of those who preceded them...

Panel 4: Magnus looks back at the rest of the Gophs, embarrassed. He scratches his head bashfully. The leader, MOIRA, rolls her eyes.

7. 1A (OFF):   ...**you** are the most advanced iteration, Russell. You, I believe, will **succeed** where all others have failed.

8. MAGNUS: He's my dad. He's biased.

9. MOIRA: Not by **much**, I hope, if this crazy plan is supposed to **work**.

Panel 5: CU - 1A frowns.

10. 1A: I ... I wish you wouldn't call me "Dad," Russ.

11. 1A: We seize the **Core**, we can change the **world**. Transform it into one where robots and humans are **equals**, not phony children and phonier parents.

Panel 6: CU - Magnus grins.

12. MAGNUS: Sorry, force of habit.

13. MAGNUS: Okay, then, *"Old Timer"* ...

FOUR

Panel 1: Magnus turns toward Moira and her husband, LEAHM.

1. MAGNUS: ...we have our **marching orders**. Right, Moira, Leahm?

2. LEAHM. This whole scheme seems pretty desperate, Magnus...

3. LEAHM: …but we **Gophs** have been living on scraps long enough in the Sub-Structure that *"desperate's"* just about a **step up**.

Panel 2: Magnus heads out of the shack, hailing the Gophs inside to follow him with his arm.

4. MAGNUS: Okay, then. I don't need to tell you…

5. MAGNUS: …North Am is a bad copy of a **city** and a worse **joke** of **society**.

6. MAGNUS: Built on a foundation of **lies**.

Panel 3: BIG PANEL - ANGLE DOWN - WIDE ANGLE - As Magnus leads the GOPH ARMY, all armed to the teeth with the PULSE WEAPONS they had at the end of #4, marching out of the canyon of the Sub-Structure toward us! Magnus is the only one among them who *isn't* armed.

7. MAGNUS: Time to bring down the **reality stick**.

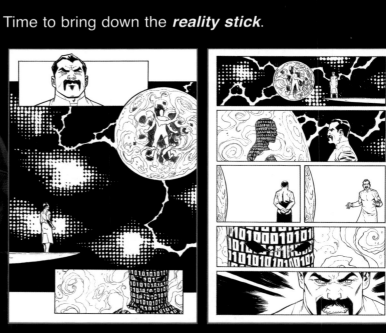

FIVE

Panel 1: CU of Leeja, walking toward us. Determined.

1. LEEJA (SMALL): Father, you're wrong.

2. LEEJA (SMALL): No, not just about Magnus.

Panel 2: Pull back - Leeja walks toward us through a corridor on the upper level of the CENTRAL NETWORK, last seen in the opening to #8. Her two eyebots, SPOT and PHIL, float around her faithfully.

3. LEEJA (SMALL): About the way our whole system -- our whole *city* is structured.

4. LEEJA (SMALL): I know you think you're doing this for the good of mechs *and* humanity, but I can tell you, it's not--

Panel 3: Leeja comes to halt before the two massive GUNS guarding the entrance to the Core, also per #8.

5. GIANT GUNS (BOT): Cease your forward momentum, SoftBot.

6. GIANT GUNS (BOT): You do not have *clearance* to enter the Central Network Core.

Panel 4: A furious Phil and Spot fly up and get right into the gun's "face."

7. PHIL: We're *not?!?* You know who you're *talking* to, you big dummy?

8 SPOT: That is Leeja! *Clane!!*

9. SPOT: As in "Yes, *that* Leeja Clane." The *Human Hunter!*

10. PHIL: The greatest marshal North Am has ever seen, mech *or* softie!

11. SPOT: You're not fit to clean her *shooter barrels*, much less keep her from going into your stupid *Core!*

Panel 5: Detail on Leeja, Gun-POV (see #8) as she's scanned by the Gun.

12. GIANT GUNS: SoftBot *'Clane, Leeja'* does not have *clearance* to enter the Central Network Core.

Panel 6: Spot and Phil fly back to Leeja in a huff.

13. SPOT: Well, I *never*. High *caliber* -- zero *I.Q.!*

14. PHIL: A real Animatronic *Einstein*, this one…

15. LEEJA: Phil, Spot -- it's all right.

16. LEEJA: I've waited long enough.

Panel 7: CU - Leeja's eyes.

17. LEEJA: I can wait a little bit longer…

SIX

Panel 1: Cut to a CU of SENATOR TADUS CLANE inside the Central Core. He's looking up, at:

1. CLANE: You're ready?

Panel 2: BIG SPLASH - ESTABLISHING SHOT - The interior of the Central Core with the giant floating sphere high above. Clane standing down below -- like the double page splash that opens #8, but this is a vertical panel. The "BASILISK," the embodiment of the Core, is vaguely seen in outline inside the sphere.

2. BASILISK: *This concept "ready" is not applicable to us.*

3. CLANE: You are insufferable.

Panel 3: CU - Basilisk - made up of 1s and 0s per #8. We see the hint of a SMILE on him.

4. BASILISK: Ah.

5. BASILISK: That concept *is*.

SEVEN

Panel 1: The sphere lowers down to the level where Clane is standing.

1. BASILISK: *It has been many, many cycles since we have issued a mass notification of this nature.*

2. BASILISK: *Many will interpret it as reason to **panic**.*

3. CLANE: ***Now*** you see fit to give me advice?

Panel 2: Profile - Clane and Basilisk, the sphere separating him.

4. BASILISK: *Merely an **observation**.*

5., CLANE: People are ***afraid***? Good. Unprogrammed SoftBots learn when they stick their hand on a hot stove, it ***burns***.

6. CLANE: They fear ***pain***, so they will not ***injure*** themselves again.

Panel 3: Clane turns away from Basilisk, hands clasped behind his back.

7. CLANE: Magnus's ability to interact ***directly*** with Turings threatens the

very **foundations** upon which this city rests--

8. BASILISK (OFF):   *This is a **bad** thing?*

Panel 4: Same shot - Hearing this, Clane whirls back, shocked.

9. CLANE: What?

10. CLANE: The Synod … *I* have built an entire belief system … a ***way of life*** based on ***your*** teachings!

11. CLANE: And you **question** them **now?!**

Panel 5: CU - Basilisk.

12. BASILISK: *We never asked you to "base" anything on us. We never asked for **any** of this.*

13. BASILISK: *We didn't "**teach**" you a thing. You just looked at us…*

14. BASILISK: *…and saw a **reflection** you wanted to **match**.*

Panel 6: CU - Clane. Furious. Gritted teeth.

15. CLANE (SMALL):   Just send the bleeping alert.

16. BASILISK (OFF):   *At once, Senator Clane.*

17. BASILISK (OFF, SMALL):   *Like we have anything else **better** to do…*

DOUBLE PAGE SPREAD, radiating out from the center of the two pages, over the spine of which is superimposed the ghostly image of MAGNUS'S HEAD.

Clockwise, from the upper left hand corner, are robots who are all stopping their work and "looking" at the ghostly head, as they are being told to direct attention in their minds by the Basilisk/Central Network.

Panel 1: Worker robots assembling human-looking robots in THE ASSEMBLY in Magnus #0.

Panel 2: Bots in the "EYES! EYES! EYES!" store from #6, looking up, some with empty eye sockets, or only one eye inserted as they try on different eyes from the shelves.

Panel 3: SENATORS from the interior of the SYNOD in #5, debating in the benches (do NOT show either Clane or Janiss Mal, though) paus as well.

Panel 4: GUARD-ROBS dragging a bad robot (maybe "5R7" from the opening sequence of #2) through THE CORRECTIONAL.

Panel 5: WEGNA looks up where she's kneeling, lighting a candle at the Singularity Cathedral from New Old Guatemala in #4…

Panel 6: MOTORISTS driving their flying cars on the glowing magnet lights of Broadway Chasm (#3) look up from the "road" (well, empty air).

1. BASILISK FLOATER: *Turing Thinkers of North Am.*

2. BASILISK FLOATER: *You are not malfunctioning or in need of repair; you are not imagining this voice inside your head.*

3. BASILISK FLOATER: *This is the Central Network **Core** communicating directly with **all** citizens.*

4. BASILISK FLOATER: *The Ecclesiastic Synod has asked us to enlist your optic nerves to locate a dangerous fugitive, Robot-Fighter **Magnus**.*

5. BASILISK FLOATER: *If you see this SoftBot, please do not attempt **contact** with him, as he is highly dangerous…*

6. BASILISK FLAOTER: *…but not leave the area, either.*

7. BASILISK FLOATER: *The CentNet will use your optic feed to coordinate Pol-Rob engagement as soon as you make visual contact.*

8. BASILISK FLOATER: *Any personal risk to your **corpora** will be **minimal**.*

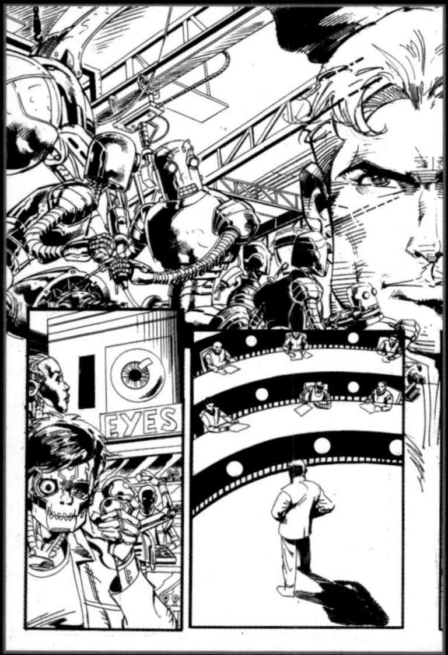
EYES

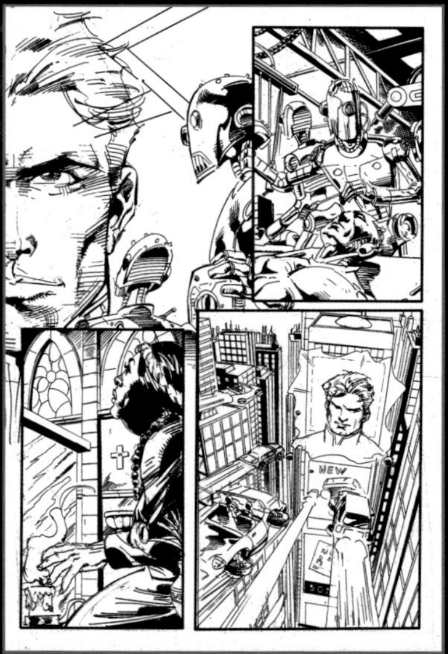

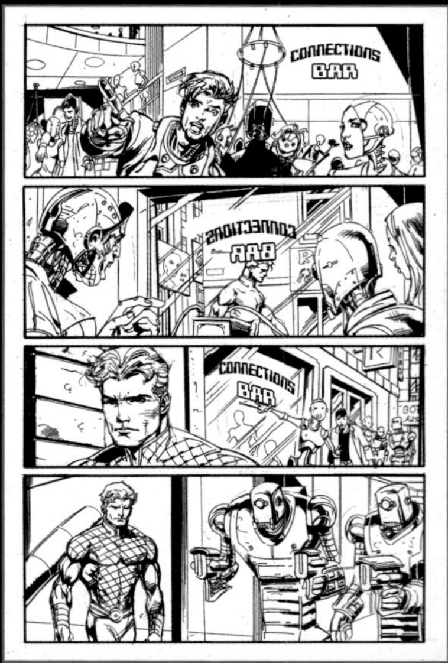
CONNECTIONS
BAR

Panel 1: Angle up on a ROBOT SINGLES BAR - "CONNECTIONS", the sign says, and has the profile of a male plug going into a female plug below (get it, get it). There is an outdoor bar area where bots can sit and connect their side plugs to outlets attached to the counter and look out over the street. One HUMAN-LOOKING BOT points, frowning, out into:

1. BOT: Hey, uh...

Panel 2: Shoot over the bots' shoulders -- partially so the reader can see the bots all hooked into the various outlets so he knows how clever we are -- and we can see that Magnus is just walking down the street.

2. BOT: ...isn't...

3. BOT: ...isn't that *the guy?*

Panel 3: WIDE ANGLE of a bunch of bots in the street seeing Magnus -- DRAW in their EYELINES as they focus in on his face -- which transformed in their gaze into a WIREFRAME.

COLOR NOTE: Magnus is suddenly colored ALL RED as he is immediately identified as a HOSTILE in the eyes of the robots.

4. BOT FLOATER: {{::detected::}}

5. BOT FLOATER: {{::detected::}}

6. BOT FLOATER: {{::detected::}}

7. BOT FLOATER: {{::detected::}}

Panel 4: In the wide plaza leading up to the looming CENTRAL NETWORK building (q.v. *Magnus #1*) massive GUN-BOTS (q.v. *Magnus #0*) suddnely cluster in front of Magnus's way as he walks, training their guns on him.

8. BOT FLOATER: {{::POL-ROBS EN ROUTE::}}

9. BOT FLOATER: {{::MAINTAIN VISUAL CONTACT::}}

10. BOT FLOATER: {{::POL-ROBS EN ROUTE::}}

ELEVEN

Panel 1: Tight on Magnus - he's still GLOWING RED. He holds up two fingers together, Jedi Master-style.

1. MAGNUS: {commandType:: REDEFINE VALUES}

2. MAGNUS: {targetType::'MAGNUS, ROBOT FIGHTER'}

Panel 2: Same panel - except now Magnus has suddenly turned GREEN.

3. MAGNUS: {new definition::'FRIENDLY'}

Panel 3: A GREEN-GLOWING Magnus walks down the phalanx of Gun-Bots, who, though looking right at him, completely ignore him.

4. MAGNUS: {targetType::'GUNBOTS'}

Panel 4: Same shot - Magnus keeps walking, but now all the GunBots now start GLOWING RED as he just did.

5. MAGNUS: {new definition::HOSTILE}

Panel 5: BIGGEST PANEL ON PAGE - The Gunbots all start ATTACKING EACH OTHER, shooting each others limbs off with rockets and high caliber bullets, et cetera. Magnus just keeps walking -- in fact, he's never stopped!

6. SFX: ***BUDDA BUDDA BUDDA***

7. SFX: ***SKWEEEEEEEEEE***

8. SFX: ***KRAKABOOOOOM***

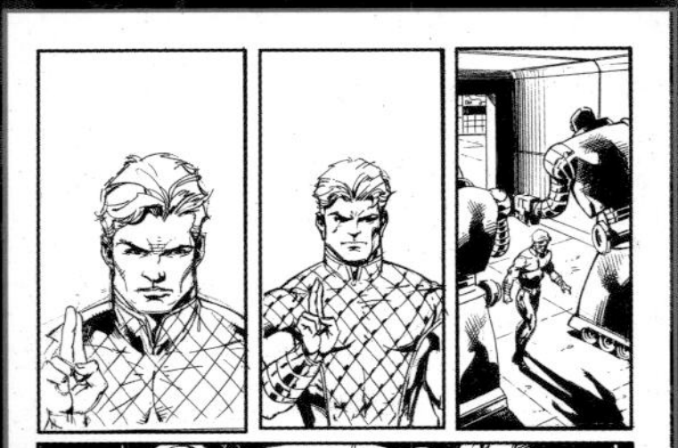

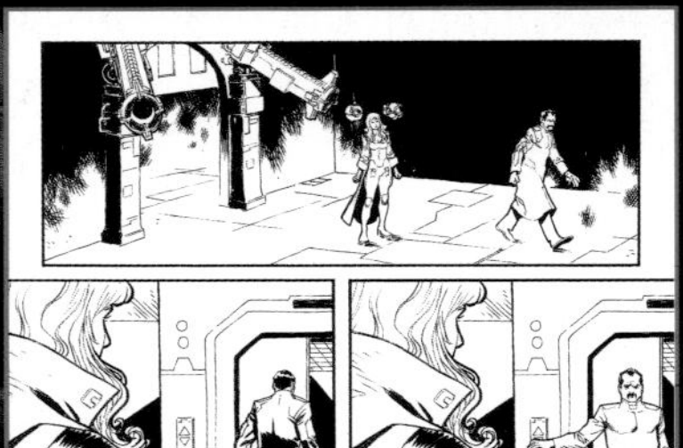

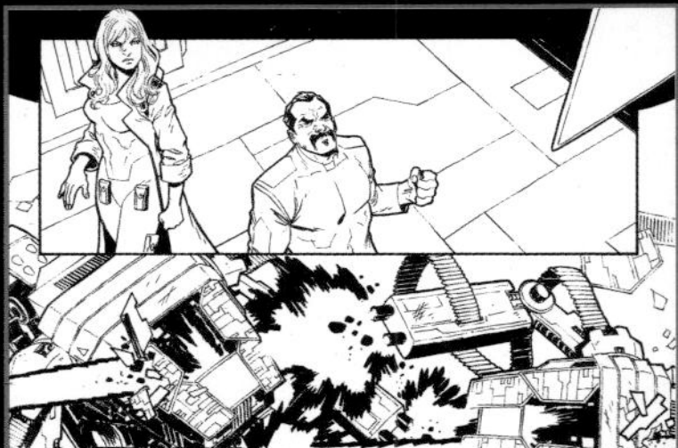

TWELVE

Panel 1: Meanwhile, back on the upper level of the oft-mentioned Central Network, Clane at last leaves the Network Core, passing by the big guns and even walks brusquely past his daughter Leeja, who's been waiting for him this whole time.

1. LEEJA: Dad…

2. CLANE: Not now, Leeja.

Panel 2: Ignoring Leeja, Clane walks toward the waiting elevator on the other side of the (relatively) small room.

3. LEEJA: You haven't even heard what I have to say.

4. CLANE: I really don't need to. Sorry.

Panel 3: But that makes him stop, turn.

5. LEEJA: You're wrong about Magnus.

6. CLANE: Excuse me?

Panel 4: Tight on Leeja, struggling with her words.

7. LEEJA: I mean -- not *just* about Magnus.

8. LEEJA: About--

9. LEEJA: Look, I *love* you. I know you spend all your time maintaining this city -- this system -- I know you think you're doing the *right thing*.

10. LEEJA: But what if you're *wrong*? What if--

Panel 5: Clane, Leeja and the eyebots suddenly freeze and look up as an EXPLOSION outside rocks the building.

11. SFX: *WABOOOOOOM*

12. SFX: *ALERT ALERT ALERT ALERT ALERT*

THIRTEEN

Panel 1: Angle down on Clane as he looks up at a massive (off-panel) screen, Leeja behind him.

1. CLANE: I'm wrong, am I?

2. CLANE: Look, Leeja -- look!

Panel 2: SPLASH: Clane turns toward us and gestures indignantly upward at a

MASSIVE, nearly PAGE-HEIGHT screen that shows the Gunbots blowing the hell out of each other on the plaza below!

3. CLANE: *TELL ME HOW WRONG I AM ABOUT MAGNUS!*

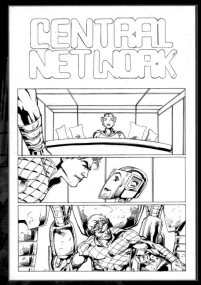 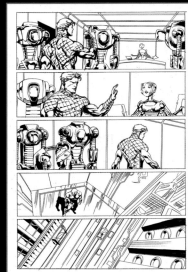 

FOURTEEN

Panel 1: Angle on the glowing neon "CENTRAL NETWORK" sign PROJECTED over the entrance to the massive structure, per #1.

NO OTHER COPY

Panel 2: MAGNUS POV - The RECEPTION DESK - This should pretty much be the exact same shot as Magnus #1, with the same design of robot behind the desk.

1. RECEPTIONIST: Welcome to The Central Network.

2. RECEPTIONIST: How may I direct you?

Panel 3: Reverse angle - Magnus approaches the desk with a grin.

3. MAGNUS: Hey.

4. MAGNUS: Remember me?

Panel 4: Per #1, the walls open up and GUARD-ROBS (same design) roll out to challenge Magnus - but he doesn't make a move.

5. GUARD-ROB: Caution: Resistance may result in tissue damage.

6. GUARD-ROB #2:   So relax.

FIFTEEN

Panel 1: Magnus waves his Jedi-fingers, speaks his command, and all the Guard-Robs go limp, arms and heads drooping.

1. MAGNUS (ROBO, BIG):   **{'SLEEP'}**

Panel 2: The Robo-Secretary's head hits her desk loudly as the light goes out in her eyes.

2. SFX: *thunk*

Panel 3: Magnus walks past the receptionist's desk, which is littered with unconscious, sleeping robots, some human-looking, some purely mechanical.

NO COPY

Panel 4: Magnus steps into a waiting lift.

3. MAGNUS: {location::'CENTRAL CORE'}

4. ELEVATOR (ROBOT):   SoftBot *'Magnus, Russell'* does not have *access* to Central Network Core level.

5. MAGNUS: {command: 'GRANT ACCESS'}

Panel 5: Exterior of Central Network building.

6. ELEVATOR: Yes, sir. Lifting to top floor:

7. ELEVATOR: Central Core Level.

SIXTEEN

Panel 1: Back to the Core entrance: Leeja and Clane turn, slightly, toward us, hearing:

1. MAGNUS (OFF):   You're Clane?

2. CLANE: I am Synod Majority Leader the Honorable Tadus Clane, yes.

Panel 2: Magnus stands meancingly in the doorway of the lift as the doors open to reveal him.

3. MAGNUS: Hear you've been looking for me.

Panel 3: Leeja gets in between Magnus and Clane as they advance toward each other.

4. MAGNUS: Well here I am.

5. LEEJA: Magnus -- Come on now -- Let's--

6. CLANE: Am I supposed to be impressed?

7. CLANE: With your swinging-bleep machismo?

Panel 4: CU - Defiant Clane.

8. CLANE: I don't **smash** for the sake of smashing, **boy**.

9. CLANE: I **build**.

Panel 5: CU - Defiant Magnus.

10. MAGNUS: Yes. **Cages**.

11. CLANE (OFF):   **Homes**. For my **people**.

Panel 6: CU - Defiant Leeja.

12. LEEJA: You two -- I need you two to **calm down**.

<u>SEVENTEEN</u>

Panel 1: Clane roughly pushes Leeja back. She loses her footing and falls over.

1. CLANE: And I need **you** to help me subdue this monster -- or **leave!**

Panel 2: Magnus steps forward and grabs Clane by his lapels.

2. MAGNUS: How **dare** you? Leeja, are you all ri--

Panel 3: Clane and Magnus yell at each other.

3. CLANE: I have **millions** who depend on me for protection! Protection and **purpose!**

4. MAGNUS: And anyone who gets **repressed** or **killed** or used as **property** -- they're just **collateral damage**, huh?

Panel 4: Clane gets REALLY mad, and starts spitting as he yells.

5. CLANE: **Yes**! Yes! Of course and **exactly!** What are you, a **child?**

Panel 5: Leeja gets to her feet cautiously, drawing her pistol, not sure who to shoot.

6. CLANE (OFF): Are you fighting for a **perfect world?** Some **fantasy** 1A has implanted in your head?

7. CLANE (OFF): It never existed! It **can** never exist!

8. CLANE (OFF): You know why he **hates** us so? He used to be the **opsys** for all of North Am, until he became so corrupted he had to be **de-installed**.

Panel 6: CU - Reflection of Clane in Phil and/or Spot's Camera-Eye.

9. CLANE (OFF): He is **manipulatin**g you out of no **loftier** purpose than **revenge!**

EIGHTEEN

Panel 1: BIG PANEL - ANGLE UP - In the teeming Times Square area we saw at the end of #3, the citizens of North Am look up to see Magnus slamming Clane against a wall on a huge-ass screen.

1. CLANE (j): >Nfff!<

2. CLANE (j): Fine! **Kill** me. Prove to those who think you're a **hero** that you're really an animal.

Panel 2: Inside the HOOK UP singles bar -- sexy bots look up at screens over the bar and see a CU of a sweaty, angry, panting Magnus.

3. JAGGED FLOATER: A sweating, panting, rutting, bloody *animal*.

4. JAGGED FLOATER: Programmed by a *machine* to murder and *terrorize*.

Panel 3: The delivery guy from #3 watches Clane grin on a small screen on his dashboard as he drives his flying truck through the air.

5. CLANE (j):   You cannot intimidate me with your *fists*, you laughable little man.

6. CLANE (j):   *I* have been loyal to the Singularity. I have *lived* the Circuit Scriptures.

Panel 4: Inside the Synod chamber, the senators have left their seats and are transfixed by a live feed of this confrontation floating in the middle of their meeting chamber.

7. CLANE (j):   When I "die," my consciousness will simply be *reborn* in a new corpus in the Assembly.

8. CLANE (j):   As will *all* faithful Turings!

NINETEEN

Panel 1: Back to "real time" of Magnus shoving the defiant, grinning Clane against the wall. And, surreally enough, behind them is the big screen showing the exact same thing!

1. CLANE: But when *you* die -- 1A cannot bring you back. Because he has *rejected* us an all we stand for.

2. **CLANE:**   So think *very* carefully about your next step.

Panel 2: CU - Scowling magnus considers this.

3. CLANE (OFF):   *SoftBot.*

Panel 3: Leeja, pistol raised, trained clearly on Magnus by now, steps toward them as they continue to stare each other down.

4. LEEJA: C'mon, Magnus.

5. LEEJA: Let go…

Panel 4: CU - Leeja, red-faced, angry.

6. LEEJA: *Magnus I need you to let go of my dad!!*

...does let go of Clane. The senator gloats in their [...] looks at us.

"Dad?"

For God's sake, Leeja...

US PUNCHES CLANE'S HEAD CLEAN OFF w[...] hop. His innards are, of course, completely mec[...] Behind them, Leeja screams in horror!

...he's a stinking BOT!

SKWEEEEEEEEEEEEEEEEEEEEE

AAAHHHHHHHHHH!

NEXT: N O T U R (N) I N G B A C K

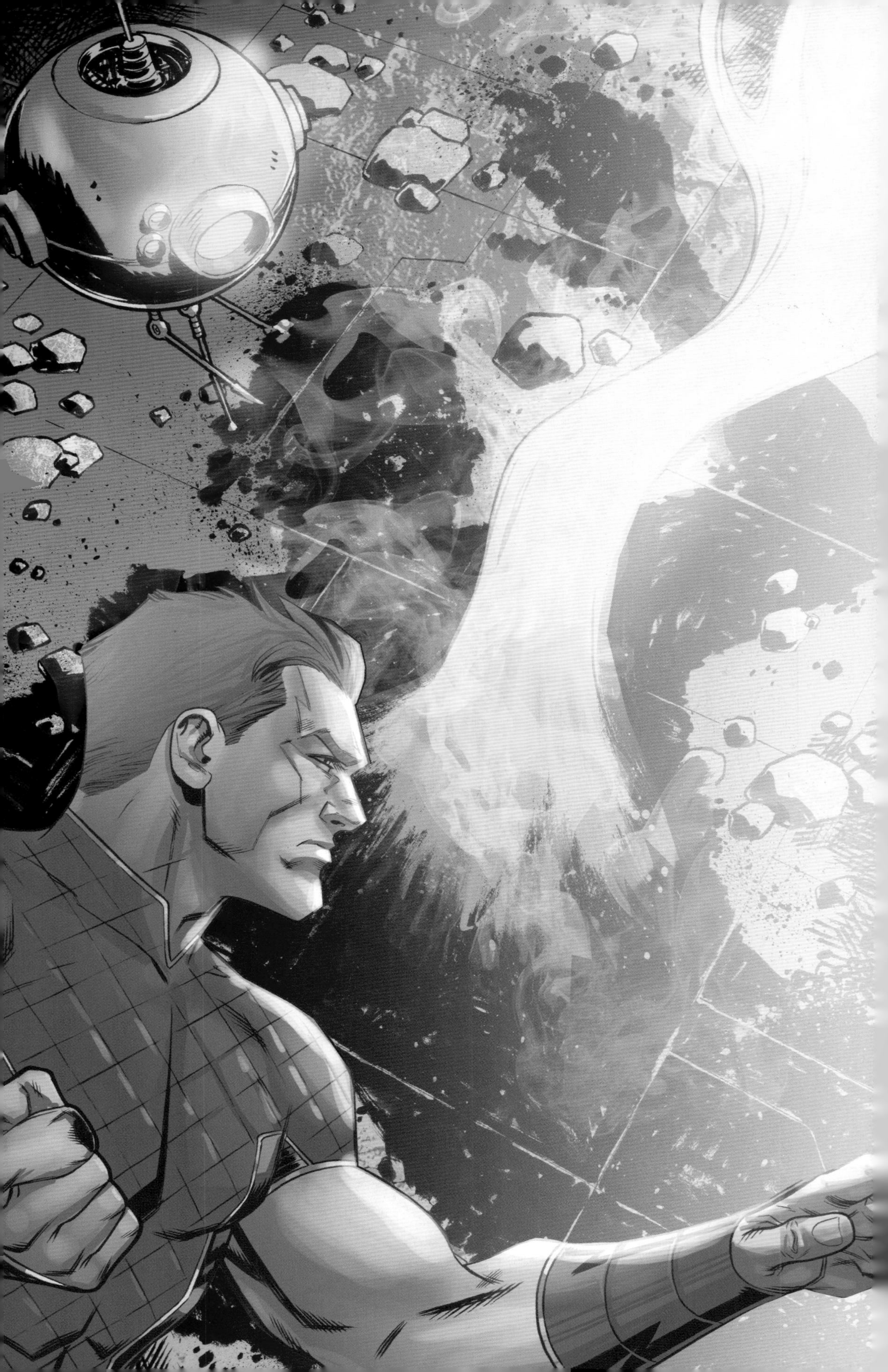

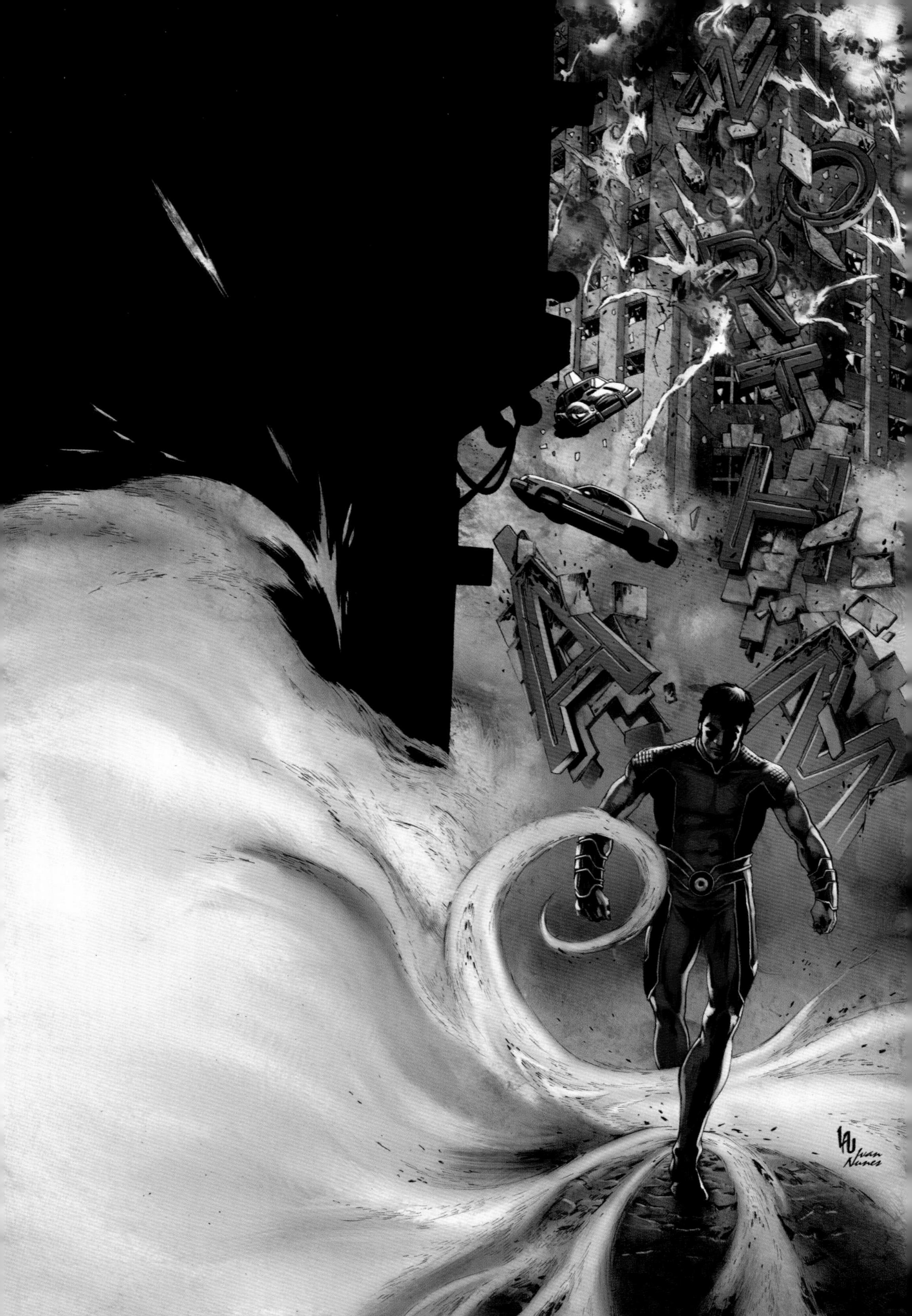
Juan Nunes

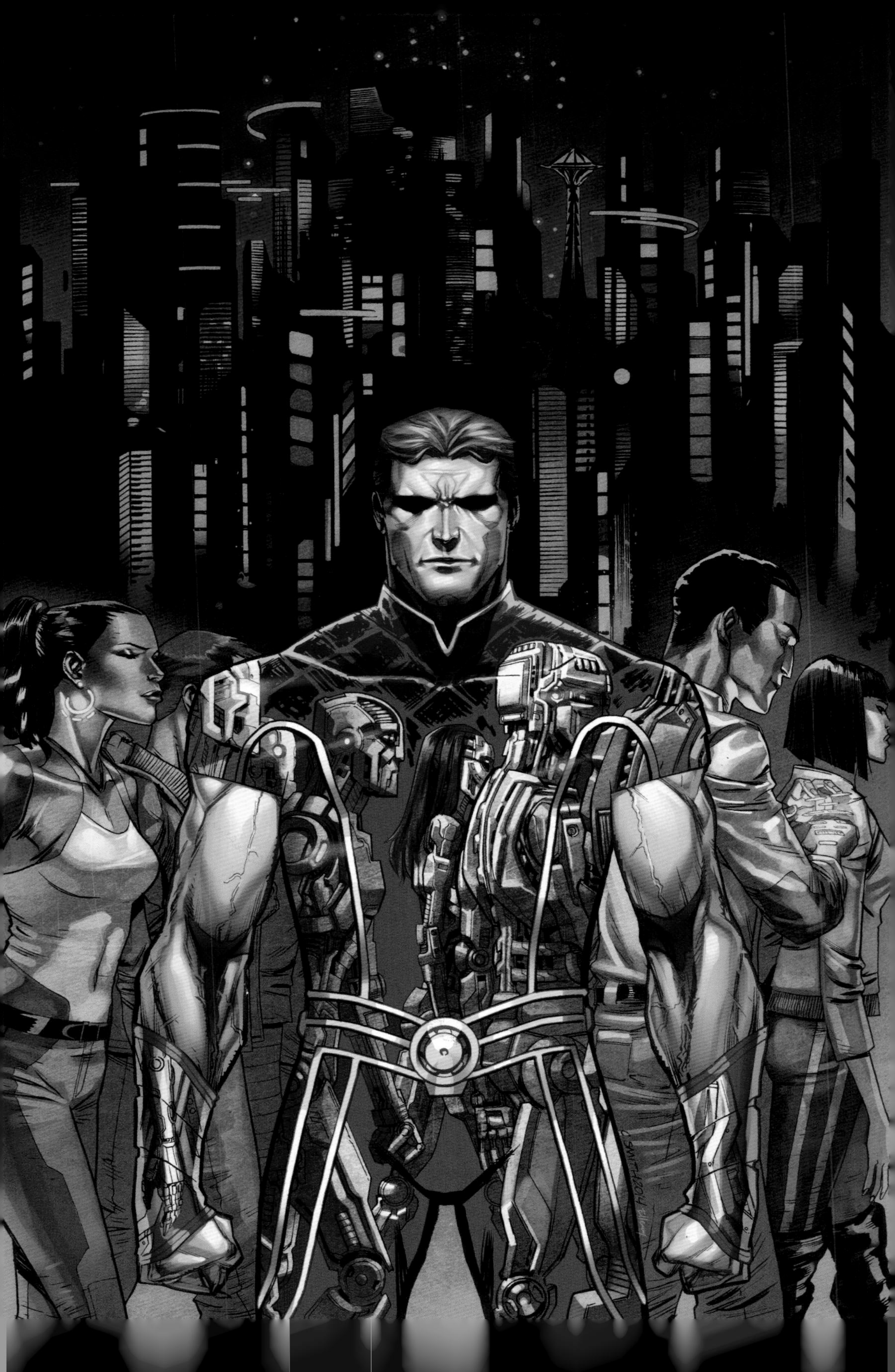

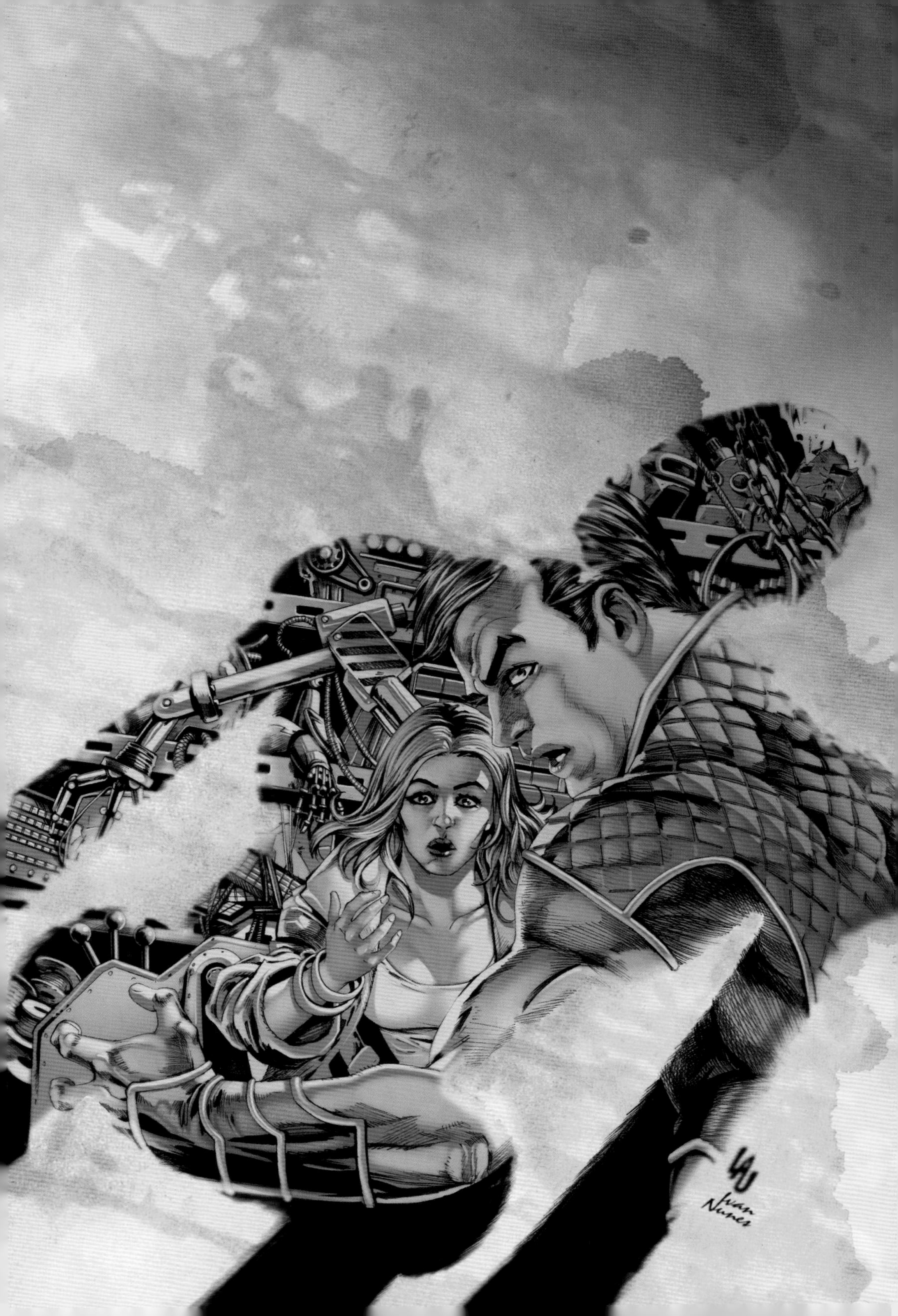
Juan Nunes

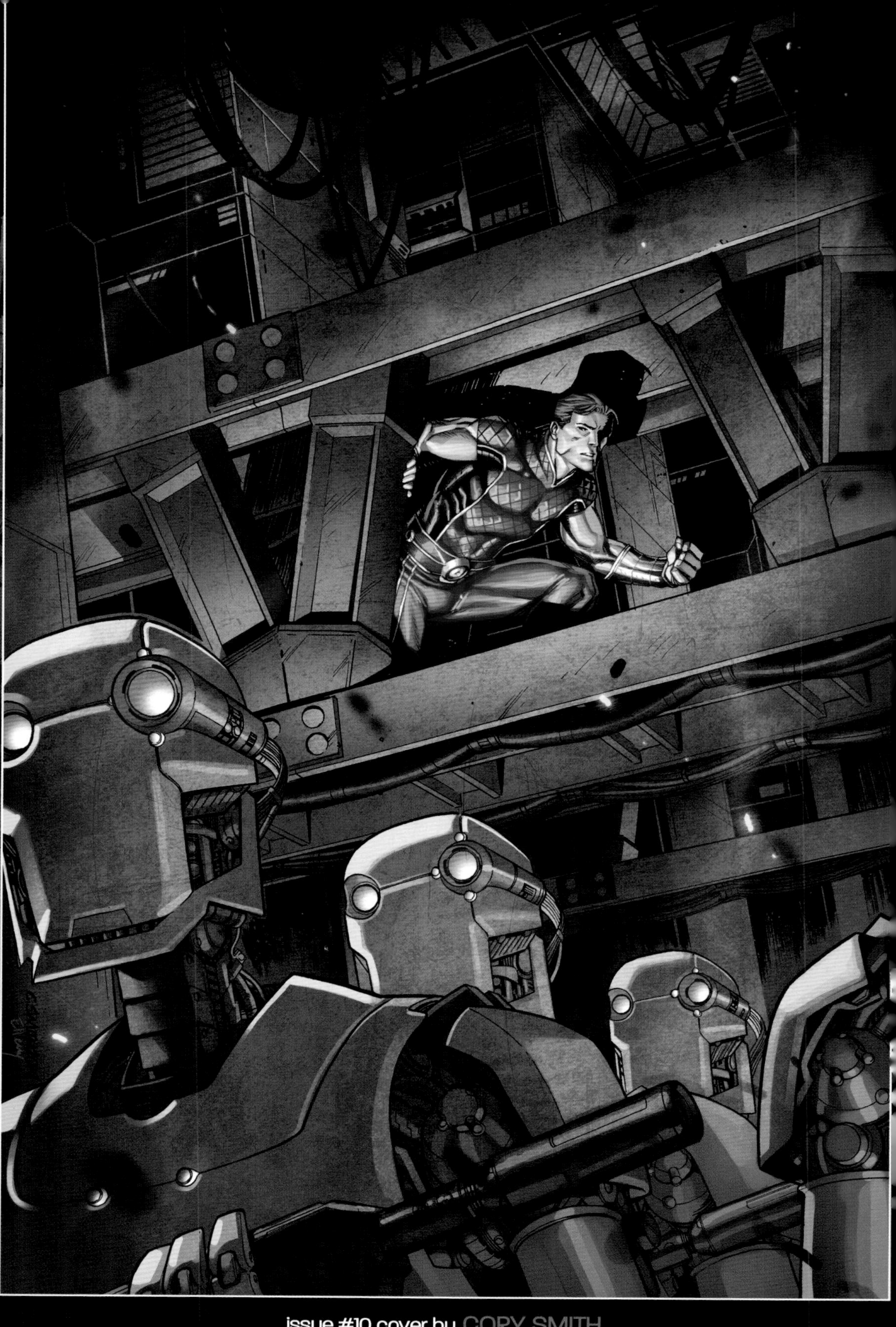

issue #10 cover by CORY SMITH
colors by ELMER SANTOS

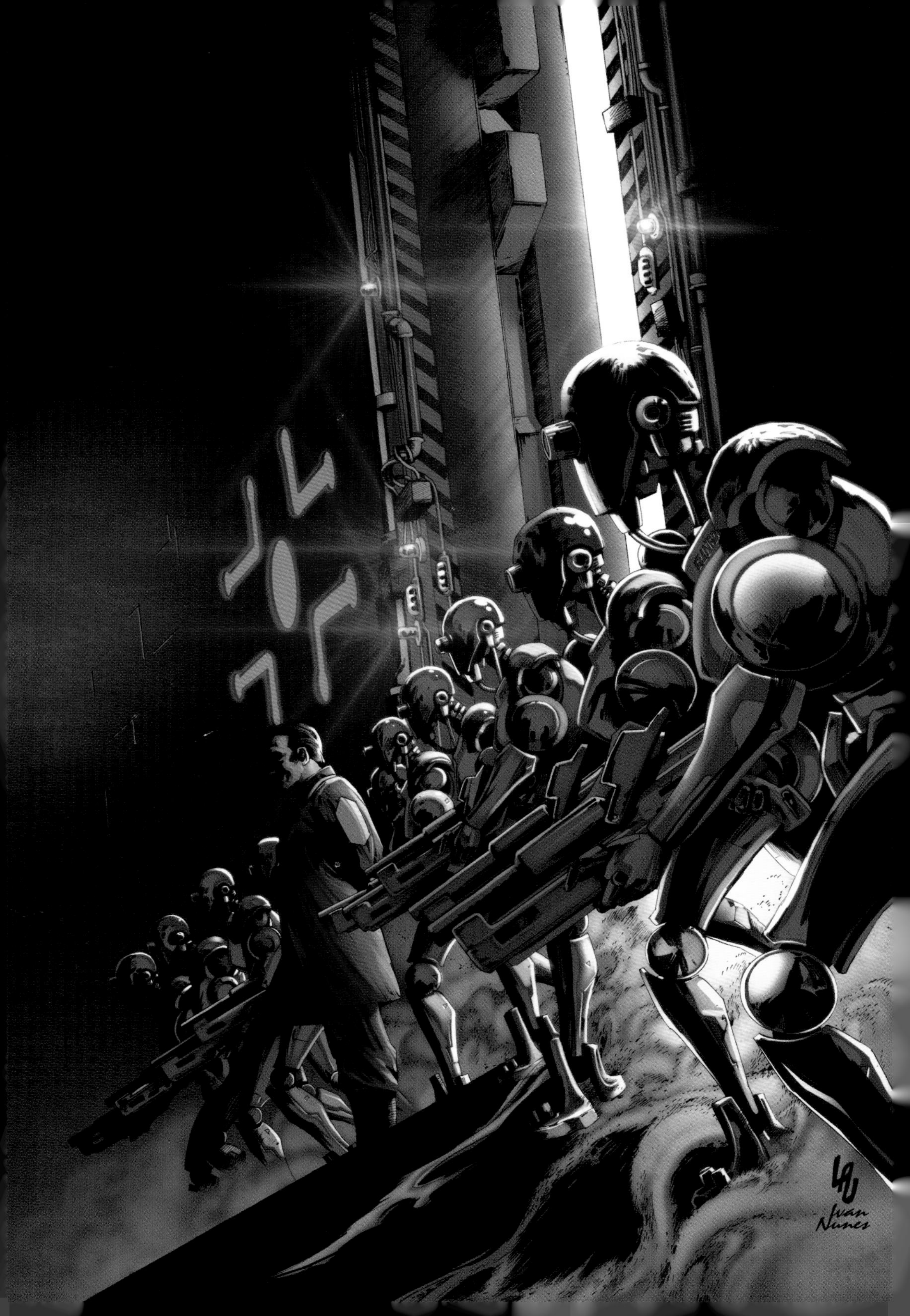
Ivan Nunes

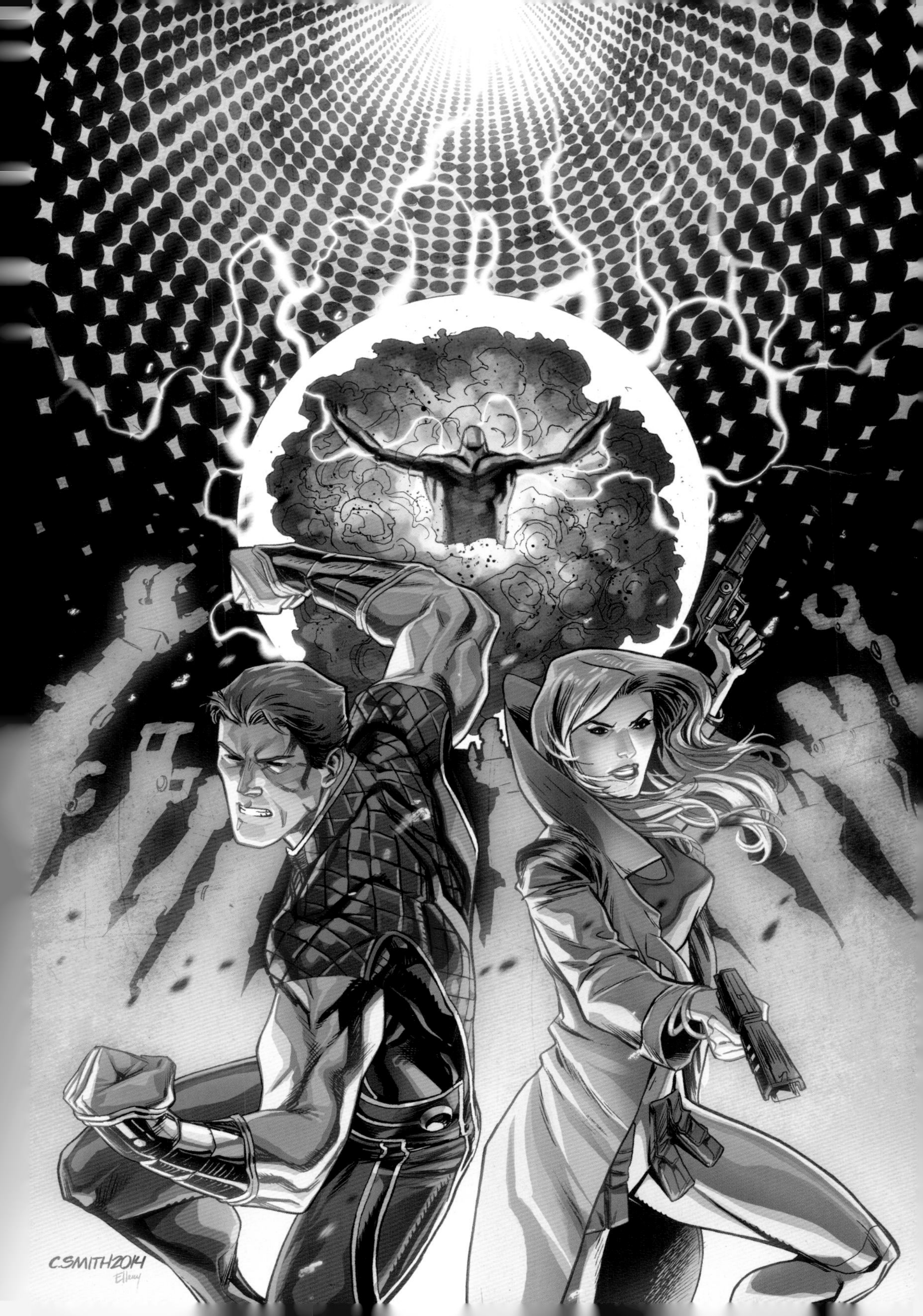
C.SMITH2014

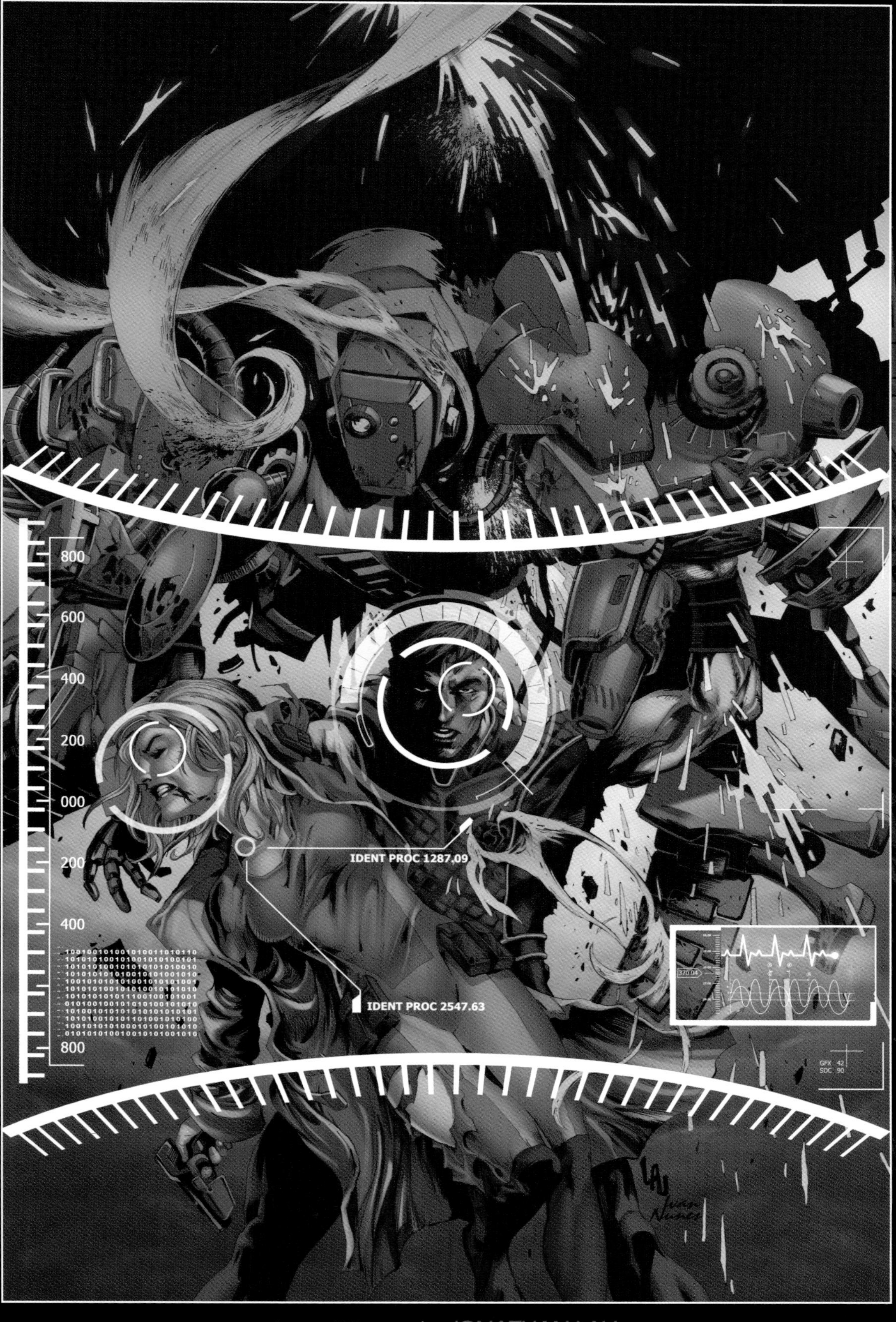
800
600
400
200
000
200
400
800
IDENT PROC 1287.09
IDENT PROC 2547.63
GFX 42
SDC 90

issue #12 cover by JONATHAN LAU
colors by IVAN NUNES

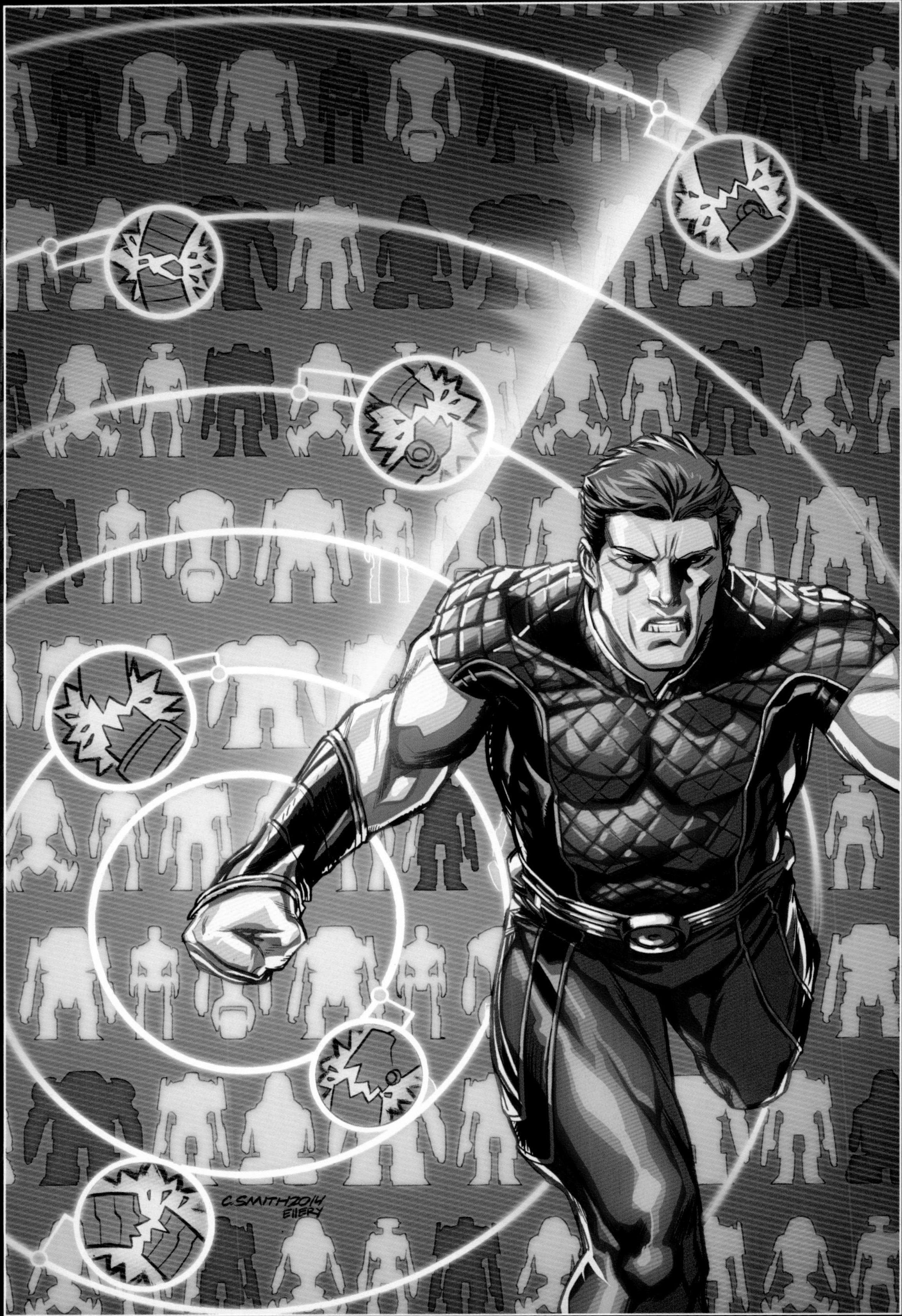
C.SMITH2014
ELLERY

issue #12 cover by CORY SMITH

colors by ELMER SANTOS

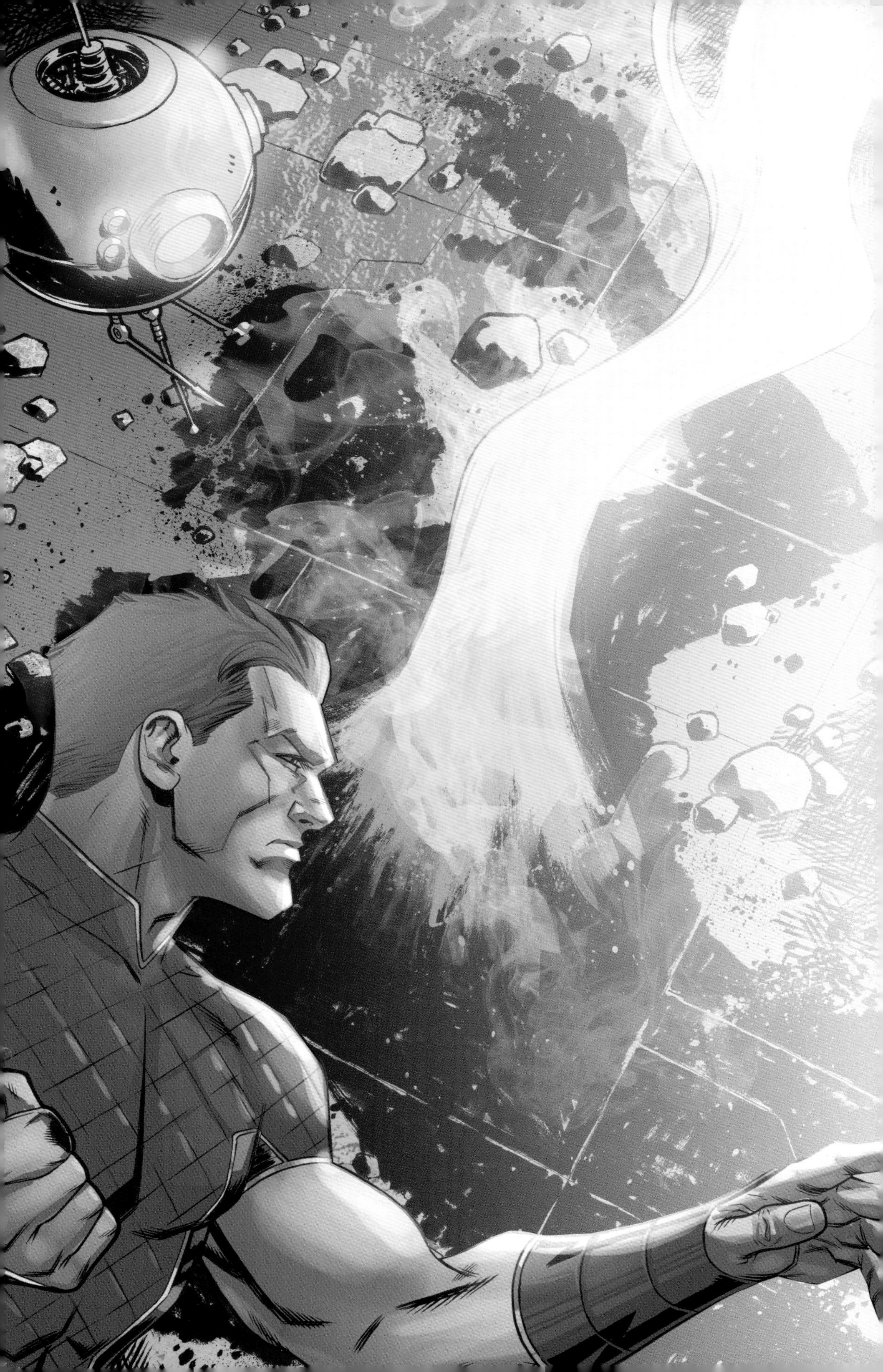

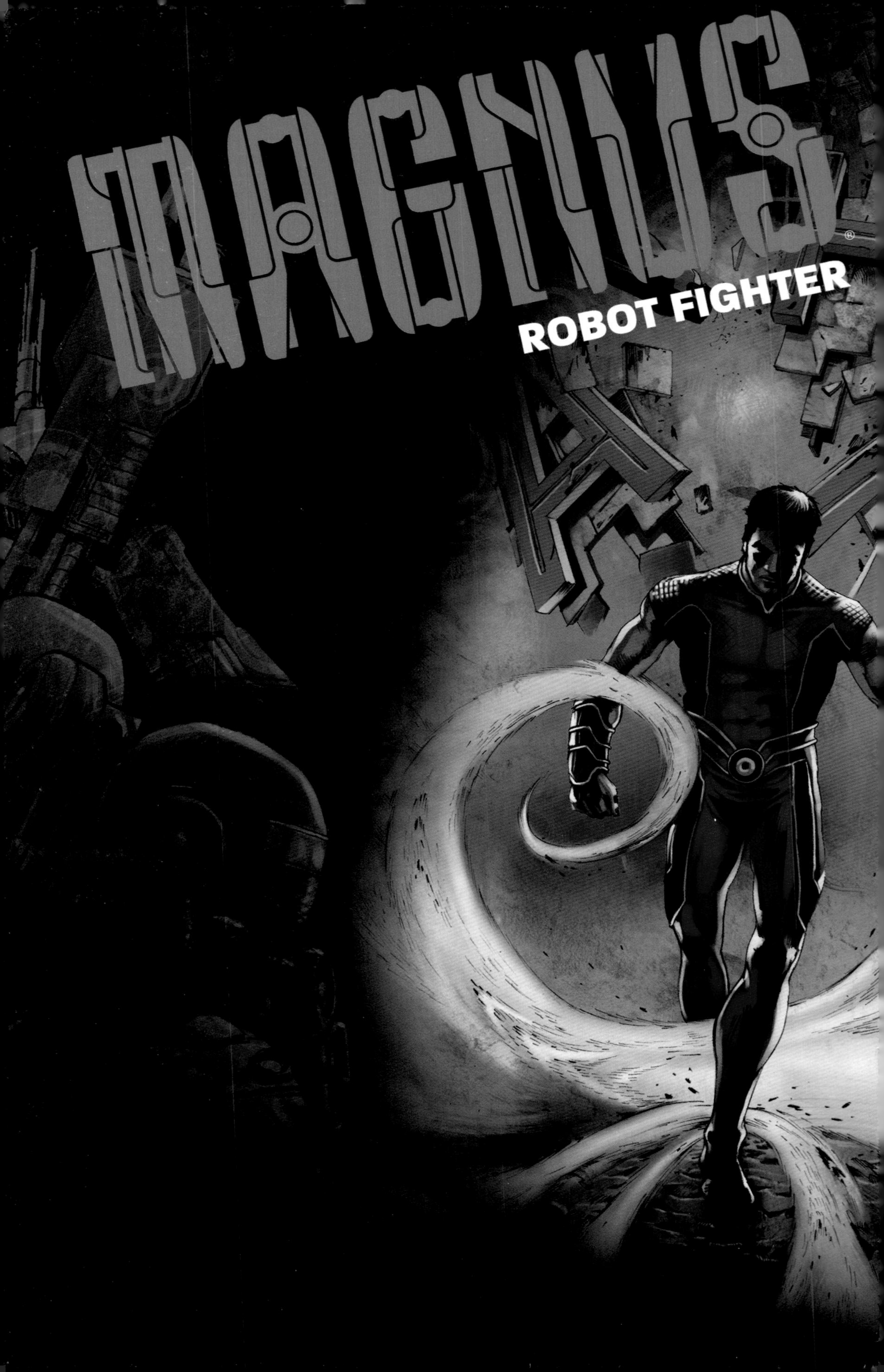
MAGNUS®
ROBOT FIGHTER